DATABASE TUNIN

DATABASE TUNING

A Principled Approach

Dennis E. Shasha

*Courant Institute
of Mathematical Sciences
New York University*

UNIX System Laboratories

Prentice Hall, Englewood Cliffs, New Jersey 07632

Library of Congress Cataloging-in-Publication Data

Shasha, Dennis Elliott.
    Database tuning : a principled approach / Dennis Shasha.
        p.   cm.
    Includes bibliographical references and index.
    ISBN 0-13-205246-6
    1. Data base management.   I. Title.
QA76.9.D3S52   1992
005.74–dc20   92-7141
                                                    CIP

Editorial/production supervision: *Harriet Tellem*
Cover design: *Karen Stephens*
Prepress buyer: *Mary McCartney*
Manufacturing buyer: *Susan Brunke*
Acquisitions editor: *Paul W. Becker*
Editorial assistant: *Noreen Regina*
Cover black/white illustration: *Ed Scarisbrick, Image Bank*
Cover photograph: *Joe Bator, Stock Market*
Composition & art: *Chiron, Inc., using ZzTEX*

Published by Prentice Hall, Inc.
A Simon & Schuster Company
Englewood Cliffs, New Jersey 07632

The publisher offers discounts on this book when ordered in bulk quantities.
For more information, write: Special Sales/Professional Marketing, Prentice Hall, Inc.
Professional & Technical Reference Division, Englewood Cliffs, New Jersey 07632

Prentice-Hall International (UK) Limited, *London*
Prentice-Hall of Australia Pty, Limited, *Sydney*
Prentice-Hall Canada Inc., *Toronto*
Prentice-Hall Hispanoamericana, S.A., *Mexico*
Prentice-Hall of India Private Limited, *New Delhi*
Prentice-Hall of Japan, Inc., *Tokyo*
Simon & Schuster Asia Pte, Ltd., *Singapore*
Editora Prentice-Hall do Brasil, Ltda., *Rio de Janeiro*

Dedication

To Karen and Cloe
for their love and support.

Contents

Chapter 6   Choosing a System   153

Chapter 7   Performance Troubleshooting— What to Test, What to Do   168

Preface

GOAL OF BOOK

Database tuning is the activity of making a database application run more quickly. "More quickly" usually means higher throughput, though it may mean lower response time for some applications.

To make a system run more quickly, the database tuner may have to change the way applications are constructed, the data structures and parameters of a database system, the configuration of the operating system, or the hardware. The best database tuners therefore like to solve problems requiring broad knowledge of an application and of computer systems.

This book aims to impart that knowledge to you. It has three operational goals.

1. To help you tune your application on your database management system, operating system, and hardware.

2. To give you performance criteria for choosing a database management system.

3. To help you build performance into a home-built database management system, should you be so courageous as to construct one.

The best way to achieve the first goal is to read this book in concert with the tuning guide that comes with your particular system. These two will complement one another in several ways.

- This book will give you tuning ideas that will port from one system to another and from one release to another. The tuning guide will mix such general techniques with system- and release-specific ones.
- This book embodies the experience and wisdom of professional database tuners, suggesting more ideas and strategies than you'll find in your system's tuning guide.
- This book has a wider scope than most tuning guides as it addresses such issues as the allocation of work between the application and the database server, the design of transactions, and the purchase of hardware.

Note to Teachers.   Although this book is aimed primarily at practicing professionals, it may have a place in an advanced university database curriculum. Suppose your students have learned the basics of the external views of database systems, query languages, object-oriented concepts, and conceptual design. You then have the following choice:

- For those of your students who will *design* a database management system in the near future, the best approach is to teach them query processing, concurrency control, and recovery. That is the classical approach.
- For those students who will primarily *use* or *administer* database management systems, the best approach may be to teach them some elements of tuning.

The two approaches complement one another well if taught together. In the classical approach, for example, you might teach the implementation of B-trees. In the tuning approach, you might teach the relevant benefits of B-trees and hash structures as a function of query type. To give a second example, in the classical approach, you might teach locking algorithms for concurrency control. In the tuning approach, you might teach techniques for chopping up transactions to achieve higher concurrency without sacrificing serializability.

I have tried to make the book self-contained inasmuch as I assume only a reading knowledge of SQL,[1-5] an advanced undergraduate-level course in data

Possible references for that material include the following:

[1] Chris Date, *A Guide to the SQL Standard*, 2nd ed. Reading, Mass.: Addison-Wesley, 1989.

[2] Hank Korth and Avi Silberschatz, *Database System Concepts*, 2nd ed. New York: McGraw-Hill, 1991.

[3] Gottfried Vossen, *Data Models, Database Languages and Database Management Systems*. Reading, Mass.: Addison-Wesley, 1991.

[4] Jeff Ullman, *Principles of Database and Knowledge-Based Systems*. New York: Computer Science Press, division of W. H. Freeman, 1988.

[5] Ramez Elmasri and Sham Navathe, *Fundamentals of Database Systems*. Redwood City, Calif.: Benjamin/Cummings, 1989.

structures, and, if possible, an undergraduate-level course in operating systems. The book discusses the principles of concurrency control, recovery, and query processing to the extent needed.

If you are using this book as a primary text for a portion of your classes, then send me electronic mail at shasha@cs.nyu.edu. I may be able to provide you with lecture notes.

SOME RELEVANT HISTORY

From telephone network troubleshooting to stock arbitrage to medical information systems to the production of newspapers, nearly every major application of computers makes extensive use of data. Although this was as true in the middle 1980s as it is today, something important has changed.

Workers in all these fields have discovered that buying a database management system is usually a better idea than developing one from scratch. The old excuse—"The performance of a commercial system will not be good enough for my application"—has given way to the new realization that the amenities offered by database management systems (especially, the standard interface, tools, transaction facilities, and data structure independence) are worth the price. This change of view has its analogue in the earlier movement from assembly language to high-level languages. In both cases, application development time and software reliability improve at some (increasingly small) cost in performance.

As the market for database management systems has grown, the systems have improved. In the mid-1980s, IBM was accused of introducing the DB2 product to sell more computers, so poorly did it perform. By 1990, DB2 and its relational competitors—INFORMIX, INGRES, ORACLE, RDB, SYBASE, UNIFY, and others—had achieved high enough performance, so that all but the lowest functionality, most time-critical, and most stable data processing applications had switched to relational systems. This may explain why approximately 80% of the software packages sold today are relational.

In the early 1990s, object orientation became fashionable. As of this writing, talk of objects is spreading across the database management landscape like tumbleweed on the Nevada desert. In this book, I take a sympathetic but cautious attitude toward this new development.

For the most part, I agree with the virtues of object orientation as a methodology for *designing* systems. For example, it is often useful to talk about network management in terms of the operations that can be performed on a switch node (turn it on, turn it off, change its routing, etc.). It is also convenient to speak of classes of switches of different types and to organize those classes in a hierarchy.

Similarly, it is useful to talk about operations on financial bond history objects and to group bonds into a class hierarchy.

Because this book is about performance, however, my interest in object-oriented database systems centers on the question: "For what kind of application is an object-oriented system likely to perform better than a relational one?" I will discuss application criteria to consider, e.g., the importance of pointer-based access to an application or the length of transactions, when discussing whether to consider an object-oriented system as an *implementation* platform.

HOW TO READ THIS BOOK

The tone of the book is informal, though I try to give you the reasoning behind every suggestion. Occasionally, you will see quantitative rules of thumb to guide you to rational decisions after qualitative reasoning reaches an impasse.

The systems used as examples run on platforms ranging from microsystems (e.g., OS/2 Extended Edition) to workstations (e.g., SYBASE, INGRES, ORACLE) to mainframes (e.g., DB2). It turns out that most tuning principles have general applicability. For this reason, I have tried to separate universally applicable (i.e., system and model-independent) principles and considerations from specific ones. This gives you several different ways of reading this book.

1. If you are interested primarily in relational database management systems, then read chapters 1 through 4.

2. If you are interested in object-oriented database management systems, then read chapters 1, 2, 3, and 5.

3. If you have to choose a database management system for your application, then read chapter 6.

4. If you must troubleshoot a performance problem, refer to chapter 7. That will give you rules of thumb as well as pointers to relevant background material in the rest of the book.

ACKNOWLEDGMENTS

Many people have contributed to this book. Heartfelt thanks go to the industrial collaborators listed on the cover. They have generously shared their experience and wisdom to make this a more useful book. (Of course, I have interpreted that wisdom, so any errors are my fault.)

Special thanks go to David DeWitt, Narain Gehani, Dusan Mocko, Steve Rozen, and Gerhard Weikum for reading large portions of the manuscript and offering much useful criticism. Eric Amiel, Veronique Benzaken, Georges Gardarin, Patrick O'Neil, and Patrick Valduriez each read a single chapter and offered many helpful comments.

This book draws on my experiences teaching students at New York University and consulting in various parts of AT&T Bell Laboratories, Unix System Laboratory, and Wall Street. I would like to thank these colleagues in industry, universities, and national laboratories for the knowledge I gained while working with them, especially Rakesh Agrawal, Brian Anderson, Juan Andrade, Marie-Jo Bellosta, Mokrane Bouzeghoub, Steve Buroff, Mark Carges, Jozef Chou, Terry Dwyer, Steve Felts, Christoph Freytag, Olivier Gruber, Stephane Grumbach, Richard Hull, Zvi Kedem, Kurt Kovach, Jishnu Mukerji, Carol Raye, Daniel Richard, Dave Rorke, Art Sabsevitz, Tom Vaden, Victor Vianu, Gottfried Vossen, and Alex Wolf.

I also wish to thank all those who helped with the production and editing of the book: Fabienne Cirio for applying her artistry in the construction of the figures; Elisabeth Baque for her help in innumerable ways; and Eric Simon for his hospitality and his perspicacious comments regarding transaction chopping.

At Prentice Hall, I would like to thank my editor Paul Becker, friendly contact Bill Zobrist, technical documentation editor Phyllis Bregman, production editors Karen Bernhaut and Harriet Tellem, and copy editor Andrea Hammer.

The U.S. National Science Foundation and other funding agencies in the United States and in other countries deserve thanks—not for directly supporting the creation of this book—but for the support that they provide many researchers in this field. Many commercial products have grown out of university research prototypes. My special thanks go to INRIA (Institut National de Recherche en Informatique et en Automatique) in France for providing me with a pleasant and productive environment during the writing of this book.

Last but not least, I would like to thank Nat Goodman who, when I asked him what he thought of this book project idea, answered, "You've had a lot of crazy ideas that have worked out OK."

1

Basic Principles

1.1 WHY A PRINCIPLED APPROACH?

Tuning rests on a foundation of informed common sense. This makes it both easy and hard.

Tuning is easy because the tuner need not struggle through complicated formulas or theorems. Many academic and industrial researchers have tried to put tuning and query processing generally on a mathematical basis. The more complicated of these efforts have generally foundered, because they rest on unrealizable assumptions. The simpler of these efforts offer useful qualitative and simple quantitative insights that we will exploit in the coming chapters.

Tuning is difficult because the principles and knowledge underlying that common sense require a broad and deep understanding of the application, the database software, the operating system, and the hardware. Most tuning books offer practical rules of thumb but don't mention their limitations.

For example, a book may tell you *never* to use aggregate functions (such as AVG) when transaction response time is critical. The underlying reason is that such functions must scan substantial amounts of data and therefore may block other queries. So the rule is generally true, but it may not hold if the average applies to a few tuples that have been selected by an index. The point of the example is that the tuner must understand the reason for the rule, viz., long transactions that access large portions of shared data may delay concurrent online transactions. The well-informed tuner will then take this rule for what it is: good advice in most situations.

This book adopts the view that you can best apply a rule of thumb if you understand the underlying principles. In fact, understanding the principles will lead you to invent new rules of thumb for the unique problems that your application presents. Let us start from the basic principles—the ones to which all others implicitly appeal.

1.2 FOUR BASIC PRINCIPLES

Four principles pervade performance considerations.

1. Think globally; fix locally.
2. Partitioning breaks bottlenecks.
3. Start-up costs are high; running costs are low.
4. Render onto server what is due onto server.

We describe each principle below and give examples of its application. Some of the examples will use terms that are defined in later chapters and in the glossary.

1.2.1 Think Globally, Fix Locally

Effective tuning requires a proper identification of the problem and a minimalist intervention. This entails measuring the right quantities and coming to the right conclusions. Doing this well is challenging as any medical professional can attest.

Because the first part of chapter 7 is devoted to the question of localizing the source of a performance problem, I will present here only two examples that illustrate common pitfalls.

- A common approach to global tuning is to look first at hardware statistics to determine processor utilization, input-output (I/O) activity, paging, and so on. The naive tuner might react to a high value in one of these measurements (e.g., high disk activity) by buying hardware to lower it (e.g., buy more disks). There are many cases, however, in which that would be inappropriate. For example, there may be high disk activity because some frequent query scans a table instead of using an index or because the log shares a disk with some frequently accessed data. Creating an index or moving data files among the different disks may be cheaper and more effective than buying extra hardware.

- Tuners frequently measure the time taken by a particular query. If this time is high, many tuners will try to reduce it. Such effort, however, will not pay off if the query is executed only seldom. For example, speeding up a query that takes up 1% of the running time by a factor of two will speed up the system by at most 0.5%.

Thus, localizing the problem to one query and fixing that one should be the first thing to try. But make sure it is an important query.

1.2.2 Partitioning Breaks Bottlenecks

A slow system is rarely slow because all its components are saturated. Usually, one part of the system limits its overall performance. That part is called a *bottleneck*.

A good way to think about bottlenecks is to picture a highway traffic jam. The traffic jam usually results from the fact that a large portion of the cars on the road must pass through a narrow passageway. Another possible reason is that the stream from one highway merges with the stream from another. In either case, the bottleneck is that portion of the road network having the greatest number of cars per lane. Clearing the bottleneck entails locating it and then adopting one of two strategies:

> **1.** Make the drivers drive faster through the section of the highway containing the fewest lanes.
>
> **2.** Create more lanes to reduce the load per lane or encourage drivers to avoid rush hour.

The first strategy corresponds to a local fix (e.g., the decision to add an index or to rewrite a query to make better use of existing indexes) and should be the first one you try. The second strategy corresponds to partitioning.

Partitioning in database systems is a technique for reducing the load on a certain component of the system either by dividing the load over more resources or by spreading the load over time. Partitioning can break bottlenecks in many situations. Here are a few examples. The technical details will become clear later.

- A bank has N branches. Most clients access their account data from their home branch. If a centralized system becomes overloaded, a natural solution is to put the account data of clients with home branch i into subsystem i. This is a form of partitioning in space (of physical resources).
- Lock contention problems usually involve very few resources. Often the free list (the list of unused database buffer pages) suffers contention before the data files. A solution is to divide such resources into pieces, in order to reduce the number of concurrent accesses to each lock. In the case of the free list, this would mean creating several free lists, each containing pointers to a portion of the free pages. A thread in need of a free page would lock and access a free list at random. This is a form of logical partitioning (of lockable resources).

- A system with a few long transactions that access the same data as many short ("online") transactions will perform badly because of lock contention and resource contention. Deadlock may force the long transactions to abort and the long transactions may block the shorter ones. Also, the long transactions may use up large portions of the buffer pool, thereby slowing down the short transactions, even in the absence of lock contention. One possible solution is to perform the long transactions when there is little online transaction activity and to serialize those long transactions (if they are loads) so they don't interfere with one another (partitioning in time). A second is to allow the long transactions (if they are read-only) to apply to out-of-date data (partitioning in space).

Mathematically, partitioning means dividing a set into mutually disjoint (non-intersecting) parts. These three examples (and the many others that will follow) illustrate partitioning either in space, in logical resource, or in time. Unfortunately, partitioning does not always improve performance. For example, partitioning the data by branches may entail additional communication expense for transactions that are initiated away from the home branch.

So, partitioning—like most of tuning—must be done with care. Still, the main lesson of this subsection is simple.

When you find a bottleneck, first try to speed up that component. If that doesn't work, then partition.

1.2.3 Start-up and Running Costs

Most man-made objects devote a substantial portion of their resources to starting up. This is true of cars (the ignition system), of certain kinds of light bulbs (whose lifetimes depend principally on the number of times they are turned on), and of database systems.

- It is expensive to begin a read operation on a disk, but once the read begins, the disk can deliver data at high speed. Thus, reading a 64-kilobyte segment from a single disk track will probably be less than twice as expensive as reading 512 bytes from that track. This suggests that frequently scanned tables should be laid out consecutively on disk.

- In a distributed system, the latency of sending a message across a network is very high compared with the incremental cost of sending more bytes in a single message. The net result is that sending a 1-kilobyte packet will be little more expensive than sending a 1-byte packet. This implies that it is good to send large chunks of data rather than small ones.

- The cost of parsing, performing semantic analysis, and selecting access paths for even simple queries is significant (more than 10,000 instructions on most systems). This suggests that often executed queries should be compiled.

- Suppose that a program in a standard programming language such as C++, Pascal, Ada, COBOL, or PL/1 makes calls to a database system. In some systems (e.g., most relational ones), each call incurs a significant expense. So, it is much better for the program to execute a single SELECT call and then to loop on the result than to make many calls to the database (each with its own SELECT) within a loop of the standard programming language.

These four examples illustrate different senses of start-up costs: obtaining the first byte of a read, sending the first byte of a message, preparing a query for execution, and sending a query across an interface. Yet in every case, the lesson is the same.

Obtain the effect you want with the fewest possible start-ups.

1.2.4 Render onto Server What Is Due onto Server

Obtaining the best performance from a data-intensive system entails more than merely tuning the database management portion of that system. An important design question is the allocation of work between the database system (the server) and the application program (the client).

Where a particular task should be allocated depends on three main factors.

1. *The relative computing resources of client and server:* If the server is overloaded, then, all else being equal, tasks should be off-loaded to the clients. For example, many object-oriented database systems will allow the application programmer to move database buffers to the client site. This is a good idea for low-contention, compute-intensive applications.

2. *Where the relevant information is located:* Suppose some response should occur (e.g., writing to a screen) when some change to the database occurs (e.g., insertions to some database table). Then a well-designed system should use a trigger facility within the database system rather than poll from the application. A polling solution periodically queries the table to see whether it has changed. A trigger by contrast fires only when the change actually takes place, entailing much less overhead.

3. *Whether the database task interacts with the screen:* If it does, then the part that accesses the screen should be done outside a transaction. The reason is that the screen interaction may take a long time (several seconds at least). If a transaction T includes the interval, then T would prevent other transactions from accessing the data that T holds. So, the transaction should be split into three steps:

(a) A short transaction retrieves the data.

(b) An interactive session occurs at the client side outside a transactional context (i.e., no locks held).

(c) A second short transaction installs the changes achieved during the interactive session.

We will return to similar examples in the next chapter and in the appendix when we discuss ways to chop up transactions without sacrificing isolation properties.

1.3 BASIC PRINCIPLES AND KNOWLEDGE

Database tuning is a knowledge-intensive discipline. The tuner must make judgments based on complex interactions between buffer pool sizes, data structures, lock contention, and application needs. That is why the coming chapters mix detailed discussions of single topics with scenarios that require you to consider many tuning factors as they apply to a given application environment. Chapter 7 synthesizes the information of chapters 2 through 5 into a methodology for diagnosing and fixing performance problems.

Here is a brief description of each chapter. As you can see, you can skip chapter 5 or chapter 4 if you are primarily interested in relational or object-oriented systems, respectively.

- Chapter 2 discusses lower level system facilities that underlie all database systems.

  - Principles of concurrency control and recovery that are important to the performance of a database system and tuning guidelines for these subcomponents.
  - Aspects of operating system configuration that are important to tuning and monitoring.
  - Hardware modifications that are most likely to improve the performance of your system.

- Chapter 3 discusses the selection of indexes.

  - Query types that are most relevant to index selection.
  - The data structures that most database systems offer (B-trees, hash, ISAM, and heap structures) and some useful data structures that applications may decide to implement (tries, 2-3 trees, frequency-ordered linked lists, multidimensional search structures).
  - Sparse versus dense indexes.
  - Clustering (primary) versus nonclustering (secondary) indexes.

- Multicolumn (composite) indexes.
- Distribution considerations.
- Maintenance tips.

Again the discussion applies to virtually all database management systems, though the chapter uses relational terminology.

- Chapter 4 studies those factors of importance to relational systems.

  - The comparative advantage of relational systems.
  - Design of table schema, and the costs and benefits of normalization, vertical partitioning, and aggregate materialization.
  - Clustering tables and the relative benefits of clustering versus denormalization.
  - Record layout and the choice of data types.
  - Query reformulation including methods for minimizing the use of DISTINCT and for eliminating expensive nested queries.
  - Stored procedures.
  - Triggers.
  - Interfaces with hierarchical systems and with fourth-generation languages.

- Chapter 5 considers the tuning problem for object-oriented systems.

  - The comparative advantage of object-oriented systems.
  - Features to look for.
  - Object layout and the choice of data types.
  - Computation layout between the client and the server.
  - Extensions to relational systems to support some of the same applications.
  - Prospectus for object-oriented database systems.

- Chapter 6 discusses the choice of a system to suit an application.

  - Questions to ask when designing an application.
  - Designing your own benchmark.
  - Transaction processing and order-entry benchmarks.
  - Relational query benchmarks including benchmarks for decision support ("data mining").
  - Benchmarks for engineering and hypermedia databases.

- Chapter 7 consists of a performance troubleshooting guide.

  - Diagnostic measurements and suggested interpretations.
  - Cross-references to appropriate chapters for techniques to eliminate bottlenecks.
  - Tools offered by various relational vendors and operating system vendors for monitoring database applications.

- The appendices discuss specialized performance hints for real-time and on-line transaction processing systems.

  - Description of considerations concerning priority, buffer allocation, and related matters, for real-time database applications.
  - Systematic technique to improve performance by chopping up transactions without sacrificing isolation properties.

- A glossary and an index will attempt to guide you through the fog of tuning terminology.

2

Universal Tuning Considerations

2.1 GOAL OF CHAPTER

This chapter discusses tuning considerations having to do with the underlying components common to most database management systems. Each component carries its own tuning considerations.

- Concurrency control—how to minimize lock contention.
- Recovery and logging—how to minimize logging and dumping overhead.
- Operating system—how to optimize buffer size, process scheduling and so on.
- Hardware—how to allocate disks, random access memory, and processors.

Figure 2.1 shows the common underlying components of all database systems.

Warning about this chapter

This is the most difficult chapter of the book. The reason is that I have written it under the assumption that you have only a passing understanding of concurrent systems. I want to lead you to a level where you can make subtle tradeoffs

- Between speed and concurrent correctness.
- Between speed and fault tolerance.
- Between speed and hardware costs.

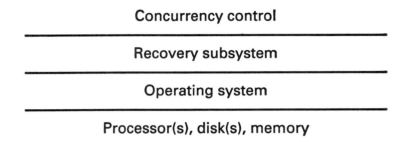

Figure 2.1 Common Underlying Components of All Database Systems.

So, it may be tough going in spots. If you have trouble, then take a break and read another chapter.

2.2 LOCKING AND CONCURRENCY CONTROL

Database applications divide their work into *transactions*. When a transaction executes, it accesses the database and performs some local computation. The strongest assumption that an application programmer can make is that each transaction will appear to execute in isolation—without concurrent activity. Because this notion of isolation suggests indivisibility, transactional guarantees are sometimes called *atomicity guarantees*.[1] Database researchers, you see, never bothered to study twentieth century physics.

The sequence of transactions within an application program, taken as a whole, enjoys no such guarantee however. Between, say, the first two transactions executed by an application program, other application programs may have executed transactions that modified data items accessed by one or both of these first two transactions. For this reason, the length of a transaction can have important correctness implications.

Example: The Length of a Transaction

Suppose that an application program processes a purchase by adding the value of the item to inventory and subtracting the money paid from cash. The application specification requires that cash never be made negative, so the transaction will roll back (i.e., undo its effects) if subtracting the money from cash will cause the cash balance to become negative.

[1] Two excellent references on this subject are the following:

1. Phil Bernstein, Vassos Hadzilacos, and Nat Goodman, *Concurrency Control and Recovery in Database Systems*. Reading, Mass.: Addison-Wesley, 1987.

2. Christos Papadimitriou, *The Theory of Concurrency Control*. New York: Computer Science Press, division of W. H. Freeman, 1986.

To reduce the time locks are held, the application designers divide these two steps into two transactions.

1. The first transaction checks to see whether there is enough cash to pay for the item. If so, the first transaction adds the value of the item to inventory. Otherwise, abort the purchase application.

2. The second transaction subtracts the value of the item from cash.

They find that the cash field occasionally became negative. Can you see what might have happened?

Consider the following scenario. There is $100 in cash available when a first application program begins to execute. An item to be purchased costs $75. So, the first transaction commits. Then some other execution of this application program causes $50 to be removed from cash. When the first execution of the program commits its second transaction, cash will be in deficit by $25.

So, dividing the application into two transactions can result in an inconsistent database state. Once you see it, the problem is obvious, though no amount of sequential testing would have revealed it. Most concurrent testing would not have revealed it either, because the problem occurs rarely.

So, cutting up transactions may jeopardize correctness even while it improves performance. This tension between performance and correctness extends throughout the space of tuning options for concurrency control. You can make the following choices.

- The number of locks each transaction obtains (*fewer tends to be better for performance, all else being equal*).
- The kind of locks those are (*read locks are better for performance*).
- The length of time that the transaction holds them (*shorter is better for performance*).

Because a rational setting of these tuning options depends on an understanding of correctness goals, the next subsection describes those goals and the general strategies employed by database systems to achieve them. Having done that, we will be in a position to suggest ways of rationally trading performance for correctness.

2.2.1 Correctness Considerations

Two transactions are said to be *concurrent* if their executions overlap in time. That is, there is some point in time in which both transactions have begun, and

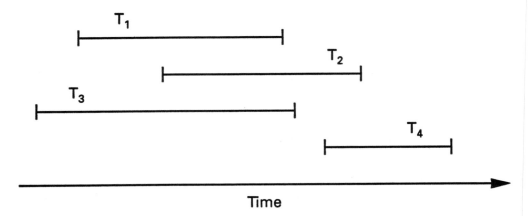

Figure 2.2   Concurrency: T_1 Is Concurrent with T_2 and T_3 Only; T_2 Is Concurrent with T_1, T_3, and T_4.

neither has completed. Notice that two transactions can be concurrent even on a uniprocessor. For example, transaction T may begin, then may suspend after issuing its first disk access instruction, and then transaction T' may begin. In such a case, T and T' would be concurrent. Figure 2.2 shows an example with four transactions.

    Concurrency control is, as the name suggests, the activity of controlling the interaction among concurrent transactions. Concurrency control has a simple correctness goal.

- Make it *appear* as if each transaction executes in isolation from all others. That is, the execution of the transaction collection must be *equivalent* to one in which the transactions execute one at a time. Two executions are equivalent if

  - one is a rearrangement of the other; and
  - in the rearrangement, each read returns the same value, and each write stores the same value as in the original.

    Notice that this correctness criterion says nothing about what transactions do. Concurrency control algorithms leave that up to the applications programmer. That is, the applications programmer must guarantee that the database will behave appropriately provided each transaction appears to execute in isolation. What is appropriate depends entirely on the application so is outside the province of concurrency control theory.

    Concurrent correctness is usually achieved through mutual exclusion. Operating systems allow processes to use semaphores for this purpose. Using a semaphore S, a thread (or process) can access a resource R with the assurance that no other thread (or process) will access R concurrently.

A naive concurrency control mechanism for a database management system would be to have a single semaphore S. Every transaction would acquire S before accessing the database. Because only one transaction can hold S at any one time, only one transaction can access the database at that time. Such a mechanism would be correct but would perform so badly that no system uses it.

Example: Semaphore Method

Suppose that Bob and Alice stepped up to different automatic teller machines (ATMs) serving the same bank at about the same time. Suppose further that they both wanted to make deposits but into different accounts. Using the semaphore solution, Bob and Alice would not be able to execute their deposits concurrently. That is, Bob would have to wait until Alice released the semaphore or vice versa. Modern banking would be completely infeasible.

An overreaction to this example would be to do away with the semaphore and to declare that no concurrency control at all is necessary. That can produce serious problems, however.

Example: No Concurrency Control

Imagine that Bob and Alice have decided to share an account. Suppose that Bob goes to a branch on the east end of town to deposit $100 in cash and Alice goes to a branch on the west end of town to deposit $500 in cash. Once again, they reach the automatic teller machines at about the same time Before they begin, their account has a balance of 0. Here is the progression of events in time.

1. Bob selects the deposit option.
2. Alice selects the deposit option.
3. Alice puts the envelope with her money into the machine at her branch.
4. Bob does the same at his branch.
5. Alice's transaction begins and reads the current balance of $0.
6. Bob's transaction begins and reads the current balance of $0.
7. Alice's transaction writes a new balance of $500, then ends.
8. Bob's transaction writes a new balance of $100, then ends.

Naturally, Bob and Alice would be dismayed at this result. They expected to have $600 in their bank balance but have only $100, because Bob's transaction read the same original balance as Alice's. The bank might find some excuse ("excess static electricity" is one favorite), but the problem would be due to a lack of concurrency control.

So, semaphores on the entire database give ruinous performance and a complete lack of control gives manifestly incorrect results. Locking is a good compromise. There are two kinds of locks.

- *Write* (also known as exclusive) locks.
- *Read* (also known as shared) locks.

Write locks are like semaphores in that they give the right of exclusive access, except that they apply to only a portion of a database, e.g., a page. Any such lockable portion is variously referred to as a *data item*, an *item*, or a *granule*.

Read locks allow shared access. Thus, many transactions may hold a read lock on a data item x at the same time, but only one transaction may hold a write lock on x at any given time.

Usually, database systems acquire and release locks implicitly using an algorithm known as *Two-Phase Locking*, invented at IBM Almaden research by K. P. Eswaran, J. Gray, R. Lorie, and I. Traiger in 1976. That algorithm follows two rules (Figure 2.3):

1. A transaction must hold a lock on x before accessing x. (That lock should be a write lock if the transaction writes x and a read lock otherwise.)

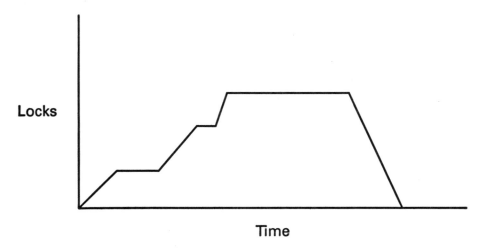

Figure 2.3 Two-Phase Rule: Once a Lock Is Released, No New Lock Can Be Acquired.

Table 2.1 ORIGINAL
DATABASE STATE

Account Owner	Balance
Ted	4000
Bob and Alice	100
Carol	0

2. A transaction must not acquire a lock on any item x after releasing a lock on any item y. (In practice, locks are released when a transaction ends.)

The second rule may seem strange. After all, why should releasing a lock on, say, Ted's account prevent a transaction from later obtaining a lock on Carol's account? Consider the following example.

Example: The Second Rule and the Perils of Releasing Shared Locks

Table 2.1 represents the original database state.

Suppose that there are two transactions. One transfers $1000 from Ted to Carol, and the other computes the sum of all deposits in the bank. Here is what happens.

1. The sum-of-deposits transaction obtains a read lock on Ted's account, reads the balance of $4000, then releases the lock.

2. The transfer transaction obtains a lock on Ted's account, subtracts $1000, then obtains a lock on Carol's account and writes, establishing a balance of $1000 in her account.

3. The sum-of-deposits transaction obtains a read lock on Bob and Alice's account, reads the balance of $100, then releases the lock. Then that transaction obtains a read lock on Carol's account and reads the balance of $1000 (resulting from the transfer).

So, the sum-of-deposits transaction overestimates the amount of money that is deposited.

————

The previous example teaches two lessons.

- The two-phase condition should apply to reads as well as writes.
- Many systems (e.g., ORACLE) give a default behavior in which write locks are held until the transaction completes, but read locks are released as soon as the data item is read (degree 2 isolation). This example shows that this

can lead to faulty behavior. *This means that if one wants concurrent correctness, one must sometimes request nondefault behavior.*

2.2.2 Lock Tuning

Lock tuning should proceed along several fronts.

1. Eliminate locking when it is unnecessary.

2. Take advantage of transactional context to chop transactions into small pieces.

3. Weaken isolation guarantees when the application allows it.

4. Use special system facilities for long reads.

5. Select the appropriate granularity of locking.

6. Change your data description data during quiet periods only. (Data Definition Language statements are considered harmful.)

7. Think about partitioning.

8. Circumvent hot spots.

9. Tune the deadlock interval.

You can apply each tuning suggestion independently of the others, but you must check that the appropriate isolation guarantees hold when you are done. The first three suggestions require special care, because they may jeopardize isolation guarantees if applied incorrectly. For example, the first one offers full isolation (obviously) provided a transaction executes alone. It will give no isolation guarantee if there can be arbitrary concurrent transactions.

Eliminate unnecessary locking

Locking is unnecessary in two cases:

1. When only one transaction runs at a time, e.g., when loading the database.

2. When all transactions are read-only, e.g., when doing decision support queries on archival databases.

In these cases, users should take advantage of options to reduce overhead by suppressing the acquisition of locks. (The overhead of lock acquisition consists of memory consumption for lock control blocks and processor time to process lock requests.) This may not provide an enormous performance gain, but the gain it does provide should be exploited.

Make your transaction short

The correctness guarantee that the concurrency control subsystem offers is given in units of transactions. At the highest degree of isolation, each transaction is guaranteed to appear as if it executed without being disturbed by concurrent transactions.

An important question is: How long should a transaction be? This is important because transaction length has two effects on performance:

- The more locks a transaction requests, the more likely it is that it will have to wait for some other transaction to release a lock.
- The longer a transaction T executes, the more time another transaction will have to wait if it is blocked by T.

Thus, in situations in which blocking can occur (i.e., when there are concurrent transactions some of which update data), short transactions are better than long ones. Short transactions are generally better for logging reasons as well, as we explain subsequently in the recovery section (pp. 27).

Sometimes, when one can characterize all the transactions that will occur during some time interval, one can "chop" transactions into shorter ones without losing isolation guarantees. The appendix presents a systematic approach to achieve this goal. Here are some motivating examples along with some intuitive conclusions.

Example: Update Blob with Credit Checks

A certain bank allows depositors to take out up to $1000 a day in cash. At night, one transaction (the "update blob" transaction) updates the balance of every accessed account and then the appropriate branch balance. Also, throughout the night, there are occasional credit checks (read-only transactions) on individual depositors that touch only the depositor account (not the branch). The credit checks arrive at random times, so are not required to reflect the day's updates. The credit checks have extremely variable response times, depending on the progress of the updating transaction. What should the application designers do?

Solution 1   Divide the update blob transaction into many small update transactions, each of which updates one depositor's account and the appropriate branch balance. These can execute in parallel. The effect on the accounts will be the same, because there will be no other updates at night. The credit check will still reflect the value of the account either before the day's update or after it.

Solution 2   You may have observed that the update transactions may now interfere with one another when they access the branch balances. If there are no other transactions, then those update transactions can be further subdivided into an update depositor account transaction and an update branch balance transaction.

Intuitively, each credit check acts independently in the previous example. Therefore breaking up the update transaction causes no problem. Moreover, no transaction depends on the consistency between the account balance value and the branch balance, permitting the further subdivision cited in Solution 2. Imagine now a variation of this example.

Example: Updates and Balances

Instead of including all updates to all accounts in one transaction, the application designers break them up into minitransactions, each of which updates a single depositor's account and the branch balance of the depositor's branch. The designers add an additional possible concurrent transaction that sums the account balances and the branch balances to see if they are equal. What should be done in this case?

Solution   The balance transaction can be broken up into several transactions. Each one would read the accounts in a single branch and the corresponding branch balance. The updates to the account and to the branch balance may no longer be subdivided into two transactions, however. The reason is that the balance transaction may see the result of an update to a depositor account but not see the compensating update to the branch balance.

———

These examples teach a simple lesson: *Whether or not a transaction T may be broken up into smaller transactions depends partially on what is concurrent with T.*

Informally, there are two questions to ask. (We present a formal characterization in the appendix. That characterization is not difficult but requires some graph theory.)

1. Will the transactions that are concurrent with T cause T to produce an inconsistent state or to observe an inconsistent value if T is broken up?

That's what happened when the purchase transaction was broken up into two transactions in the example *The Length of a Transaction* (p. 10). Notice, however, that the purchase transaction could have been broken up if it had been reorganized slightly. Suppose the purchase transaction first subtracted money from cash (rolling back if the subtraction made the balance negative) and then added the value of the item to inventory. Those two steps could become two transactions given the concurrent activity present in that example. The subtraction step can roll back the entire transaction before any other changes have been made to the database. Thus, rearranging a program to place the update that causes a rollback first may make a chopping possible.

2. Will the transactions that are concurrent with T be made inconsistent if T is broken up?

That's what would happen if the balance transaction ran concurrently with the finest granularity of update transactions i.e., where each depositor-branch update transaction was divided into two transactions, one for the depositor and one for the branch balance.

Here is a rule of thumb that often helps when chopping transactions (the appendix will present a systematic method for chopping up transactions):

Suppose transaction T accesses data X and Y, but any other transaction T' accesses at most one of X or Y. Then T can often be divided into two transactions, one of which accesses X and the other of which accesses Y, as illustrated in Figure 2.4.

This rule of thumb led us to break up the balance transaction into several transactions, each of which operates on the accounts of a single branch. This was possible, because all the small update transactions worked on a depositor account and branch balance of the same branch.

Caveat—warning: Transaction chopping as advocated here and in the appendix works correctly if properly applied. The important caution to keep in mind

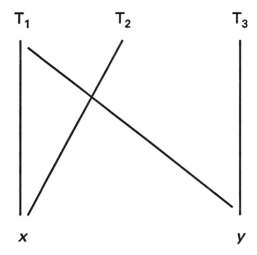

T_1 accesses x and y

T_2 accesses x

T_3 accesses y

Figure 2.4 When It Is Good to Split: Splitting T_1 into Two Transactions, One Accessing x and One Accessing y, Will Not Disturb Consistency of T_2 or T_3.

is that adding a new transaction to a set of existing transactions may invalidate all previously established choppings.

Weaken isolation guarantees carefully

Quite often, weakened isolation guarantees are sufficient. SQL I offers the following options:

1. *Degree 0:* Reads may access *dirty data*, i.e, data written by uncommitted transactions. If an uncommitted transaction aborts, then the read may have returned a value that was never installed in the database. Also, different reads by a single transaction to the same data will not be *repeatable*, i.e., they may return different values. Writes may overwrite the dirty data of other transactions. A transaction holds a write lock on x while writing x, then releases the lock immediately thereafter.

2. *Degree 1:* Reads may read dirty data and will not be repeatable. Writes may not overwrite other transactions' dirty data.

3. *Degree 2:* Reads may access only committed data, but reads are still not repeatable. In a classical locking implementation with a single version of each data item, write locks are acquired and released in a two-phased manner. A transaction holds a read lock on x when it reads it. Relational systems offer a slightly stronger guarantee known as *cursor stability*: During the time a transaction holds a "cursor," it holds its read locks. This is normally the time that it takes a single SQL statement to execute.

4. *Degree 3:* Reads may access only committed data, and reads are repeatable. Writes may not overwrite other transactions' dirty data. It appears as if each committed transaction executes in isolation, one at a time.

Some transactions do not require exact answers and, hence, do not require degree 3 isolation. For example, consider a statistical study transaction that counts the number of depositor account balances that are over $1000. Because an exact answer is not required, such a transaction need not keep read locks. Degree 2 or even degree 1 isolation may be enough.

The lesson is: *Begin with the highest degree of isolation (degree 3 in relational systems). If a given transaction (usually a long one) either suffers extensive deadlocks or causes significant blocking, consider weakening the degree of isolation, but do so with the awareness that the answers may be off slightly.*

Another situation in which correctness guarantees may be sacrificed occurs when a transaction includes human interaction and the transaction holds hot data.

Example: Airline Reservations

A reservation involves three steps:

1. Retrieve the list of seats available.
2. Determine which seat the customer wants.
3. Secure that seat.

If all this were encapsulated in a single transaction, then that transaction would hold the lock on the list of seats in a given plane while a reservations agent talks to a customer. At busy times, many other customers and agents might be made to wait.

To avoid this intolerable situation, airline reservation systems break up the act of booking a seat into two transactions and a nontransactional interlude. The first transaction reads the list of seats available. Then there is human interaction between the reservation agent and the customer. The second transaction secures a seat that was chosen by a customer. Because of concurrent activity, the customer may be told during step 2 that seat S is available and then be told after step 3 that seat S could not be secured. This happens rarely enough to be considered acceptable. Concurrency control provides the lesser guarantee that no two passengers will secure the same seat.

Use facilities for long reads

Some relational (e.g., ORACLE, RDB) and object-oriented systems (e.g., Gem-Stone) provide a facility whereby read-only queries hold no locks yet appear to execute at degree 3 isolation. The method they use is to save an old version of any data item that is changed after the read query begins.

Using this facility has the following implications:

- Read-only queries entail no locking overhead.
- Read-only queries can execute in parallel and on the same data as short update transactions without causing blocking or deadlocks.
- There is some time and space overhead, because the system must write and hold old versions of data that have been modified. The only data that will be saved, however, is that which is updated while the read-only query runs.

My guess is that most vendors will soon provide this facility, because of its evident usefulness. Two caveats should be kept in mind, however.

1. Read-write queries may execute incorrectly using this facility so should opt for full degree 3 isolation (e.g., the SERIALIZABLE option in ORA-CLE). To understand why, consider again the example *The Length of a Transaction* (p. 10). Suppose that the original application is written as one transaction, but the read portion holds no locks. Then the two transactions

in the scenario of that example can commit if they both read cash simultaneously. This would result in a negative cash balance.

2. In some cases, the space for the saved data may be too small. One may then face an unpleasant surprise in the form of a return code such as "snapshot too old."

Control the granularity of locking

Most modern database management systems offer different "granularities" of locks. That is, a transaction may obtain a table-level lock, a page-level lock, or, increasingly often, a record-level lock. A *page-level lock* will prevent concurrent transactions from accessing (if the page-level lock is a write lock) or modifying (if the page-level lock is a read lock) all records on that page. A *table-level lock* will prevent concurrent transactions from accessing or modifying (depending on the kind of lock) all pages that are part of that table and, by extension, all the records on those pages. Record-level locking is said to be *finer grained* than page-level locking, which, in turn, is finer grained than table-level locking.

If one were to ask the average application programmer on the street whether, say, record-level locking were better than page-level locking, he or she would probably say, "Yes, of course. Record-level locking will permit two different transactions to access different records on the same page. It must be better."

By and large this response is correct for online transaction environments. A rule of thumb backed by experience and theory is the following:

If every transaction accesses well under 1% of the records of any table and each of these records is on a different page, then record-level locking is better than page-level or table-level locking. Thus, the rule of thumb applies to any environment with many short transactions, each of which accesses a few random pages. In fact fine-granularity locking in this environment will give less blocking and fewer deadlocks than coarser granularity locking.

Fine-grained locking is not always good, however. Consider the following situations.

- One transaction wants to read and update the balance of every bank depositor and perform the appropriate updates to the branch balances.

This transaction would acquire far too many locks if it performed record-level locking. Also, if there were concurrent short update transactions, these would either abort, be blocked, or cause the balance update transaction to abort. (For example, the long transaction might scan and update Ted's account before Alice's (table 2.1, p. 15), whereas a transfer transaction may update those accounts in reverse order, creating a deadlock. One of the two transactions would then have to abort.) Thus, table granularity locking may help reduce lock management overhead as well as reduce the risk of deadlock-induced aborts.

- A transaction wishes to do a query, e.g., find all listings with last name "Robin" and modify their status. Assume there is a clustering index on last name.

In this case, the transaction would tend to acquire many record locks on the same data pages (because all the records with last name "Robin" will be colocated on a few pages). Page-level locking would incur less overhead without increasing the contention among transactions appreciably.

The conclusion is simple: *Long transactions should use table locks, medium length transactions based on clustering indexes should use page locks, and short transactions should use record locks.* Transaction length here is relative to the size of the table at hand: a long transaction is one that accesses nearly all the pages of a table in question.

Technical Digression: the size of locking granules

Y. C. Tay[2] of the University of Singapore presented a mathematical model to show when refining granularity is good. It went like this: Suppose that D is the number of lockable data items now (e.g., the number of pages) and D' would be the the number using a refined locking granularity (e.g., the number of records). Similarly, suppose that k is the average number of locks obtained by a transaction now and k' is the number required using the refined locking granularity. Refining the granularity, Tay showed, is worthwhile if $(k'/k)^2 < D'/D$. For example, if the accesses of certain applications access one record per page, then $D'/D > 1$, yet $k' = k$. Refining granularity would definitely help in that case. Thomasian and Ryu of IBM Watson Research have extended these results in various ways.

———

There are basically three tuning knobs that the user can manipulate to control granule size.

1. *Explicit control of granularity:* Some systems allow database programmers to specify the lock granularity they want. For example, in ORACLE, a long update transaction might precede its table access with the command

- LOCK TABLE ACCOUNT IN EXCLUSIVE MODE

[2] Y. C. Tay, *Locking Performance in Centralized Databases.* Orlando: Academic Press, 1987.

2. *Setting the escalation point:* Some systems such as INGRES will acquire the default (finest) granularity lock until the number of acquired locks exceeds some threshold set by the database administrator. At that point, the next coarser granularity lock will be acquired. This is called "escalation." The general rule of thumb is to set the threshold high enough so that in an online environment of relatively short transactions, escalation will never take place.

3. *Size of the lock table:* If the administrator selects a small lock table size, the system will be forced to escalate the lock granularity. This will be bad if there is a lot of concurrent contention.

Suggestion: A Stress Test on Your System's Concurrency Control Mechanism:
Put ten indexes on a table. Then bombard the table with inserts. For example, perform fifty concurrent insert transactions per second.
You may find that your system deadlocks, unless you escalate locks to the table level. That is a bad sign if this scenario may occur in your application.

Data description language (DDL) statements are considered harmful

Data description data (also known as the system catalog or metadata) is information about table names, column widths and so on. DDL is the language used to access and manipulate the system catalog. Catalog data must be accessed by every transaction that performs a compilation, adds or removes a table, adds or removes an index, or changes an attribute description. As a result, the catalog can easily become a hot spot and therefore a bottleneck. My general recommendation therefore is to avoid updates to the system catalog during heavy system activity, especially if you are using dynamic SQL.

Think about partitioning

One of the principles from chapter 1 held that partitioning breaks bottlenecks. Overcoming concurrent contention requires frequent application of this principle.

Example: Insertion to History

If all insertions to a data collection go to the last page of the file containing that collection, then the last page will be a concurrency control bottleneck. This is often the case for history files and security files. A good strategy is to partition insertions to the file across different pages and possibly different disks.

This strategy requires some criterion for distributing the inserts. Here are some possibilities.

1. Set up many insertion points and insert into them randomly. This will work provided the file is essentially write-only (like a history file) or whose only readers are scans.

2. Set up a clustering index based on some interesting attribute that is not correlated with the time of insertion. (If the attribute's values are correlated with the time of insertion, then use a hash data structure as the clustering index, as we describe in the next chapter.) In that way, different inserted records will likely be put into different pages.

One might wonder how much partitioning to specify. A good rule of thumb is to specify at least $n/4$ insertion points where n is the maximum number of concurrent transactions writing to the potential bottleneck.

––––––

Example: Free Lists

Free lists are data structures that govern the allocation and deallocation of real memory pages in buffers. Locks on free lists are held only as long as the allocation or deallocation takes place, but free lists can still become bottlenecks.

The rule of thumb is to specify a number of free lists equal to the maximum number of concurrent threads of control. For example, in ORACLE, you can specify this tuning parameter, called FREE_LIST_PROC, for each table.

––––––

Circumventing hot spots

A *hot spot* is a piece of data that is accessed by many transactions and is updated by some. Hot spots cause bottlenecks, because each updating transaction must complete before any other transaction can obtain a lock on the hot data item. (Use

monitoring tools, such as those discussed in chapter 7, section 4, to find hot spots.)
There are three techniques for circumventing hot spots.

1. Use partitioning to eliminate it, as discussed earlier.
2. Access the hot spot as late as possible in the transaction.

Because transactions hold locks until they end, rewriting a transaction to
obtain the lock on a hot data item as late as possible will minimize the time
that the transaction holds the lock.

3. Use special database management facilities.

Here is an example. In many applications, transactions that insert data associate a unique identifier with each new data item. When different insert
transactions execute concurrently, they must somehow coordinate among
themselves to avoid giving the same identifier to different data items.

One way to do this is to associate a counter with the database. Each insert
transaction increments the counter, performs its insert and whatever other
processing it must perform, and then commits. The problem is that the
counter becomes a bottleneck, because a transaction will (according to two-
phase locking) release its lock on the counter only when the transaction
commits.

Some systems, for example ORACLE and IMS/FastPath, offer a facility that
enables transactions to hold a lock on the counter only while accessing the
counter and not until the transaction completes. This eliminates the counter
as a bottleneck but may introduce a small problem.

Consider an insert transaction I that increments the counter then aborts. Before I aborts, a second transaction I' may increment the counter further.
Thus, the counter value obtained by I will not be associated with any data
item. That is, there may be gaps in the counter values. Most applications
can tolerate such gaps

Tune the deadlock checking interval

The two-phase locking algorithm, used in most database systems, is vulnerable to
deadlock. (See appendix A1 concerning real-time databases for methods to avoid
deadlock when you know your transaction population very well.) Some systems
offer the possibility of setting the time interval between checks for deadlocks.
Other systems allow users to set the waiting timeout threshold; the threshold is
the maximum time a transaction will wait for a lock before aborting.

Extreme cases give the major idea behind any tuning effort of these times.

1. If there is little update activity and the transactions are short, then there is little probability of deadlock, so the deadlock interval (or timeout threshold) should be long.

2. If deadlocks happen frequently, then it is good to break them quickly, otherwise the blocked transactions in the deadlock will cause other transactions to block as well. In this case, the deadlock interval (or timeout threshold) should be short.

2.3 LOGGING AND THE RECOVERY SUBSYSTEM

Many database management systems make a claim like the following:

Our system has an integrated physical and logical recovery mechanism that protects database integrity in case of hardware and software failures.

The claim is exaggerated, to say the least. After all, an arbitrary software failure could transform a good database state to an arbitrarily erroneous one. Similarly, enough hardware failures could cause data to be lost or corrupted. For the best database management systems, the truth is much closer to the following:

Our system can protect database integrity against single hardware failures (of a processor, network or any disk drive) and a few software failures (failures of the client, a few addressing errors within the server, and fail-stop crashes of the operating system).

In practice, two kinds of hardware failures can be tolerated:

1. A *fail-stop* failure of a processor and erasure of its random access memory. (Fail-stop means that when the processor fails, it stops. On the hardware of many vendors such as IBM, Tandem Stratus, and Sequoia, redundant checking circuitry stops the processor upon detection of failure.)

2. The fail-stop failure of a disk, provided enough redundant disks are available.

Systems that use mirrored disks, dual-powered controllers, dual-bus configurations and back-up processors can essentially eliminate the effect of such errors. For example, Jim Gray reports that Tandem Non-Stop systems have relegated hardware failures to under 10% of their system outages.[3]

As a side benefit, certain facilities (like database dumps to remote backups and process pairs) used to protect against hardware failures can be used to recover a database state, at least partially, even in the face of software failures. Most (over

---

[3] J. Gray, "A Census of Tandem System Availability, 1985-1990," *IEEE Trans. on Reliability*, vol. 39, no. 4, pp. 409-418, 1990.

99%) software failures occur only once and cause the system to stop. They are called "Heisenbugs."[4]

From the viewpoint of speed and hardware cost, however, the recovery subsystem is pure overhead and significant overhead at that. To understand how to tune to minimize this overhead, you should understand the basic algorithms for recovery.

2.3.1 Principles of Recovery

Theseus used a string to undo his entry into the labyrinth. Two thousand years later, the Grimm brothers report a similar technique used by Haensel and Gretel who discovered that the log should be built of something more durable than bread crumbs.[5]

Recall that transactions are the unit of isolation for the purposes of concurrency control. Transactions are also the unit of recovery in the following two senses:

1. The effects of *committed* transactions should be permanent. That is, changes should persist even after the completion of the transactions that make those changes.

2. Transactions should be *atomic*. That is, following the recovery from a hardware failure, it should be possible to reconstruct the database to reflect the updates of all *committed* (i.e., successfully completed) transactions. It should also be possible to eliminate the effects of any updates performed by aborted (i.e., rolled back) or unfinished transactions.[6] Figure 2.5 shows the states of transactions.

Achieving the first objective requires putting the data of committed transactions on *stable storage*—storage that is immune to failures. Complete immunity is impossible to achieve, but a good approximation is possible. As a first step, stable storage must be built out of media (e.g., disks, tapes, or battery-backed random access memory) that survive power failures. Such media are called *durable*. As a second step, in order to survive failures of durable media, such as disk crashes, the data must be replicated on several units of durable media, such as redundant disks.

---

[4] Most such "Heisenbugs," occur because of some unusual interaction between different components according to E. Adams's article "Optimizing Preventive Service of Software Products," *IBM Journal of Research and Development*, vol. 28, no. 1, 1984.

[5] Jim Gray and Andreas Reuter, *Transaction Processing: Concepts and Techniques.* San Mateo Calif.: Morgan-Kaufmann, 1992.

[6] These two rules imply, in practice, that no committed transaction should depend on the updates of an unfinished or aborted transaction. That is ensured by the locking algorithms.

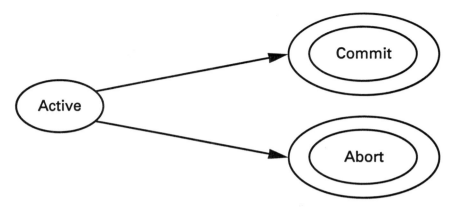

Figure 2.5   States of Transactions: Once a Transaction Enters Commit or Abort,
It Cannot Change Its Mind.

Achieving transaction atomicity

Algorithms to achieve transaction atomicity are based on two simple principles.

1. Before a given transaction commits, it must be possible to undo the effects of that transaction, even if random access memory fails. This implies that the *before images* of the updates of the transaction (i.e., the values of the data items before the transaction writes them) must remain on stable storage until commit time. On failure, they can be written to the database disks if they are not already there.

2. Once a transaction commits, it must be possible to install the updates that the transaction has made into the database, even if random access memory fails. Therefore the *after images* of the updates of the transaction (i.e., the values of the data items that the transaction writes) must be written to stable storage sometime before the commit actually takes place. In that way, if there is a failure any time after the database commit takes place, it will be possible to "redo" the effects of those updates (i.e., install the updates into the database).

The sharp (but still uneducated) reader may wonder how it is possible to have both the before and after images on stable storage before the commit point. After all, there is room for only one of them on the database disks.[7]

It is true that the database disks can store only one of the two kinds of images. So, stable storage must contain more than just the database. The other

---

[7] We use "database disks" as shorthand for "the durable media on which the database is stored." Until we discuss disk failures, we will assume that the database disks are stable.

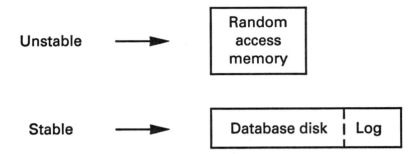

Figure 2.6   Stable Storage Holds Log as Well as Database.

area on stable storage is called the *log* (Figure 2.6). It may contain after images, before images, or both.

Commercial logging algorithms work as follows:

- The recovery subsystem writes the after images of each transaction's updates to the log before the transaction commits in order to satisfy principle 2 above. An important tuning decision is to determine whether the transaction's after images should be written to the database disks immediately after commit or whether those updates can be delayed. Delaying is better for failure-free performance, but may slow down recovery time as we will discuss in section 2.3.2 (p. 34).

- Most systems also write uncommitted after images to the database disks when there is no room left in the database buffer (section 2.4.2 contains a detailed discussion of the buffer). In order not to jeopardize principle 1, the recovery subsystem must ensure that the log contains the before image of each data item. It can do this by explicitly writing the before image or by using the value written by the last committed write on that data item. This is known as a *redo-undo* logging algorithm.

Every logging algorithm establishes the following guarantee:

(i)   *current database state = current state of database disks + log*

The current database state is the state reflecting all committed transactions. By contrast, the database disks reflect only the committed transactions physically on the database disks. During normal operation, some transactions may have been committed on the log, but some of their updates may not yet have been written to the database disks.

Logging variants

Most commercial systems log an entire page whenever a portion of a page is modified. This is called *page-level logging*. It is also possible to log just a portion of a page, e.g., divide the page into some number of portions and log all modified portions. This is called *byte-level logging*. This saves log disk space, especially if the page size is large. A third possibility is to log each changed record. This is called *record-level logging*. Some object-oriented systems use *object-level logging*. All these approaches log the "state" of a new (or old) page, so are called "state-based."

By contrast, there is a technique known as *logical logging* in which the log information is the operation and argument that caused an update. For example, the logged operation might be "insert into employee," and the argument may be "(143-56-9087, Hackett, . . .)." This technique saves log space because it omits detailed information about index updates. A group at IBM Almaden research, led by C. Mohan, has studied logical logging for this purpose. Systems from IBM and Tandem have incorporated logical logging and the idea will surely become widespread in the near future.

Checkpoints

To prevent the log from growing too large, the recovery subsystem periodically copies the latest committed updates from the log to the database disks. This act is called a *checkpoint*. Setting the interval between checkpoints is a tuning parameter as we will discuss in section 2.3.2 (p. 35). Checkpoints cause overhead, but save space in some cases and reduce recovery time.

Database dumps

A *database dump* is a transaction-consistent state of the entire database at a given time. A *transaction-consistent* state is one that reflects the updates of committed transactions only. Note that, in contrast to a checkpoint, the database dump consists of the entire database (rather than the latest updates only).

If a failure corrupts the database disks, then it is possible to reconstruct the correct state of the database from the previous database dump combined with the log. (In the absence of a dump, a failure of a database disk entails a loss of data, unless the data on that disk is duplicated on at least one other disk.) That is, the dump offers the following guarantee:

(ii)   *current database state = log + database dump*

Because the log enters into both equations (i) and (ii), make sure it is reliable. You might consider mirroring the log, i.e., replicating the log on two disks. Also, since the equations show that recreating the current database state requires the presence of either the disk database or the dumped database, separate the dumped data from the disk database.

Database dumps offer an important side benefit that can be relevant to an application that can afford hardware but has trouble fitting all its long transactions into the batch window. The database dump can be used to populate an archival database against which queries can be posed that do not require extremely up-to-date information, e.g., decision support queries or statistical queries.

Applications for which the data must be available virtually all the time may require that the entire system be mirrored. In that case, database dumps are rarely necessary, because one of the two mirrored systems is likely to survive any single failure.

Group commit

If every committing transaction causes a write to the log, then the log disk(s) may become a bottleneck. Therefore, many systems use a strategy known as *group commit*. According to this strategy, the updates of many transactions are written together to a log. If your application must support many concurrent short update transactions, then ensure that your database management system offers group commit and that it is turned on.

The only conceivable disadvantage of group commit is that a transaction's locks cannot be released until its updates have been written to the log. Because group commit delays those updates, group commits will cause locks to be held longer. This may cause a problem with very hot data items.

2.3.2 Tuning the Recovery Subsystem

There are the four main ways to tune the recovery subsystem. They can be applied individually or in combination.

1. Put the log on a dedicated disk or disks to avoid seeks.
2. Delay writing updates to database disks as long as possible.
3. Trade desired recovery time against time and space overhead when setting checkpoint and database dump intervals.
4. Reduce the size of large update transactions.

Put log on separate disk

Because the log is on stable storage and because, for many systems, stable storage means disk, transactions that update must perform disk writes to the log. This is bad news. The corresponding good news is that, in the absence of a failure, the log can be written sequentially and in large chunks. Therefore, if a disk has nothing but the log on it, then the disk rarely does seeks and hence can maintain a very high I/O rate. So, the very first use of an extra disk should be to segregate log data onto a disk of its own (or several disks if you are mirroring). As mentioned earlier, reliability considerations suggest separating the database disks from the log in any case.

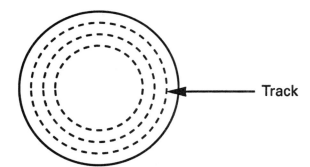

Figure 2.7 Surface of Platter on Disk. Concentric Dashed Circles Are Called Tracks.

Technical Digression: background comment on disks

A disk is a collection of circular platters placed one on top of the other and rotating around a common axis (called a spindle). Each platter, except the top and bottom platters, has two read-write surfaces. (The top surface of the top platter and the bottom surface of the bottom platter are unused.) The data on each surface is held on *tracks*, each of which is a circle. Each platter is associated with a disk *head*. To access the data on track *i* of a given platter, the disk head must be over track *i*. At any time, all disk heads associated with a disk are over the same track on their respective platters. The set of track *i*'s is called the *i*th *cylinder*. Thus, the set of disk heads moves from cylinder to cylinder (Figure 2.7).

The time that it takes to access a disk is made up of three significant components.

1. *Seek time*: the time it takes to move the disk head (the reading and writing device) to the proper track (about 10 milliseconds).

2. *Rotational delay*: the time to wait until the proper portion of the spinning track is underneath the disk head (about 10 milliseconds).

3. *Read/Write time*: the time to read or write the data on the spinning track (between 1 and 10 kilobytes per millisecond).

Rotational delay can be minimized by reading or writing large chunks of data at a time. In fact the time to read or write a track is not much greater than the time to read or write a portion of the track. This explains why reading pages in advance of their need and group commits are important optimizations—an application of the principle that start-up costs are high, but running costs are low.

Seek time can be minimized in two ways.

1. The best way is to ensure that subsequent accesses continue from where previous ones left off. This explains why it is good to keep log data on a disk of its own. When writing such data, the operating system will ensure that after one track is filled, writing proceeds on a different track of the same cylinder.

2. The next best way is to put frequently accessed data on the middle track of the disk if the disk is magnetic. If the disk is optical and has more data on outer tracks than inner tracks (CLV format), then put frequently accessed data a little closer to the outermost track than to the innermost one.[8]

The effects of seeks and rotational delay can be substantial. A good quality disk can perform 50 random disk accesses per second at best. (A random disk access is one that accesses a cylinder and track irrespective of previous accesses. So, most of these accesses will involve seek time and rotational delay.) If each access retrieves a 4-kilobyte page, then the total throughput is 200 kilobytes per second. If read (or written) sequentially, the same disk can offer a throughput between 1 and 10 megabytes per second. Thus, a well-organized disk can be a factor of ten or more faster than a poorly organized one for applications that do a lot of scanning.

Buffered commits

As you already know, before a database transaction commits, it writes the after images of the pages (or records, in some cases) it has updated onto the log. The question is: What should happen immediately after commit?

There are two options.

- *Unbuffered commit strategy:* Write the after images into the database after committing.
- *Buffered commit strategy:* Keep each after image x in random access memory until it is "convenient" to write it. Normally, this means waiting until the database disk heads are over the cylinder containing x.

Using the unbuffered commit strategy, recovery from random access memory failures is fast. The reason is that almost all the updates of committed transactions are already on the database disks.

The buffered commit strategy gives much higher performance during normal (failure-free) operation, however. There are two reasons for this.

1. Writing all the updates of a committing transaction onto the log disk constitutes a sequential write (therefore no seeks), whereas those same updates

---

[8] D. A. Ford and S. Christodoulakis at the University of Waterloo in Canada have an ongoing research project on this subject. See for example, their paper in the 1991 Very Large Data Base (VLDB) conference.

may be distributed widely on the database disks. Writing those updates immediately to the database disks, as done by the unbuffered commit strategy, will cause the database disks to do many random writes (therefore many seeks). On the other hand, a buffered commit strategy can schedule writes to avoid seeks, thus reducing the load on the database disks.

The database administrator must tune buffered commit to achieve two conflicting goals

- The database buffer should not fill up with committed pages that have not been flushed to disk. (This suggests writing recently committed pages to disk sooner rather than later.)
- There should be few random writes to the database disks. (This suggests writing such pages later rather than sooner.)

Each database management system offers its own tuning tools for this facility. For example, INGRES allows the database administrator to specify the number of asynchronous "daemon" threads that write committed pages to the database disks. By contrast, ORACLE (using the DBWR parameters) allows the administrator to specify when the system should write committed pages to the database disks based on the number of such pages that haven't yet been written.

2. The buffered commit strategy can sometimes avoid writing an update to the database disks altogether. For example, if many transactions write the same data item, then that item needs to be written to the database disks only at checkpoint time as opposed to once each time it is updated. Again, this reduces the load on the database disks.

Setting intervals for database dumps and checkpoints

Setting database dump intervals is a tradeoff between recovery time following a failure of one or more database disks and online performance. The more often the dump is performed, the less data will have to be read from the dumped database following a disk crash. Very few applications require dumps to occur more frequently than once or twice a day.

Some system administrators wonder whether it is worthwhile to perform dumps at all. Dumps offer the following benefits:

- If a database disk fails and there is no dump, then the system will lose data irretrievably. Thus, the dump is an insurance against database disk failure. Note, however, that a log failure will cause data to be lost whether or not there is a dump.

- A dump can be used for data mining queries that do not require completely up-to-date information.

A dump has two costs:

- It increases response time while it occurs.
- It requires space to store. The dump should not be stored on the database disks. If it is, then the dump may be corrupted at the same time as the database, causing a loss of data.

Recall that a checkpoint forces data that is only on the log and in the database buffer to the database disks. Thus, a checkpoint is only necessary when using a buffered commit strategy. A checkpoint offers two benefits:

1. A checkpoint reduces the time and log space needed to recover when there is a failure of random access memory, because committed updates will already be on the database disks.

2. A checkpoint does not reduce the log space needed to recover from database disk failures. To recover from such failures, the log must hold all the updates since the last database dump.

The main disadvantage is that a checkpoint degrades online performance, though much less than a dump. Applications that demand high availability should do checkpoints every 20 minutes or so. Less demanding applications should perform checkpoints less frequently.

From batch to minibatch

A transaction that performs many updates without stringent response time constraints is called a *batch* transaction. If such a transaction is excessively long, the buffer may become full, and a rollback resulting from a failure may be very costly. An approach around this problem is to break the transaction into small transactions (minibatch). Each minitransaction updates a persistent variable saying how much it has accomplished.

For example, suppose the task is to update a set of customer accounts in sorted order based on customer_ID. Each minibatch transaction can update a set of account records and then put the customer_ID of the last account modified into a special database variable called, say, lastcustomerupdated. These minibatch transactions execute serially. In case of failure, the program will know to continue modifying accounts from lastcustomerupdated onward.

Caveat. Because this transformation is a form of transaction chopping, you must ensure that you maintain any important isolation guarantees, as discussed in this chapter's section 2.2.2 (pp. 16 ff) and in the appendix.

2.4 OPERATING SYSTEM CONSIDERATIONS

The operating system performs several functions that can have a significant impact on database application performance.

- The operating system schedules *threads* of control (called processes in some operating systems), the fundamental units of execution in a computer system. Issues here include the amount of time needed to schedule a new thread (the less the better); the time slice of a database thread (should be long); and whether different threads should have different priorities (database threads should all run at the same priority for most applications).
- The operating system manages virtual and physical memory mappings. The issue here is how big to make the portion of virtual memory that is shared by all database threads, called the *database buffer* and how much random access memory to devote to that buffer.
- The operating system sets the number of user threads of control that can access the database concurrently. The goal is to have enough to accommodate the available users while avoiding thrashing.
- The operating system manages files. Issues here include whether the files can span devices (necessary for large databases); whether the files can be built from contiguous portions of the disk (helpful for scan performance); whether file reads can perform lookahead (also helpful for scan performance); whether accessing a page of a large file takes, on the average, more time than accessing a page of a small file (obviously should be avoided); and whether a process can write pages asynchronously (useful for the buffered commit strategy discussed earlier).
- The operating system gives timing information. This can help determine whether an application is I/O-bound or processor-bound.
- The operating system controls communication between address spaces on the same site (i.e., the same processor or another processor within the same shared memory multiprocessor) and address spaces on different sites. The main issue here is the performance of messages. If they are fast, then database performance will be better. Otherwise, database performance will be worse. There is little you can do about this as a tuner, except take the speed into account when deciding on a distribution strategy.

2.4.1 Scheduling

Each time an operating system schedules a different thread of control, it goes through some computation that is useless to the database application. Therefore the database tuner should try to minimize the amount of time spent switching contexts. There are two obvious ways to do this.

1. Choose an operating system that has a lightweight thread-switching facility. Many newer operating systems offer this facility. IBM's CICS, although not itself an operating system, introduced this notion in the late 1960s.

2. Minimize the number of such switches. A switch is inevitable when an application makes an I/O request, but optional reasons for switches should be avoided. This means that time slice-driven interrupts should be infrequent for the great majority of database applications that are concerned primarily with high throughput rather than low response time. A good compromise on modern microprocessors is to give each thread a 1-second time slice. This is enough computation time for most applications and will prevent an infinite loop from hanging the system.

A second aspect of scheduling has to do with thread priorities. Two bad priority decisions can hurt database performance.

1. *Obviously bad decision*: The database system runs at a lower priority than other applications. When those applications consume a lot of resources, the database applications will perform badly.

2. *Subtly bad decision*: Transactions do not all run at the same priority. You may be tempted to give threads that execute transactions with greater importance higher priorities. Unfortunately, this strategy may backfire if transactions with different priorities access and may conflict on the same data item. Consider the following example:

Example: Priority Inversion
Suppose that transaction T_1 has the highest priority, followed by T_2 (which is at the same priority as several other transactions), followed by T_3.

1. Transaction T_3 executes and obtains a lock on some data item x.

2. Transaction T_1 starts to execute and requests a lock on x but is blocked because T_3 has a lock on x.

3. Transaction T_2 now starts to execute (without accessing x). Other transactions of its same priority continue to execute for a long time, thereby precluding T_3 from executing to completion.

Indirectly, T_2 and other transactions of its same priority prevent T_1 from executing. This is called *priority inversion* (Figure 2.8).

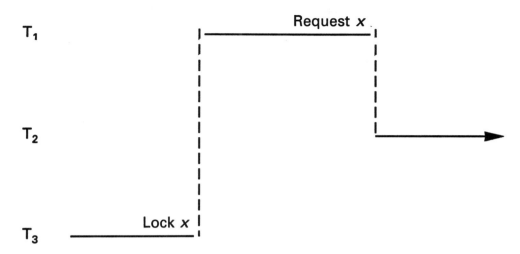

Figure 2.8   Priority Inversion: T_1 Waits for Lock that Only T_3 Can Release. T_2 Runs Instead, However.

Some database systems handle this problem by a method known as *priority inheritance*. The idea is that once a thread acquires a lock, its scheduling priority increases to the maximum level of any thread that is waiting for that lock. As you can see by reviewing the previous example, priority inheritance protects against priority inversion.

- If your system does not protect against priority inversion, then give the same priority to all pairs of transactions that may conflict.

- If your system does protect against priority inversion, then you may choose to give higher priority to online transactions than to batch ones. However, this may generate additional thread-switching overhead thus hurting throughput.

2.4.2 Database Buffer

Because accesses to disk take much longer than accesses to random access memory, the database tuner must try to minimize the number of disk accesses. One way to do this is to store the entire database in random access (electronic) memory. This is feasible only for certain applications, however (see appendix A1 on real-time databases for example). The goal of memory tuning for all other applications is to ensure that frequently read pages rarely require disk accesses.[9]

---

[9] This discussion concerns the data page buffer, but similar considerations apply to the stored procedure buffer and the other buffers that many database systems offer.

Database processes

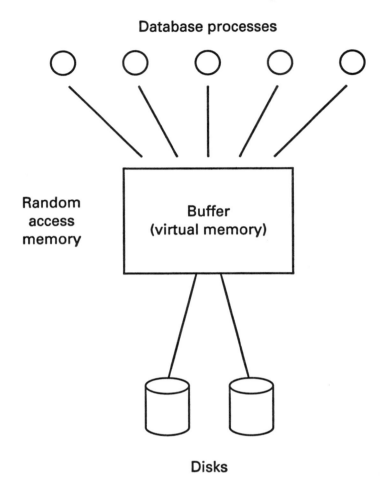

Random access memory

Buffer (virtual memory)

Disks

Figure 2.9   Buffer Is in Virtual Memory, Though Its Greater Part Should Be in Random Access Memory.

Concurrent transactions in a database application share data in a certain portion of virtual memory known as the *database buffer*, *buffer*, or sometimes the *database cache*. The purpose of the buffer is to reduce the number of physical accesses to secondary storage (usually disks). Figure 2.9 shows the components of the buffer.

The impact of the buffer on the number of physical accesses depends on three different parameters.

1. *Logical reads and writes*: These are the pages that the database management system accesses via system read and write commands. Some of these pages will be found in the buffer. Others will translate to physical reads and writes.

2. *Database Management System (DBMS) page replacements*: These are the physical accesses to secondary storage that occur when a page must be brought into the buffer and there are no free pages. By increasing the number of asynchronous paging daemons as discussed in this chapter's section 2.3 (pp. 34 ff), the tuner can ensure that replacements occur rarely.

3. *Operating system paging.* These are physical accesses to secondary storage (in some systems, a swap disk) that occur when part of the buffer space lies outside random access memory. The tuner should ensure that such paging occurs rarely too.

Assuming that paging and page replacements occur rarely, the important question is how many logical accesses become physical accesses. The *hit ratio* is defined by the following equation:

$$hit\ ratio = \frac{number\ of\ logical\ accesses - number\ of\ physical\ accesses}{number\ of\ logical\ accesses}$$

That is, the hit ratio is the number of logically accessed pages found in the buffer divided by the total number of logically accessed pages.

The tuning parameter that determines the hit ratio is the size of buffer memory. To tune the buffer size, run a typical load for an hour. Check to see whether the hit ratio is too low. Systems with ample random access memory should aim for a hit ratio of more than 90%. This may be impossible, however, for systems with extremely large databases and lots of random I/O. For example, if 30% of the accesses may touch any page in the database with equal likelihood and the database contains hundreds of billions of bytes, then even a system with a gigabyte-sized buffer will have a hit ratio of 70% or less. So, the best strategy is to *increase the size of the buffer until the hit ratio flattens out, while making sure that DBMS page replacements and operating system paging are low.* Some systems, such as ORACLE, offer a utility that will tell the user what the hit ratio would be if the buffer were larger.

The second tuning parameter is to buy additional random access memory. This should be considered when two factors hold.

1. Increasing the size of the buffer within the currently available random access memory would cause significantly more paging.

2. Increasing the buffer size would increase the database access hit ratio significantly. That is, significantly more logical I/O's would access pages in the buffer.

If some set of applications X have much more demanding response time requirements than the rest of the applications Y and access different data, then consider dedicating a database buffer to X and a different one in Y. (This facility is available in DB2, for example.) However, if all applications have basically the same requirements, then use a single buffer.

2.4.3 How Much Memory Is Economical

Even ignoring performance considerations, you may want to move some data into main memory from disk if you access it often enough. Here is some quantitative guidance derived from a paper by Jim Gray and Frank Putzolu.[10]

The question they pose is when does it make sense to keep a particular page of data in random access memory as opposed to bringing it into memory periodically from disk?

Clearly, the more frequently the page is accessed, the more useful it is to put the page in memory. Similarly, the less expensive random access memory is compared with the cost of disk accesses, the more pages should be kept in random access memory. Now let us derive simple equations to guide this decision.

Quantitative Discussion:

Consider a selection of technology with the following cost characteristics (I've given the numbers solely for the purposes of illustration):

- A high-quality (but slow) 1-gigabyte disk offers 20 random page accesses per second and costs $10,000. That is $500 per access per second and $0.01 per kilobyte.
- Each access per second costs $1,000 in processor, channel, and controller cost. Taking these two points per second, we conclude that the access cost A is $1,500 per access per second.
- Random access memory (including support circuitry and packaging hardware) costs $0.1 per kilobyte.
- The page size B is 4 kilobytes.

Suppose page p is accessed every $I = 3,000$ seconds. Should you keep it permanently in random access memory, considering cost factors alone?

- You save A/I dollars in accesses per second, i.e. $1,500/3,000 = $0.5.
- You spend $0.4 for the 4 kilobytes of extra random access memory and $0.04 for 4 kilobytes of disk storage as backing store.

---

[10] J. Gray and F. Putzolu, "The 5 minute rule for trading memory for disc accesses and the 5 byte rule for trading memory for CPU time," ACM SIGMOD Conference, 1987.

So, it would be worth it to keep p in random access memory. If the inter-access time is greater than 3,410 seconds, however, then keeping the page on disk is more economical.

In general, it is better to keep a page in memory if A/I is greater than the cost of the random access memory to store the page (the cost of storage on disk is usually negligible by comparison).

2.4.4 Multiprogramming Level

Many system administrators believe that the more concurrent users their system supports the better. It is true that increasing the number of threads of control (usually, in this case, within the database system's server) helps consume idle cycles of underutilized processor(s). However, high multiprogramming levels can actually hurt performance if either of the following limitations is reached.

1. The amount of random access memory the users occupy exceeds the real memory of the system, causing paging either in process space or in the buffer.

2. Lock conflicts arise from the large number of concurrently running transactions.

Various workers have proposed conflicting rules of thumb for setting the amount of concurrency. It turns out that no rule of thumb is valid in all cases, so a better approach if you have a stable application environment is to use the Incremental Steps method:[11]

• Start with a low bound on the maximum number of concurrent transactions allowed.

• Increase the bound by one and then measure the performance.

• If the performance improves, then increase the bound again. Otherwise, you have reached a local performance maximum. (Theoretical and practical studies indicate that the first local maximum is probably also an absolute maximum.)

If your application is stable but has different transaction profiles at different times during the day, then your bound should change with your application's profiles. Efforts to automate the selection of multiprogramming level are in progress at various research centers including Hans-Juerg Schek and Gerhard Weikum's group at Zurich's ETH, and Alex Thomasian at IBM.

[11] Hans-Ulrick Heiss and Roger Wagner, "Adaptive Load Control in Transaction Processing Systems," in Barcelona, September 1991, *Proceedings of the 17th International Conference on Very Large Data Bases*, pp. 47-54.

2.4.5 Files: Disk Layout and Access

File systems allow users to create, delete, read and write files (which are sequences either of bytes or records). The main tunable parameters for file systems you are likely to encounter follow:

- *The size of disk chunks that will be allocated at one time*: Some file systems call these *extents*. If many queries tend to scan portions of a file, then it is good to specify track-sized (or larger-sized) extents for the sake of performance. Write performance can also be improved by using extents. For example, logs and history files will benefit significantly from the use of extents or other slicing techniques. If access to a file is completely random, then small extents are better, because small extents give better space utilization.

- *The usage factor on disk pages*: Some systems, such as ORACLE, offer users the control of how full a page can be and still allow insertions. The higher the *usage factor*, the fuller the page can be when insertions occur. If there are many updates to rows that may make them larger (e.g., conversions of NULLS to non-NULLS) or insertions to a table having a clustering index, then it is good to make the usage factor low (70% or less). Otherwise, use a high usage factor (90% or higher) to improve the performance of table scans.

- *The number of pages that may be prefetched*: Again, prefetching is useful for queries that scan files. Unless random access memory is scarce, the number of pages to be prefetched should correspond to a large portion of a track.

- *The number of levels of indirection to access a particular page*: This is an important issue for UNIX-based systems. Because the UNIX file index structure interposes more levels of indirection for pages towards the end of a file than for pages near the beginning of the file, it may take much longer to access the former than the latter. To avoid this, many database management systems built on top of UNIX use "raw slices."

2.5 HARDWARE TUNING

The world would be much simpler if tuning the hardware could be done independently from tuning the software. Unfortunately, the two are intimately related. Although expert tuners often begin with an analysis of processor utilization, I/O activity, and paging, they rarely stop there.

The reason is simple: The fact that a resource is overloaded does not imply that you have to buy more of it. It may be better to add indexes to support important queries for example. That is, fixing the software may lessen the load on the hardware.

This section addresses what to do after you have determined (through the techniques of chapter 7) that more hardware may help. As the subsections indicate, the order in which to enhance the hardware configuration is first to purchase memory, then disks, then processing power, then network bandwidth.

2.5.1 Add Memory

In most systems, the cheapest hardware improvement is to add memory and then to increase the size of the buffer pool. This will reduce the load to the disks if it increases the hit ratio without increasing paging.

2.5.2 Add Disks If Saturated

If adding (reasonable amounts of) memory doesn't help, then buy disks and controllers if all the disks are overloaded. A disk is overloaded whenever there is significant queueing, usually at around 35 random accesses per disk spindle. Here are some uses of extra disks (and controllers).

1. Put the log on a separate disk to ensure that writes to the log are sequential, as we discussed in the recovery section.

2. Use disk mirroring as a mechanism to improve read throughput. Most disk mirroring subsystems divide the read load among the mirrored disks. So, disk mirroring can help read-intensive applications that are disk-bound. (Technical point: Some database management systems such as SYBASE allow writes to mirrored disks to occur in parallel, if they go through independent controllers, but force the writes to occur one at a time if they go through the same controller. Parallel writes will be much faster.)

3. Partition large tables across several disks. Perhaps even under-utilize the space on your disks to ensure that they can handle the access load. Depending on your application, you may choose two different partitioning strategies.

- Write-intensive applications should move nonclustering (i.e., secondary) indexes to a disk other than the one on which the data resides. The reason is that each modification will have to update most of the indexes as well as the table, thus balancing the load.
- Read-intensive applications should partition frequently accessed tables across many disks. This balances the read load across the disks.

2.5.3 Add Processors

In a single processor system, an 85% utilization rate on the processor indicates that the processor is overloaded. (The corresponding number for a multiprocessor system is 80%.) If adding memory has not reduced this load and your software architecture is tuned as well as possible, then your system needs more processing power.

It is cheaper to buy more processors than to buy a bigger one.[12] Two processors of X MIPS (millions of instructions per second) may be significantly less effective for an application than one processor of $2X$ MIPS if they must communicate with one another, however. This communications overhead (approximately 2,000 instructions to send a 1 byte message across a LAN) is sometimes called the *MIPS penalty*.

When laying out the application, then, you should observe the following partitioning rules:

- If possible, offload the non-database applications onto a single processor.

  Reason. These applications will not have to communicate at all with the database application.

- Consider a dumped database for decision support.

  If your system has many long read queries, then consider having two redundant systems. One will be dedicated to long read-only transactions against the data gathered at the last database dump. The other will perform online transactions. This will eliminate the network communication between the two systems except at the moment of the dump itself.

- Allow read-only transactions to span server sites before allowing update transactions to span several sites.

  Reasons. First, some systems will not guarantee transaction atomicity if updates occur at several sites. Second, read-only transactions incur less overhead when they span sites than update transactions. (The overhead of the "two-phase commit" protocol may be as much as four messages per site for updates, whereas the protocol is completely unnecessary if the transaction is known to be read-only.)

- Examine the form of data sharing your application does when choosing among the following three hardware architectures (Figure 2.10):

  - Have several processors, but a single logical main memory and set of disks. Such an architecture is called *tightly-coupled* and is typical of bus-based

----

[12] Trends indicate that a microprocessor will cost 100 times less per MIP than a mainframe by the year 2000.

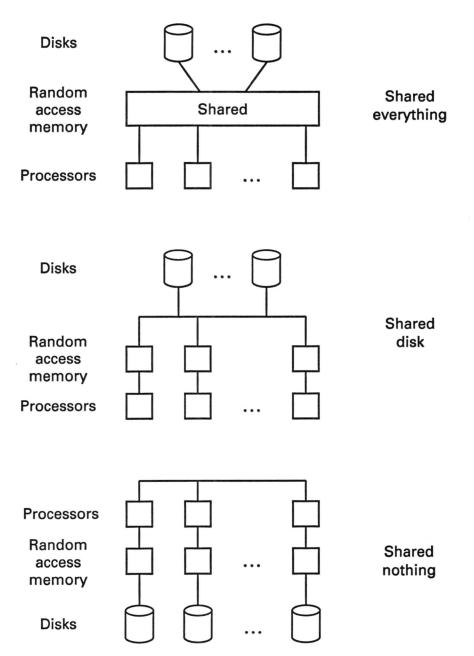

Figure 2.10   Possible Processor–Disk–Random Access Memory Configurations.

multiprocessors. This is a good architecture for applications in which all the data is shared (e.g., a large centralized accounting application).

- Have several processors, each with its own main memory and disks. Such an architecture is called *shared-nothing* and is the one to use in an application that requires geographical distribution, (e.g., a multinational bank) or an application that can be decoupled into independent subapplications.
- Have several processors, where each has its own main memory but the processors share disks. This architecture is called *shared-disk* and should be used when a tightly-coupled architecture would be ideal, but the application overpowers a single tightly-coupled site.

2.6 TROUBLESHOOTING

As a kind of self-test, see if you can figure out what to do in the following situations. All situations begin when someone tells you that their application runs too slowly.

Scenario 1

The Employee table is on disk 1, the Student table is on disk 2, and the log is on disk 2. The Student table is smaller than the Employee table but is accessed more often. Disk 2 supports more than twice the I/O rate of disk 1. The customer is willing to buy a new disk. What should you do with it?

Action. Probably the best thing to do is to put the log on the third disk. The log works much better in that case (i.e., as a sequential storage medium) and the system can tolerate the failure of a database disk, if there is also a database dump on tape.

Scenario 2

Response time is quite variable. You learn that new tables are added to the database concurrently with online transactions. Those new tables are irrelevant to the online transactions.

Action. Suggest that those new tables be added outside of the online window. The reason is that any DDL statement will tend to interfere with online transactions that must access table description (catalog) information.

Scenario 3

A new credit card offers large lines of credit at low interest rates. Setting up a new card customer involves the following three-step transaction:

1. Obtain a new customer number from a global counter.
2. Ask the customer for certain information, e.g., income, mailing address.

3. Install the customer into the customer table.

The transaction rate cannot support the large insert traffic.

Action.   The interview with the customer should not take place while holding the lock on the customer number counter. Instead, step 2 should occur first outside a transactional context. Then steps 1 and 3 should be combined into a single transaction. If obtaining the customer number causes lock contention, then obtain it as late as possible or use a special facility as described in section 2.2 of this chapter (p. 26).

Scenario 4

A brokerage house wishes to print out a monthly stock report for every client. In a first implementation, they perform their transaction in the following way (using pseudocode):

```
begin transaction

for every account print out value
of position in each stock

end transaction
```

There is no concurrent modification activity, but they observe that their lock table size is insufficient.

Action.   Because there is no concurrent activity, the transaction should run at the lowest isolation degree available (degree 0 or degree 1). No locks should be necessary.

Scenario 5

The accounting department would like to determine the average salary by department to include in a management report. While they run this transaction, arbitrary updates may occur.

In a first implementation, they do the following:

```
begin transaction
  SELECT dept, avg(salary) as avgsalary
  FROM employee
  GROUP BY dept
end transaction
```

Because of concurrent updates to the employee table, the query tends to deadlock or to block other transactions.

Action.   Partition in time or space.

1. If your database management system has a facility to perform read-only queries without obtaining locks, then use it.

2. Pose this query when there is little update activity, e.g., at night.

3. Execute this query on a slightly out-of-date copy of the data.

If none of the preceding is feasible, then use degree 1 or 2 isolation. This may result in an inconsistent result. For example, if there is an across-the-board raise to the sales department that is executed after the query reads salesman A's salary, but before the query reads saleswoman B's salary, then the result will be inconsistent.

Scenario 6

Consider again the previous scenario with three added constraints:

1. The only updates will be updates to individual salaries. No transaction will update more than one record.

2. The answer must be consistent.

3. The query must execute on up-to-date data.

Action.   Using degree 2 isolation will achieve concurrent correctness in this case. The reason is that each concurrent update transaction accesses only a single record.

Scenario 7

An application supports thousands of inserts per hour and hundreds of thousands of short update-only transactions per hour. The inserts come packaged as large transactions every 20 minutes or so and last for 5 minutes. When the inserts enter, update response time goes up to 15 to 30 seconds, deadlocks occur, and one of the disks shows exceedingly high utilization. In between the insert bursts, response time is subsecond.

Action.   The inserts appear to monopolize the system and the data appears to be poorly partitioned. Two changes in conjunction or in isolation are likely to help.

1. Smooth out the insert traffic by chopping the large insert transactions into small ones (if this is possible as far as concurrent correctness is concerned) and issuing them one at a time.

2. Repartition the data, so that the insert traffic is spread to different disks, but the updates still enjoy fast access. A clustering index on a nonsequential key (see chapter 3 pp. 69 ff) will work well.

Scenario 8

The system is slow due to excessive processor utilization. An important (relational) transaction executes an SQL query that accesses a single record from within a loop in the programming language.

Action. Replace the loop by a single query that accesses the records and then allows the programming language code to iterate based on a cursor. This will save time because programming language to database interactions are expensive, whereas cursor-based access is less so.

Scenario 9

The disks show high access utilization but low space utilization. The log is on a disk by itself. The application is essentially read-only and involves many scans. Each scan requires many seeks. Management refuses to buy more disks.

Action. Consider reorganizing the files on disk to occupy large sequential portions of disk. (On UNIX systems, consider using raw slices.) Raise the prefetching level and increase the page utilization. This will reduce the seek time and the number of disk accesses.

Scenario 10

The new credit card company is now established. It bills its customers on the last Thursday of each month. The billing transaction takes all night, so other necessary batch jobs cannot be accomplished during this time.

Action. The first question to ask is whether the application has to work this way. If 1/20 of the bills could be sent out every working day, then the billing application would create fewer demands on the system each day (partitioning in time). Another approach is to run the billing job as a big batch job but only on the weekend. We will consider table clustering as a solution to such a problem in chapter 4.

Scenario 11

Many capital markets (stock exchanges, commodity exchanges, etc.) distribute "ticks" containing information about positions and trades. A tickerplant takes these streams of ticks and distributes them to a community of brokers, traders, and so on. Ticks come in at rates of 500 to 1000 per second. The system should not lose any.

Tickerplants support a notion of watchlist (e.g., lists of stocks individuals follow), plus historical queries (e.g., Boeing's ticks over the past two hours), and some analytics (e.g., market averages).

Action.   As much data as possible should be stored in random access memory.- The only disk accesses should be to a history file of ticks and to a recovery log. Large disk extents should be used for the history file (or raw slices on UNIX).

Processing intended to broadcast data to traders should be distributed. That is, the system administrator should partition the traders into different groups and one processor should serve each group (Figure 2.11).

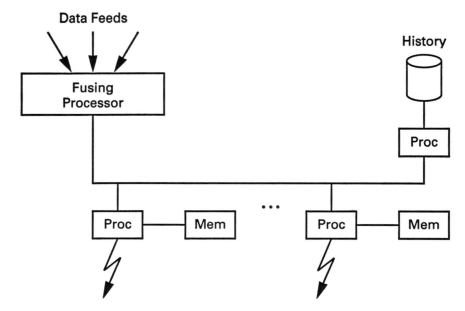

Figure 2.11   Distribution of Data to Traders

3

Tuning Indexes

3.1 GOAL OF CHAPTER

An *index* for a table is a data organization that enables certain queries to access one or more records of that table fast. Proper tuning of indexes is essential to high performance. Improper selection of indexes can lead to the following mishaps:

- Indexes that are maintained but never used.
- Files that are scanned in order to return a single record.
- Joins that take forever.
- Concurrency control bottlenecks.

This chapter gives you guidance for choosing, maintaining, and using indexes. (Figure 3.1 shows the place of indexes in the architecture of a typical database system.) The hints apply directly to relational systems. If you use a VSAM-based, hierarchical, network-based, or object-oriented database system, then you will have to translate a few of the examples in your head, but you will find that the principles remain relevant.

3.2 TYPES OF QUERIES

The usefulness of an index depends on how the queries use the index. For example, if there is an index on attribute A, but no query ever mentions A, then the index entails overhead (for maintenance on inserts and deletes) without yielding any benefit. This is obviously folly. Less obvious sources of folly can result from

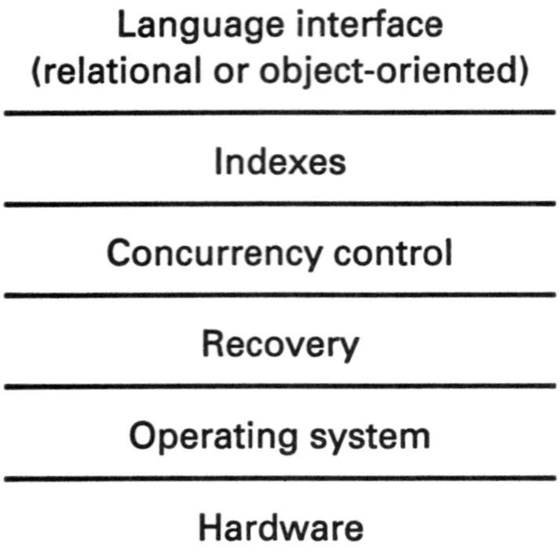

Language interface
(relational or object-oriented)
―――――――――――――――――――

Indexes
―――――――――――――――――――

Concurrency control
―――――――――――――――――――

Recovery
―――――――――――――――――――

Operating system
―――――――――――――――――――

Hardware

Figure 3.1   Indexes in Database
System Architecture.

placing the wrong kind of index on an attribute with respect to the queries performed on that attribute. Because an infinite number of queries are possible, let's abstract the queries into a few "types." Later, we'll characterize the strengths of each kind of index with respect to these types.

1. A *point query* returns at most one record (or part of a record) based on an equality selection. For example, the following returns the name field value of the single employee with ID number 8478.

```
SELECT name
FROM Employee
WHERE ID = 8478
```

2. A *multipoint query* is one that may return several records based on an equality selection. For example, if many employees may receive the salary $40,000, then the following is a multipoint query.

```
SELECT name
FROM Employee
WHERE salary = 40000
```

3. A *range query* on attribute X is one that returns a set of records whose values lie in an interval or half-interval for X consisting of more than one value. Here are two examples.

```
SELECT name
FROM Employee
WHERE salary >= 50000
AND salary < 60000
```

```
SELECT name
FROM Employee
WHERE salary >= 55000
```

4. A *prefix match query* on an attribute or sequence of attributes X is one that specifies only a prefix of X. For example, consider the attributes last name, first name, city (in that order). The following would be prefix match queries on those attributes:

- last name = 'Gates',
- last name = 'Gates' AND first name = 'George'
- last name = 'Gates' AND first name LIKE 'Ge%'
- last name = 'Gates' AND first name = 'George' AND city = 'San Diego'

The following would not be prefix match queries, because they fail to constrain a prefix of last name, first name, and city.

- first name = 'George'
- last name LIKE '%ates'

5. An *extremal query* is one that obtains a set of records (or parts of records) whose value on some attribute (or set of attributes) is a minimum or maximum. For example, the following query finds the names of employees who earn the highest salary.

```
SELECT name
FROM Employee
WHERE salary = MAX(SELECT salary FROM Employee)
```

6. An *ordering query* is one that displays a set of records in the order of the value of some attribute (or attributes). For example, the following query displays the Employee records in the order of their salaries. The first record is an employee having the lowest salary, and the last record is an employee having the highest salary.

```
SELECT *
FROM Employee
ORDER BY salary
```

7. A *grouping query* is one that partitions the results of a query into groups. Usually, some function is applied to each partition. For example, the following query finds the average salary in each department.

```
SELECT dept, AVG(salary) as avgsalary
FROM Employee
GROUP BY dept
```

8. A *join query* is one that links two or more tables. If the predicates linking the tables are based on equality, the join query is called an *equality join query*. For example, the following query finds the Social Security number of employees who are also students.

```
SELECT Employee.ssnum
FROM Employee, Student
WHERE Employee.ssnum = Student.ssnum
```

Join queries that are not equality join queries require an examination of nearly every pair of records in the two tables even when indexes are present. Whenever possible, systems process such queries as selections following an equality join query. For example, the following query finds all employees who earn more than their manager.

```
SELECT e1.ssnum
FROM Employee e1, Employee e2
WHERE e1.manager = e2.ssnum
AND e1.salary > e2.salary
```

The system will first perform the join based on

```
e1.manager = e2.ssnum
```

and then filter the result with a selection based on the salary predicate. This is a good strategy even if an index on salary were present. To see why, notice that the number of records in the join based on

```
e1.salary > e2.salary
```

is approximately $(n^2)/2$ where n is the number of Employee records. If there are 10,000 Employee records, this is 50,000,000 records. The time to assemble such a quantity of records is likely to be far longer (by a factor of 50 or more) than the time a decent database management system would take to perform the equality join, even without indexes. (The decent system would likely either create a temporary index or sort both relations and then perform a merge-join of the results.)

3.3 KEY TYPES

A *key* of an index is a set or sequence of attributes. Index searches use values on those attributes to access records of an accompanying table. Many records in the accompanying table may have the same key value.[1]

---

[1] In normalization theory, as explained in the next chapter, the notion of key is different. In that theory, the key of a relation is a set of attributes with the property that no two distinct records have the same values on those attributes.

From the viewpoint of the index designer, there are two kinds of keys with respect to a table T.

1. A *sequential key* is one whose value is monotonic with insertion order. That is, the last record inserted into T has the highest value of the key. For example, if a timestamp marking the time of insertion of a record were a key, then it would be a sequential key.

2. A *nonsequential key* is a key whose value is unrelated to the insertion order to the table. For example, if a Social Security number were a key of an Employee table, then it would be a nonsequential key, because the last record inserted will only rarely have the highest Social Security number.

In certain cases, sequential keys will cause concurrency control problems as we will see.

3.4 DATA STRUCTURES

Most database systems support at least one of the following three data structures: B-trees, hash tables, and ISAM structures. In addition there are a few useful main memory lookup structures that you should know about (beyond standard linked lists): 2-3 trees, tries, frequency-ordered linked lists, and multidimensional data structures.

3.4.1 Structures Provided by Database Systems

The access pattern on an attribute of a table should guide the choice of data structure to access it. (Other factors such as whether the attribute is clustering or not also play a role as we will see later in this chapter.) To understand what each data structure can do, you must understand a few details about its organization.

Levels, depth, and disk accesses

B-trees, ISAM structures, and hash structures can be viewed as trees. Some of the nodes in those trees are in random access memory and some are not. As a general rule, the root will often be in random access memory, and an arbitrary leaf will rarely be. In fact, the likelihood that a node will be in random access memory decreases the farther the node is from the root.

Because an access to disk secondary memory costs 20 to 30 milliseconds if it requires a seek (as these index accesses will), the performance of a data structure depends critically on the number of nodes in the average path from root to leaf. That number is known as the *number of levels* in a B-tree and ISAM structure.

One technique that database management systems use to minimize the number of levels is to make each interior node have as many children as possible (on

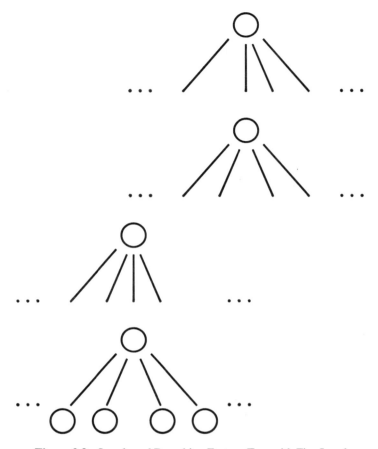

Figure 3.2   Levels and Branching Factor: Tree with Five Levels
Having Fanout of Four.

the order of 1000 for many B-tree implementations). The maximum number of
children a node can have is called its *fanout* (Figure 3.2).

When there is no room for an insert to fit in the node of a data structure, the
node is said to *overflow*. In a B-tree, an overflowing node n *splits* into two nodes
n and n' such that the distance between n' and the root is the same as the distance
between n and the root. In ISAM and hash structures, the new page n' is pointed
to from n, a technique known as *overflow chaining*. The chaining technique will
cause the distance from the root to n' to be one greater than the distance from the
root to n. (In some systems such as INGRES, a B-tree leaf page will use overflow
chaining if there are more pointers associated with some key than will fit on a
single page.)

Thus, to compute the average number of nodes that must be traversed to reach a data node.

- For B-trees, count the number of levels (plus the average number of overflows if they are allowed).
- For ISAM structures, count the number of levels plus the average number of overflows.
- For hash structures, compute the average number of overflows.

Some systems violate the tree topology of their data structures by providing right links among the leaf nodes (and possibly the interior nodes as well). That is each leaf node has a pointer to its right neighbor. Such a *link implementation* helps speed range queries in B-trees and ISAM structures.

Specialized concurrency control methods can also use the links to remove concurrency control bottlenecks from data structures, as shown originally by Peter Lehman and S. B. Yao of the University of Maryland, and later elaborated by Yehoshua Sagiv of Jerusalem University, Betty Salzberg of Northeastern, Vladimir Lanin of New York University and me. C. Mohan of IBM Almaden research proposed practical algorithms to unify this style of concurrency control and recovery considerations.[2] Several IBM products may soon adopt a variant of that algorithm.

B-Trees

A B-tree is a balanced tree whose leaves contain a sequence of key-pointer pairs. The keys are sorted by value[3] (Figure 3.3).

Evaluation. B-trees are the best general data structure for database systems in that they seldom require reorganization, and they support many different query types well. If range queries (e.g., find all salaries between $70,000 and $80,000) or extremal queries (e.g., find the minimum salary) occur frequently, then B-trees are useful, whereas hash structures are not. If inserts are frequent and the B-tree key is nonsequential, then B-trees will give more consistent response times than both ISAM structures and hash structures, because those structures may

---

[2] C. Mohan, "ARIES/KVL: A Key-Value Locking Method for Concurrency Control of Multiaction Transactions on B-Tree Indexes," 16th Very Large Data Bases conference, San Mateo: Morgan-Kauffman, 1990.

[3] What we call B-trees here are technically called B+ trees. Strictly speaking, a B-tree has pointers to data pages (or records) in its internal nodes as well as in its leaf nodes; this turns out to be a bad strategy, since it yields low fanout. Therefore, all major systems use B+ trees (which have pointers to data only at the leaves). A classical general survey about B-trees can be found in the survey article by D. Comer, "The Ubiquitous B-Tree," *ACM Computing Surveys*, vol. 11, no. 2, New York: ACM, pp. 121-137, 1979.

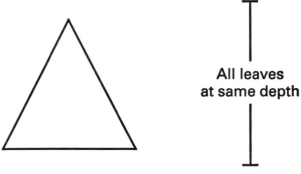

Keys are sorted at leaves

Figure 3.3　B-Tree Is Mutiary Tree Such that Every Leaf Is at Same Distance from Root and Keys (Attribute[s] Being Indexed) Are Sorted at Leaves.

have overflow chains of unpredictable length. (Please note that I am discussing the data structure alone. Later, we will see that the data pages indexed by a clustering index, B-tree or not, may have overflow pages.)

B-trees work poorly if they are based on sequential keys and there are many inserts, because all inserts will access the last page, forming a concurrency control bottleneck.

Because the fanout of a B-tree is the maximum number of key-pointer pairs that can fit on a node of the B-tree, the bigger the key is, the lower the fanout. A smaller fanout may lead to more levels in the B-tree.

Example:　Influence of Key Length on Fanout

For example, consider the number of levels deep a B-tree can be whose leaf pages contain 40 million key-pointer pairs.

If pointers are 6 bytes long and the keys are 4 bytes long, then approximately 400 key-pointer pairs can fit on a 4-kilobyte page. In this case, the number of levels (including the leaf pages) of a B-tree with 64 million key-pointer pairs would be 3. The root level would consist of one node (the root). The next level down would have 400 nodes. The leaf level would have 160,000 nodes, each with 400 key-pointer pairs giving a total of 64 million.

This assumes 100% utilization. If nodes are merged when they fall to half full, then their utilization holds at around 69%. In order to save restructuring time and increase the amount of concurrency, some systems (e.g., INGRES) never merge nodes. Studies by Ted Johnson and me have shown that for B-trees with more inserts than deletes (both random), the utilization will be in the range from 65% to 69% even if nodes are never merged.[4] That would give more than 41 million key-pointer pairs in the leaves for a 3-level B-tree.

By contrast, if keys are 94 bytes long, then only 40 can fit per page. In that case, even assuming 100% utilization,

• The root level would have one node.
• Level 2 would have 40 nodes.
• Level 3 would have 1600 nodes.
• Level 4 would have 64,000 nodes.
• Level 5 would have 2,560,000 nodes, each with at most 40 key-pointer pairs.

Thus, a five level B-tree is needed to store all these key-pointer pairs.

In this example, a large key may cause the B-tree to be two levels deeper. If the data is static, then use your system's key compression option if it has one. This will reduce the space needed and save disk accesses at a relatively small processor cost (30% per record access). A typical compression technique is called *prefix compression*. Prefix compression will store in nonleaf nodes only that part of a key that is needed to distinguish the key from its neighbors in the node. For example, if there are three consecutive keys Smith, Smoot, and Smythe, then only Smi, Smo and Smy need be held. Many systems use prefix compression.

Other forms of compression are more controversial. For example, version 5 of ORACLE had a form of compression called *front compression* in which adjacent keys had their common leading portion factored out. So, the preceding three keys would be stored as Smith, (2)o, (2)y, where the 2 indicates that the first two characters are the same as the previous key. This saved space but caused two problems.

• It entailed substantial processor overhead for maintenance.
• It made item locking within B-tree nodes more subtle—locking (2)y would have implicitly required locking Smith as well.

So, ORACLE abandoned this form of compression in version 6 with little user protest.

----

[4] T. Johnson and D. Shasha, "Utilization of B-trees with Inserts, Deletes, and Modifies," 8th ACM SIGACT-SIGMOD Conference on Principles of Database Systems, pp. 235-246, March 1989. If inserts enter in sorted order (i.e., not at all random), then utilization can fall to 50% in some systems. Check your system's tuning guide.

ISAM

ISAM (Index sequential access method) structures are similar to B-trees but are optimized for infrequently changing data. The optimization can take many forms. In some older IBM products, ISAM structures are closely tied to disk architectures. Each leaf page maps to a track, and sibling leaves are on the same or neighboring tracks. This provides very fast scan behavior, because seeks and rotational delays are minimized.

In all systems that implement them, the upper levels of ISAM structures never change, hence there are no locks on those levels. If an insertion occurs to a full page, ISAM structures use overflow chaining. Because overflow space on the same cylinder is limited, many inserts can cause the performance of an ISAM structure to degrade significantly. At that point, it is good to reorganize the structure (Figure 3.4).

Evaluation.   Provided there are few overflows, ISAM structures

- Support range queries even better than B-trees because the utilization of each page is often near 100%, reducing the number of pages that need to be retrieved.
- Reduce locking overhead, because nonleaf nodes of the structure are never locked.

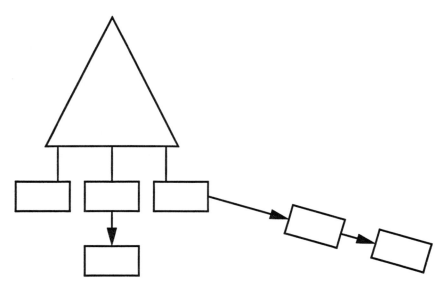

Figure 3.4   In ISAM Structures Tree Is Fixed, but
Leaves May Overflow, Forming Chains.

Their main disadvantages are the following:

- Sequential keys cause concurrency bottlenecks on ISAM structures when there are many inserts. This is also true for B-trees, but ISAM structures suffer from an additional factor: inserts will cause the last leaf page to overflow, slowing accesses to recently inserted data as well as new insertions. Because of these problems with insertions, you should drop the ISAM index when performing a large load.

- Whether inserts are sequential or not, ISAM structures will overflow under heavy insert traffic. This will eventually eliminate their advantage compared with B-trees, unless you can reorganize them before the average overflow length exceeds 1. This normally requires quiescing the system—a serious disadvantage.

- ISAM structures suffer from large key sizes, for the same reason as B-trees.

Intuitively, an ISAM structure has many of the properties of a bound personal address book. If the address book is very empty, then it wastes space. If it is very full, then it requires overflow pages. In between, its size is known, and access is quick.

Hash structures

Hash structures are a method of storing key-value pairs based on a pseudo-randomizing function called a *hash function*. The hash function can be thought of as the root of the structure. Given a key, the hash function returns a location that contains either a page address (usually on disk) or a directory location that holds a page address. That page either contains the key and associated record or is the first page of an overflow chain leading to the record(s) containing the key. The hash function will return arbitrarily different locations on key values that are close but unequal, e.g., Smith and Smythe. The implication is that the records containing such close keys will likely be on different pages. This property makes hash structures completely unhelpful for range queries.

Evaluation.   Hash structures can answer point queries (e.g., find the employee with Social Security number 247-38-294) in one disk access provided there are no overflow chains, making them the best data structures for that purpose (Figure 3.5). They are also good for multipoint queries especially if they are part of a clustering index (see section 3.6, pp. 69 ff). However, they are useless for range, prefix, or extremal queries.

If you find that your hash structure has a significant amount of overflow chaining, you should reorganize (drop and add or use a special reorganize function on) the hash structure following a large number of inserts. Avoiding overflow chaining may require you to underutilize the hash space. Some performance

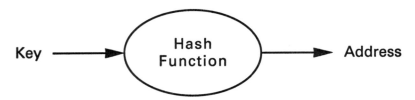

Figure 3.5   Address Returned by Hash Function Either Holds Data
Corresponding to Key or Leads to that Data through Series of Pointers.

consultants suggest that a hash table should be no more than 50% full to ensure that a single disk access will be enough in most cases. So, hash structures have the purest space utilization of any structure. Hash structures may also be very sensitive to the choice of hash function. For example, different hash functions may cause a factor of 8 difference in I/O performance on the UNIFY system.

Because hash functions convert keys to locations or page identifiers, the size of a hash structure is not related to the size of a key. The only effect of key size on a hash structure is that the hash function takes slightly longer to execute on a long key. This is only important in a processor-bound system.

Whereas hash structures with low space utilization perform well for point queries, they perform badly for queries that must scan all the data.

3.4.2 Data Structures for Lookup Tables

A *lookup table* is a table that is often read but never updated (or at least never updated during online transaction processing). Typical examples of lookup tables are conversion tables, e.g., from two letter codes to full spellings of states or countries. Putting such small tables in the database system introduces unnecessary overhead, so many application designers store these tables as unordered arrays, linked lists, or as sorted structures that are sequentially searched.

You might, however, consider different data structures. We have already discussed hash structures and B-trees. A special case of a B-tree, known as a *2-3 tree* is a good choice to maintain sorted data within random access memory. Like a B-tree, all the leaves in a 2-3 tree are the same distance from the root. The difference is that the maximum fanout is 3, and the minimum fanout is 2. This makes for a longer, less bushy tree than a normal B-tree. Research studies by Mike Carey and his colleagues at the University of Wisconsin at Madison have shown that narrow, long trees perform better than wide short trees for random access memory data structures.

Another structure that should not be neglected is the *trie* (Figures 3.6 and

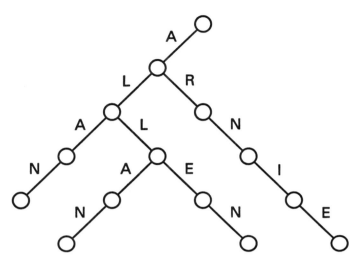

Figure 3.6   Trie for Names Alan, Allan, Allen, and Arnie.

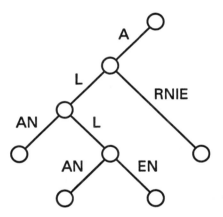

Figure 3.7   Compressed Trie for Alan, Allan, Allen, and Arnie.

3.7). This structure is a fast, simple data structure for looking up arbitrary length strings in memory.[5]

Another structure for designers who like the simplicity of linked lists is the *frequency-ordered linked list*. The idea of this structure is that the first entries of the linked list are the most frequently accessed and the last entries are the

---

[5] Recent results about tries can be found in the paper by R. Ramesh, A. J. G. Babu, and J. Peter Kincaid, "Variable-Depth Trie Index Optimization: Theory and Experimental Results" in *ACM Transactions on Database Systems*, March 1989, vol. 14, no. 1, pp. 41-74.

Figure 3.8   Frequency-Ordered List Would Place Paris before Brive.

least frequently accessed. A background algorithm keeps tracks of accesses and rearranges the list appropriately during quiet periods.

Example: Train Reservations in France

On the French Minitel service, one can reserve a seat on a long distance train by accessing a terminal. The first two questions asked are the city of origin and the city of arrival. For each city, if the client types in the name, the system inserts the city's numerical code. A naive design would be to store this as a list sorted by alphabetical order. As a result a little-known city (e.g., Brive) would be found in less time than a major city (e.g., Paris). What would be a better structure?

Action.   Suppose that you want fast response time and the ability to permit users to type in only enough of the prefix of a name to identify it uniquely. For example, they should be able to type in Toul to identify Toulouse. To achieve this goal, consider using a trie. If you are only concerned with having the speed of access be related to the frequency of access, then use a frequency-ordered list. (Figure 3.8).

––––––

If your application concerns geometry, then you should know about *multidimensional data structures*. Typical examples that can be found in the literature are quadtrees, k-d trees, K-D-B trees, R-trees, R+-trees, grid structures, and hB-trees.[6] Like composite indexes (discussed later in this chapter), multidimensional data structures apply to multiple attributes. Unlike composite indexes, multidimensional data structures apply symmetrically to their attributes, which often makes the processing of geographical queries more efficient.

––––––

[6] The following papers provide many useful backward references: J. Nievergelt, H. Hinterberger, and K. C. Sevcik, "The Grid File: An Adaptable Symmetric Multikey File Structure" in *ACM Transactions on Database Systems*, March 1984, vol. 9, no. 1, pp. 38-71. David Lomet and Betty Salzberg, "The hB-Tree: A Multiattribute Indexing Method with Good Guaranteed Performance" in *ACM Transactions on Database Systems*, December 1990, vol. 15, no. 4, pp. 625-658. Some of the other researchers who work on these structures include Timos Sellis (R+-trees) and Hanan Samet (quadtrees) of the University of Maryland, Antonin Guttman (R-trees), Oliver Guenther (cell trees) at FAW Ulm, and Peter Widmayer of the University of Freiburg.

A typical such query finds all cities having at least 10,000 inhabitants within a certain latitude and longitude range—that is, symmetrically along both dimensions.

```
SELECT name
FROM City
WHERE population >= 10000
AND latitude >= 22
AND latitude < 25
AND longitude >= 5
AND longitude <= 15
```

So far, commercial geographical information systems have mainly used R-trees and quadtrees to answer such queries.

3.5 SPARSE VERSUS DENSE INDEXES

The data structure portion of an index has pointers at its leaves to either data pages or data records.

- If there is at most one pointer from the data structure to each data page, then the index is said to be *sparse*.
- If there is one pointer to each record in the table, then the index is said to be *dense*.

Assuming that records are smaller than pages (the normal case), a sparse index will hold fewer keys than a dense one. In fact, the

number of pointers in dense index = number of pointers in sparse index
× number of records per page

If records are small compared to pages, then there will be many records per data page and the data structure supporting a sparse index will usually have one fewer level than the data structure supporting a dense index.[7] This means one less disk access if the table is large. By contrast, if records are almost as large as pages, then a sparse index will rarely have better disk access properties than dense indexes.

The main advantage of dense indexes is that they can support certain read queries within the data structure itself. For example, if there is a dense index on

---

[7] In most systems, every pointer has an associated key. However, if many keys have the same value and the key is large, an important optimization for dense indexes is to store a given key value only once followed by a list of pointers. If that optimization is used, then a dense index may not need more levels than a sparse index.

the keywords of a document retrieval system, one can count the number of key-word lists containing some term, e.g., "mountain trail," without accessing the lists themselves. (Count information is useful for that application, because queriers frequently restrict their query when they discover that their current query would retrieve too many documents.)

3.6 TO CLUSTER OR NOT TO CLUSTER

A *clustering index* (sometimes called a *primary* index) on an attribute (or set of attributes) X is an index that colocates records whose X values are "near" to one another (Figure 3.9).

Two records are colocated if they are close to one another on disk. What "near" means depends on the data structure. For B-trees and ISAM structures, two X values are "near" if they are close in their sort order. For example, 50 and 51 are near as are Smith and Sneed. For hash structures, two X values are "near" only if they are identical. That is why clustered B-trees and ISAM structures are good for partial match, range, multipoint, point, and general join queries. By contrast, hash structures are useful only for point, multipoint, and equijoin queries.

Clustering indexes are sparse in some systems (e.g., SYBASE) and dense in others (e.g., ORACLE, DB2). In yet other systems (e.g., INGRES), the clustering index is sparse if based on an ISAM or hash structure and dense if based on a B-tree. Using the sparse alternative can then reduce response time by a factor of two or more.

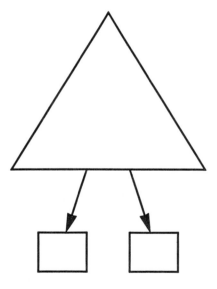

Figure 3.9   Sparse Clustering Index Holds Pointer at Leaves for Every Page of Table Being Indexed. Dense Index Holds Pointer for Every Row of Table. So, Sparse Clustering Index Will Often Have Fewer Levels.

Because a clustering index implies a certain table organization and the table can be organized in only one way at a time, there can be at most one clustering index per table.

A *nonclustering index* (sometimes called a *secondary* index) is an index on an attribute (or set of attributes) Y that puts no constraint on the table organization. The table can be clustered according to some other attribute X or can be organized as a heap (see later). A nonclustering index is always dense—there is one leaf pointer per record. There can be many nonclustering indexes per table.

Just to make sure you understand the distinction between the two kinds of indexes, consider a classical library (the kind with books). A book may be clustered by access number, e.g., Library of Congress number. The access number is the book's address in the library. Books with close access numbers will tend to be physically close to one another. In addition, there may be several nonclustering indexes, e.g., one based on last name of author and another based on title. These are nonclustering because two books with the same author name may be physically far apart. (For example, the same author may write a book about database tuning and another one about a mathematical detective.)

A *heap* is the simplest table organization of all: Records are ordered according to their time of entry. That is, new inserts are added to the last page of the data structure. For this reason, inserting a record requires a single page access. That is the good news.

The bad news is that

- Concurrent insert transactions will tend to lock one another out unless your system offers record locking, because all inserts access the same page. If your system offers record locks, then short-term page locks—held only as long as it takes to obtain the record lock—may cause a bottleneck if the insert rate is high enough.

- Deleted space cannot be reused except on the last page, because all new inserts access the last page.

With this introduction, we are now in a position to compare clustering and nonclustering indexes.

3.6.1 Evaluation of Clustering Indexes

A clustering index offers the following benefits compared with a nonclustering one:

- If the clustering index is sparse as clustering B-trees are in SYBASE or as ISAM structures are in INGRES, then it will store fewer pointers than a dense index. (Recall that nonclustering indexes cannot be sparse.) As we saw in section 3.5 (p. 67), this can save one disk access per record access if the records are small.

- A clustering index is good for multipoint queries, i.e., equality accesses to non-unique fields. For example, a clustering index is useful for looking up names in a telephone book, because all people with the same last name are on consecutive pages. By contrast, a nonclustering index on the first three digits of subscribers' phone numbers would be worse than useless for multipoint queries. A query to find all subscribers in the 497 exchange might require an access to nearly every page.

  For the same reason, a clustering index will help perform an equality join on an attribute with few distinct values. For example, consider the equality join query on first names:

  ```
  SELECT Employee.ssnum, Student.course
  FROM Employee, Student
  WHERE Employee.firstname = Student.firstname
  ```

  If the relation Employee has a clustering index on firstname, then for each Student tuple, all corresponding Employee tuples will be packed onto consecutive pages.

  If the Employee and Student tables both have a clustering index on firstname based on a B-tree or ISAM structure, then the database management system will often use a processing strategy called a *merge-join*. Such a strategy reads both relations in sorted order, thus minimizing the number of disk accesses required to perform the query. (Each page of each relation will be read in once.) This will also work if both relations have a clustering index on first name based on a hash structure that uses the same hash function.

- A clustering index based on a B-tree or ISAM structure can support range, prefix match, and ordering queries well. (Other structures that place lexicographically close values in a physically close region also have this property.) The white pages of a telephone book again provide a good example. All names that begin with 'St' will be on consecutive pages.

  A clustering index based on these data structures can also eliminate the need to perform the sort in an ORDER BY query on the indexed attribute.

- A clustering index on attribute or attributes X can reduce lock contention in two ways.

  (a) A retrieval of several records with the same X value, a prefix match query on X, or a range query on X will access and lock only a few consecutive pages of the table data. If the table is unclustered or clustered on some other attribute(s) Y (where neither X is a prefix of Y nor is Y a prefix of X) then such queries may access many more pages (i.e., a different page for each record in many cases). The fewer pages accessed, the fewer pages that are locked in systems that use page-level locking.

(b) A clustering index can eliminate a concurrency control hot spot in insert intensive environments. Such environments make a hot spot of the last page of a heap organization. A clustering index based on a hash structure will always eliminate this hot spot on the data table. A clustering index based on a B-tree or ISAM structure will also eliminate this hot spot provided the key is not sequential.

The main disadvantage of a clustering index is that its benefits can diminish if there are a large number of overflow data pages. The reason is that accessing such pages will usually entail a disk seek. Overflow pages can result from two kinds of updates.

- Inserts may cause data pages to overflow.
- Record replacements that increase the size of a record (e.g., the replacement of a NULL value by a long string) or that change the indexed key value will also cause overflows of the data page.

When there are a large number of overflow pages in a clustering index, then consider invoking a utility to eliminate them.

Redundant tables

Since there can be at most one clustering index per table, certain applications may consider establishing a redundant second table. Once again, you need to look no farther than your telephone book to see an illustration of this idea. The white pages are clustered by name. The yellow pages contain only a subset of the entries in the white pages, but are clustered by category of goods and services offered (e.g., computer dealer, acupuncturist, ski shop). The two books both contain address and telephone information—hence, they are partially redundant. Adding redundancy works well when there are few updates.

3.6.2 Nonclustering Indexes

Because a nonclustering index on a table imposes no constraint on the table organization, there can be several nonclustering indexes on a given table.

1. A nonclustering index can eliminate the need to access the table. For example, suppose there is a nonclustering index on attributes A, B, and C of

R. Then the following query can be answered completely within the index, i.e., without accessing the data pages.

```
SELECT B, C
FROM R
WHERE A = 5
```

If your system takes advantage of this possibility (as does INFORMIX, for example), nonclustering indexes will give better performance than sparse clustering ones (though equal performance to dense clustering ones). Of course updates would need to access the data pages of the *R* table.

2. Suppose the query must touch the table *R* through a nonclustering index based on *A*. Let *NR* be the number of records retrieved and *NP* be the number of pages in *R*. If *NR* < *NP*, then approximately *NR* pages of *R* will be logically read. The reason is simple: it is likely that each record will be on a different page. If *NR* > *NP*, then more than *NP* pages may be retrieved if the buffer pool is smaller than the relation size.

Thus, nonclustering indexes are good if each query retrieves significantly fewer records than there are pages in the file. We use the word "significant" for the following reason: A table scan can often save time by reading many pages at a time, provided the table is stored contiguously on tracks. For example, INGRES 5.0 normally reads 8 pages at a time on a scan. Therefore, even if the scan and the index both read all the pages of the table, the scan may complete by a factor of 2 to 10 times faster.

Consider the following two examples concerning a multipoint query.

> **(a)** Suppose a table *T* has 50-byte records and pages are 4 kilobytes long. Suppose further that attribute *A* takes on 20 different values, which are evenly distributed among the records. Is a nonclustering index on *A* a help or a hindrance?
>
> *Evaluation.*   Because attribute *A* may contain 20 different values, each query will retrieve approximately 1/20 of the records. Because each page contains 80 records, nearly every page will have a record for nearly every value of *A*. So, using the index will give worse performance than scanning the table.
>
> **(b)** Consider the same situation as in item (a), except each record is 2 kilobytes long.
>
> *Evaluation.*   In this case, a query on the nonclustering index will touch only every tenth page on the average, so the index will help at least a little.

We can draw three lessons from these examples.

- A nonclustering index serves you best if it can help you avoid touching a data page altogether. This is possible for certain selection, count, and join queries that depend only on the key attributes of the nonclustering index.
- A nonclustering index is always useful for point queries (recall that these are equality selections that return one record).
- For multipoint queries, a nonclustering index on attribute A may or may not help. A good rule of thumb is to use the nonclustering index whenever the following holds:

  number of distinct key index values $> c \times$ *number of records per page*,

  where c is the number of pages that can be prefetched in one disk read.

  This inequality would imply that the use of the nonclustering index would entail fewer disk accesses than scanning all the pages of the relation.

There are two situations when you should eliminate a nonclustering index.

- The modification frequency relative to the retrieval frequency is high (as a rule of thumb, at least one-third as frequent). Here a modification is either an insertion, deletion, or update to one of the fields in the index key. The reason is that each such modification will entail at least two disk accesses to the nonclustering index.
- Lock escalation occurs. In some systems, a table with many nonclustering indexes may cause a transaction that does a substantial number of updates to escalate to table-level locking. (As explained in chapter 2 (p. 24), escalation occurs when a transaction acquires more than a predetermined threshold of locks.)

3.6.3 Composite Indexes

A *composite index* (called a concatenated index in some systems) is an index based on more than one attribute. A composite index may be clustering or nonclustering. For example, consider a relation

$$person(ssnum, lastname, firstname, age, telnumber, \ldots)$$

One might specify a composite index on (lastname, firstname) for Person. White pages of telephone books are organized in this fashion. Thus, a data structure supporting a dense composite index on attributes $(A, B, C, \ldots)$ will store pointers to all records with a given A value together; within that collection, it will store pointers to all records with a given B value together; within that subcollection, it will store pointers to all records with a given C value together; and so on.

Composite indexes offer the following benefits compared with single attribute (i.e., "normal") indexes.

- A dense composite index can sometimes answer a query completely, e.g., how many people are there with last name 'Smith' and first name 'John'?
- A query on all attributes of a composite index will likely return far fewer records than a query on only some of those attributes. Because they are more selective, a composite nonclustering index may be useful when no combination of single-attribute nonclustering indexes would be.
- A composite index is an efficient way to support the uniqueness of multiple attributes. For example, suppose that the relation (supplier, part, quantity) records the quantity of a particular part on order from a particular supplier. There may be many records with the same supplier identifier and many records with the same part identifier, but there should be only one record with a given supplier-part pair. This can be supported efficiently by establishing a composite index on (supplier, part) in conjunction with an SQL UNIQUE option.
- A composite index can support certain kinds of geographical queries. For example, suppose we look at the relation City, having to do with cities in the Southern Hemisphere.

City(name, latitude, longitude, population)

If we use a clustering composite index (latitude, longitude) then the query

```
SELECT name
FROM City
WHERE population >= 10000
AND latitude = 22
AND longitude >= 5
AND longitude <= 15
```

will execute quickly because all such cities will be packed as closely together as possible. By contrast, the following similar query will derive much less benefit from the composite clustering index:

```
SELECT name
FROM City
WHERE population >= 10000
AND longitude = 22
AND latitude >= 5
AND latitude <= 15
```

The reason is that all cities at latitude 5 will be packed together no matter what their longitude value is. As a result, a search will access the entire fraction of the database of cities whose latitudes fall within the range between 5 and 15 degrees South. So a composite index is not as good as a multidimensional one for general spatial queries. But it is often the only choice you have.

When designing a composite index, you must specify the order of the attributes in the index. As illustrated by the last example about latitude and longitude, you should put attribute *A* before attribute *B* if your queries tend to put more constraints on *A* than on *B*. (So, a composite index on latitude, longitude will perform well on queries that specify a single latitude and a range of longitudes but not on queries that specify a single longitude and a range of latitudes.)

There are two main disadvantages of composite indexes:

- They tend to have a large key size. As we saw in the description of B-trees earlier (pp. 60 ff), this can cause B-trees and ISAM structures to be very large and to contain many levels unless some form of compression is used. Implementing a composite index as a hash structure solves the size problem but doesn't support prefix match or range queries.

- Because a composite index encompasses several attributes, an update to any of its attributes will cause the index to be modified.

3.7 JOINS AND INDEXES

A join can take advantage of an existing index when one of the following conditions hold.

- The index is on the join attribute and there is not a point or multipoint constraint as part of the qualification. For example, an index on either R.B or S.C will help for the query

```
SELECT R.A, R.D
FROM R, S
WHERE R.B = S.C
```

but not for this one

```
SELECT R.A, R.D
FROM R, S
WHERE R.B = S.C
AND S.D = 5
AND R.E = 6
```

In the second query, the selections on S.D and R.E would probably be applied first. They would create temporaries that would have no indexes in most systems.

- In the first query, a dense index on S.C may work better than a sparse clustering index, because the query can be answered without reference to the table data in S. This is called a *semijoin* condition. The semijoin condition does not hold for

```
SELECT R.A, R.D, S.E
FROM R, S
WHERE R.B = S.C
```

Here, a nonclustering index on S.C will still help, but the performance will be worse than on the first query because every match in the join query will translate to a logical page access. Even with a clustering index on S.C, every matching value will translate to a logical page access on S. Nevertheless, a clustering index may give better performance than a nonclustering one for three reasons.

> **(a)** If the clustering index is sparse, it may contain fewer levels than a dense nonclustering one.
> **(b)** If many S records hold a given matching S.C value (that is, S.C is not a unique field within S), all those records will be colocated if S is clustered on S.C, but not otherwise. This will save accesses to table data relative to a nonclustering index.
> **(c)** If the R records are clustered on R.B in the same way as S is clustered on S.C (e.g., both are sorted on their respective fields), a merge-join is possible if the index is clustering. This will minimize the number of disk accesses.

- B-tree and ISAM structures can be used when the join comparison operator is one of <, <=, >=, or >.
- Hash indexes can be used only when the join comparison operator is =. Even then, they may not be so helpful. The reason is that each time the system accesses the hash index with a new key, fetching the resulting disk page will likely require a seek, because hash functions do not colocate the locations of records with consecutive keys. Therefore, such joins are worthwhile only when the relation that is hashed is much larger than the relation with which it is joined.

3.8 AVOID INDEXES ON SMALL TABLES

Indexes on small tables can do more harm than good. Many system manuals will tell you not to use an index on a table containing fewer than, say, 200 records. However, you should know that this number depends on the size of the records compared with the size of the index key.

- An index search will require reads of at least one and possibly two index pages and one data page. By contrast, if the entire relation is held on a single track on disk, reading it may require only a single physical read (provided you set your prefetching parameter to allow the system to read an entire track at once). An index may hurt performance in this case.

- If each record occupies an entire page on the other hand, then 200 records may require 200 disk accesses or more. In this case, an index is worthwhile for a point query, because it will entail only two or three disk accesses.

- If many inserts execute on a table with a small index, then the index itself may become a concurrency control bottleneck. (Lock conflicts near the roots of index data structures can form a bottleneck. Such conflicts arise when many inserts apply to a small index.)

3.9 SUMMARY: TABLE ORGANIZATION AND INDEX SELECTION

Table organization and clustering

Cluster on the most frequently accessed field or field(s) and follow this advice (Figure 3.10):

```
if you have a transient table
  or you must do bulk loading
  or you have a small table (less than a track)
   then use a heap table organization without any indexes
else if you have a very large table
        (larger than a disk) and
        fairly frequent updates and
        little quiet time (24-hour uptime)
   then use a heap with nonclustering indexes
        and record locking

else if table undergoes frequent insertions then
    if (1) you have no quiet time (24-hour uptime), or
       (2) you access sorted subranges, extremal values
           or perform ORDER By queries on some
           nonsequential key attribute(s) X
     then cluster based on a B-tree  for X
    else /* point and multipoint queries mostly
           and you have quiet time
       */
          cluster based on a hash structure
    end if
else /* infrequent insertions, not too large */
```

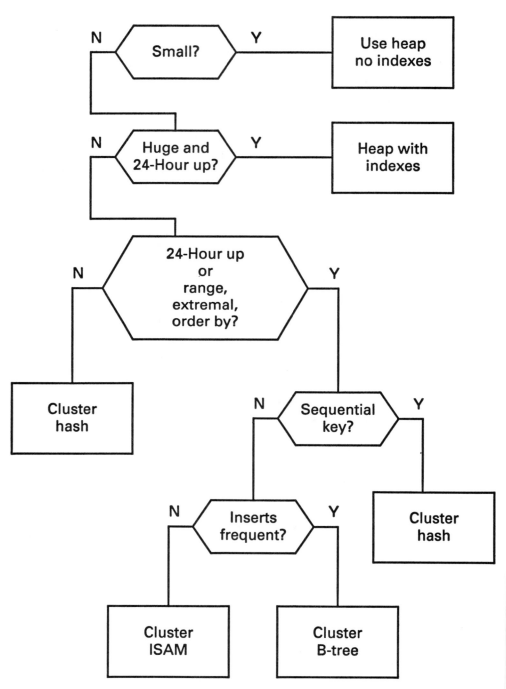

Figure 3.10   Primary and Secondary Index Selection.

```
      if application frequently accesses
        sorted subranges of key values
        or extremal values
            then cluster based on ISAM (or B-tree)
      else
                cluster based on a hash structure
      end if
end if


if you have very few updates and space
  is ample
    then create redundant tables and
        perform the above analysis
        for each frequently accessed
        set of attributes
end if
```

Nonclustering indexes

A nonclustering index on an attribute or set of attributes X that have no index currently should be established when at least one of these conditions holds.

- You want to ensure that X is unique, i.e., that no two records have the same X value.
- Selection or join retrievals on X return far fewer *records* than there are *pages* in the table or many queries can be answered by examining the index alone. In addition, insertions, deletions, or updates that modify part of X are relatively rare compared with retrievals.

Composite indexes

These indexes may be clustering or nonclustering. For concreteness, assume the composite index is on some sequence of attributes X. The phrase "if prefix matches may be useful," pertains to sequence X. For example, if $X = AB$, then a useful prefix match might perform an equality selection on A and a prefix selection on B. The reverse (equality selection on B and prefix selection on A) would not be a useful prefix match.

```
if prefix matches may be useful
   and there are few updates
       then use a composite ISAM index
else if prefix matches may be useful
       but there are many updates
```

```
            then use a composite B-tree index
else if prefix matches are not useful but
        multiple attribute exact matches are useful
            then use a composite hash index
else don't use a composite index
end if
```

Compression

Use key compression when the following conditions all hold:

- You are using a data structure other than a hash structure.
- Compressing the key will reduce the number of levels in your index.
- Your system is disk-bound but has plenty of processor power.
- Updates to the data structure are relatively rare. (Updates to the underlying table that don't affect the index cause no difficulty, but insertions and deletions do.)

Sequential keys

Sequential keys suffer from a concurrency control disadvantage compared with nonsequential keys when the following conditions all hold.

- The sequential key is on a table with many inserts—concurrent inserts perform poorly.
- The table is organized as a heap or is clustered based on a B-tree or ISAM data structure.
- Page-level locking is used either on the table or on the clustering data structure. (The problem will be reduced but not eliminated if you use record-level locking.)

Table 3.1   INDEXES OFFERED BY SOME RELATIONAL VENDORS

System	Primary Data Structures	Secondary Data Structures
DEC RDB	B-tree (dense), Hash (sparse)	B-tree
IBM DB2,	B-tree (dense)	B-tree
IBM SQL/DS	B-tree (dense)	B-tree
IBM OS/2	B-tree (dense)	B-tree
INGRES	B-tree (dense)	B-tree
	Hash (sparse), ISAM (sparse)	Hash, ISAM
ORACLE	B-tree (dense)	B-tree
SYBASE	B-tree (sparse)	B-tree

What systems offer

Virtually all commercial database management systems offer B-trees, usually with prefix compression. Systems differ in whether they offer other data structures and whether their primary (clustering) indexes are sparse or not. (Recall that secondary indexes must be dense.) Table 3.1 summarizes the facilities offered by some major relational products as of the beginning of 1992.

3.10 DISTRIBUTING THE INDEXES OF A HOT TABLE

A *hot table* is one that is accessed by many transactions concurrently. If several disks are available, then it may be worthwhile to partition accesses to that table across several disks. Depending on the access patterns, you may choose one of two organizations:

- Insert- or delete-intensive applications should move their nonclustering indexes to a disk other than the one containing the table data. The reason is that all indexes will have to be updated when an insert takes place. This partitioning balances the load between the disks having the nonclustering indexes and the disks having the clustering index and the table data. It is useful to keep the clustering index with the table data, because most read accesses and all insert accesses will use that index.
- Applications that perform many point queries and multipoint queries with few updates or with updates that modify only nonindexed attributes should spread the table, the clustering index, and the nonclustering indexes over several available disks. This maximizes the number of queries that can execute concurrently.

3.11 GENERAL CARE AND FEEDING OF INDEXES

Here are some maintenance tips on indexes.

- From time to time, your indexes need the data equivalent of a face lift. For example,
  - In a clustering index on attribute A, data page overflows have caused new pages to be placed on a different cylinder from old pages whose records have the same A values.
  - An ISAM structure (or hash structure) has long overflow chains.
  - Hash structures showing poor performance for point or multipoint queries may have insufficient space on disk. Recall that some systems suggest that hash spaces be no more than 50% utilized—check your tuning manual.

- A B-tree has many empty nodes that have not been removed (this occurs in some systems such as INGRES that do not free index nodes that are empty).

To fix these problems, you can drop the index and rebuild it perhaps allocating more space. Some systems allow you to modify an index in place.

- Drop indexes when they hurt performance. If an application performs complicated queries at night and short insert transactions during the day, then it may be a good idea to drop the indexes when the updates occur and then rebuild them when the inserts have completed.

- Run the catalog statistics update package regularly to ensure that the optimizer has the information it needs to choose the proper indexes.

When running those statistics, consider the options carefully. Some systems, such as INGRES, offer histogram options on the statistics update package. The idea is to give the density of values in a given range. For example, if many employees have salaries between $40,000 and $50,000, but only a few have salaries between $1,400,000 and $1,500,000, then the system will be smart enough to use a nonclustering salary index for queries on the higher salary range but not for the lower one. Choosing many histogram cells will help the query optimizer make the correct decision.

- Use a system utility that tells you how the system processes the query, i.e., the system's *query plan*. (Nearly every system has this facility, see chapter 7, section 7.4.) The query plan will tell you which indexes are being used. Aside from out-of-date catalog statistics, there are several reasons why a query optimizer may not use indexes that might help.

  - The use of an arithmetic expression. For example, suppose that the Employee relation stores yearly salary and you want to find those employees who earn more than $4000 per month. Here are two equivalent queries (ignoring arithmetic precision issues).

```
SELECT *
FROM Employee
WHERE salary/12 >= 4000

SELECT *
FROM Employee
WHERE salary >= 4000 * 12
```

However, in many systems, the first query will not use an index on salary, whereas the second one will.

- The use of a string function. For example, the following query may not use an index on name in some systems:

```
SELECT *
FROM Employee
WHERE SUBSTR(name, 1, 1) = 'G'
```

- If a bind variable (a variable set by the programming language) has a different type than the attribute to which it is being compared, the index might not be used, as in IBM's OS/2 EE system. So, if you compare a bind variable with a table attribute, ensure they are of the same type. This means

  – Integer with integer of same size.
  – Float with float of same size.
  – String with string of the same maximum size.

- A comparison with NULL.

```
SELECT *
FROM Employee
WHERE salary IS NULL
```

- Some systems may not use indexes effectively for certain types of queries, such as nested subqueries, selection by negation, and queries that use ORs. We discuss this further in section 4.6 of the next chapter.

3.12 TROUBLESHOOTING

The scenarios below use the following tables. (Similar scenarios would apply to collections in object-oriented systems.)

- Employee(ssnum, name, dept, manager, salary).
- Student(ssnum, name, course, grade, stipend, written_evaluation).

Scenario 1

When the Student relation was created, a nonclustering index was created on name. However, the following query does not use that index.

```
SELECT *
FROM Student
WHERE name = 'Bayer'
```

   Action.   Perhaps, the catalog statistics have not been updated recently. For that reason, the optimizer concludes that Student is small and hence the index should not be used. Try updating the statistics.

Scenario 2

You discover that the following important query is too slow. It is a simple query, and there is a nonclustering index on salary. You have tried to update the catalog statistics, but that did not help.

```
SELECT *
FROM Employee
WHERE salary/12 = 4000
```

Action.   The index is not used because of the arithmetic expression.

Scenario 3

Your customer eliminates the arithmetic expression, yielding the following query.

```
SELECT *
FROM Employee
WHERE salary = 48000
```

However, the system uses the index without improving performance.

Action.   The index is not a clustering index. Many employees happen to have a salary of $48,000. Using the index causes many random page reads, nearly one for each employee. The index may be useful for other salaries that are less common, however.

Scenario 4

Your system has a 2-kilobyte size page. The Student table records are very long (about 1 kilobyte), because of the length of the written_evaluation field. There is a clustering index on Social Security number, but the table suffers overflow chaining when new written_evaluation data is added.

Action.   The clustering index doesn't help much compared with a nonclustering one on Social Security number. The nonclustering index will be easier to maintain.

Scenario 5

Suppose there are 30 Employee records per page. Each employee belongs to one of 50 departments. Should you put a nonclustering index on department?

Action.   If such an index were used, performance would be worse, not better. The reason is that approximately 3/5 (=30/50) of the pages would have Employee records from any given department. Using the index, the database system would access 3/5 of the pages in random order. A table scan would likely be faster.

Scenario 6

Suppose there are 30 Employee records per page. However, in this case, there are 2,000 departments. Should you put a nonclustering index on department to support multipoint queries on departments?

Action. Each page has only a 30/2000 chance of having an Employee record. Using the index would be worthwhile.

Scenario 7

Auditors take a copy of the Employee file to which they wish to apply a statistical analysis. They allow no updates, but want to support the following accesses:

1. Count all the employees that have a certain salary (frequent).

2. Find the employees that have the maximum (or minimum) salary within a particular department (frequent).

3. Find the employee with a certain Social Security number (rare).

Initially, there is no index.

Action. A clustering index on salary would give less benefit than a nonclustering index, because the first query can be answered solely based on the nonclustering index on salary. That is, it won't be necessary to access the actual Employee records. By contrast, the same query using a clustering index may have to access the Employee records if the clustering index is sparse. A nonclustering composite index on (dept, salary) using a B-tree would be useful to answer the second style of query. A sparse clustering index on Social Security number will help if the Employee tuples are small, because a sparse index may be a level shorter than a dense one.

Scenario 8

Suppose that the student stipends correspond to monthly salaries whereas the employee salaries are yearly. To find out which employees are paid as much as which students, we have two choices.

```
SELECT *
FROM Employee, Student
WHERE salary = 12*stipend
```

or

```
SELECT *
FROM Employee, Student
WHERE salary/12 = stipend
```

Which is better?

Action.   Many systems will use an index on salary but not on stipend for the first query, whereas they will use an index on stipend but not on salary for the second query. If there is an index on only one of these, then it should be used.

If there are indexes on both, then the situation is a bit complicated.

- If the index on the larger table is clustering, then arrange your query to use it. This will avoid reading the larger relation.
- Even if the index on the larger table is nonclustering, but the larger table has more pages than the smaller table has records, then arrange your query to use the index on the larger table. Again, this will avoid reading all the pages of the larger relation. This will be a common case.
- By contrast, suppose the index on the larger table is nonclustering and you suspect that every page of the larger table will have at least one record that matches some record of the smaller table. In that case, using the index on the larger table may cause the query to access the same page of the larger table several times. So, it may be worthwhile to arrange your query to use the index on the smaller table.

The ideal would be that the two fields be placed on the same basis, i.e., both monthly or both yearly. Then the optimizer would make the choice.

Scenario 9

A purchasing department maintains the relation Onorder(supplier, part, quantity, price).

The department makes the following queries to Onorder.

1. Add a tuple, specifying all fields (very frequent).
2. Delete a tuple, specifying supplier and part (very frequent).
3. Find the total quantity of a given part on order (frequent).
4. Find the total value of the orders to a given supplier (rare).

Action.   If there is time to eliminate overflow pages at night, then a clustering composite index on (part, supplier) would work well. Part should come first in the composite index, because then a prefix match query on part will answer query 3. (Because of this prefix match query, the data structure in the clustering composite index should be a B-tree rather than a hash structure.)

Scenario 10

Consider a variant of scenario 9 in which the queries access an archival read-only Onorder relation.

Action.   Once again, a clustering composite index on (part, supplier) would work well. To support query 4, a nonclustering index on supplier alone would be helpful.

Scenario 11

A credit card company has a sudden inflow of new clients. Customer numbers are assigned in order of insertion. Transactions access the client table in four basic ways.

- Insert new client records. (frequent)
- Locate a client by Social Security number. (frequent)
- Locate a client by customer number. (occasional)
- Scan the table for customer billing purposes. (rare)

There is a clustering hash index on Social Security number. There is a nonclustering B-tree index on customer number. By using a system-specific facility for sequence numbers (see the section 2.2 (p. 26) of the last chapter) you ensure that customer number is not a bottleneck. Nevertheless, concurrent insert transactions appear to serialize.

Action.   All inserts modify the last page of the B-tree index. Observe that the lock contention does not occur on data pages because the data pages are clustered by Social Security number rather than by order of insertion. One solution is to use a hash nonclustering index on customer number instead of a B-tree index. Hashing will tend to place new distinct records randomly in the hash index, thus avoiding the creation of a contention bottleneck.

Scenario 12

A table has a clustering B-tree index on Social Security number and performs simple retrievals and updates of records based on Social Security number. The performance is still not good enough. What should be done?

Action.   B-trees are not as fast as hash structures for point queries.

Scenario 13

The Employee table has no clustering indexes. It is found to perform poorly when there are many concurrent inserts. What should be done?

Action.   Employee is organized as a heap, so all inserts to Employee occur on the last page, making that page a locking hot spot. The following should help:

- Find some way to even out the flow of inserts. (This may not be possible for the application, e.g. all ending stock prices are inserted at the closing of the market. In that case, group all inserts into a single threaded set of transactions and eliminate concurrent queries.)

- Use record-level locking.
- Create a hash-based clustering index based on customer number or Social Security number. (Hashing will spread records with consecutive customer numbers across the file.) Alternatively, create a B-tree-based clustering index on Social Security number. (This will also spread the records across the file.)

Scenario 14

Ellis Island is a small island south of Manhattan through which flowed some 17 million immigrants to the United States between the late 1800s and the mid-1900s. Immigration workers filled in some 200 fields on each immigrant, containing information such as last name (as interpreted by the immigration worker), first name, city of origin, ship taken, nationality, religion, arrival date, and so on. You are to design a database management system to allow the approximately 100 million descendants of these 17 million to retrieve the record of their ancestors.

To identify an immigrant, the querier must know the last name of the immigrant as well as some other information (the more the merrier). Most queriers will know the last name and either the first name or the year of arrival. What is a good structure?

Action.   Once the records are loaded, this database is never updated. So, an ISAM structure is a good possibility, if your system offers one. Otherwise use a B-tree. Because nearly all queriers know the last name of their ancestor and many know the first name as well, a clustering composite index on (last name, first name) would help. Indexes on other single fields would probably not help because they would not be selective enough. However, composite indexes on (last name, year of arrival) might be helpful. Because there are no updates, the only cost to indexes is space.

4

Tuning a Relational Database System

4.1 GOAL OF CHAPTER

Approximately 80% of the database systems sold today are relational—not bad for a data model that was dismissed as totally impractical when Ted Codd first introduced it in the early 1970s (shows you how much to trust critics). The relational model offers a simple, more or less portable, expressive language (usually SQL) with a multitude of efficient implementations.[1]

To put relational systems in perspective, let us consider the applications that each data model dominates.

- Hierarchical and network data models tend to be used for applications with simple (preferably hierarchical) data relationships that change little over time. High performance is critical. Special high performance hierarchical databases, e.g., IMS/FastPath, are about twice as fast as relational systems, e.g., DB2, for online transaction processing. This speed advantage is, however, diminishing and good tuning of a relational application can often result

[1] In 1990, according to International Data Corporation, relational database software sold for about $1.4 billion just counting IBM mainframe, DEC VMS, and UNIX platforms. Installations of the IBM mainframe market through 1990 were about evenly split between DB2 on MVS (about 6,000 copies) and SQL/DS on VM (5,000 copies). The DEC VAX/VMS market was dominated by ORACLE with 48,000 of the 74,000 copies, though DEC RDB was a strong contender (15,000 copies). INGRES, INFORMIX, and SYBASE each sold fewer than 6,000 copies. On UNIX, ORACLE and INFORMIX each sold about 40,000 copies whereas INGRES and SYBASE each sold fewer than 5,000 copies.

in the same high performance as conversion to a hierarchical data model—and at far less expense.

- Today's object-oriented database systems are best used for applications that perform graph traversal as a fundamental operation. Circuit design and newspaper layout are often-cited examples. We will discuss this comparative advantage in detail in the next chapter.
- Relational systems capture the rest of the market. This includes their well-known applications in finance, accounting, and decision support, but extends to signal processing, genetics, and medical computing.

Because of the spectrum of applications that relational systems cover, making them perform well requires a careful analysis of the application at hand. Helping you do that analysis is the goal of this chapter. The analysis will have implications for lower level facilities, such as indexes and concurrency control. This chapter, however, discusses higher level facilities (Figure 4.1). The discussion will concentrate on four topics.

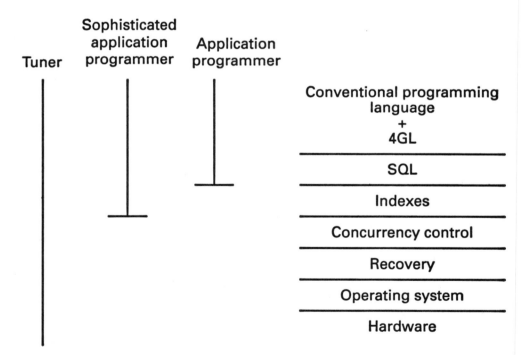

Figure 4.1   Architecture of Relational Database Systems with Tuning Responsibilities.

- Table (relation) design—tradeoffs among normalization, denormalization, clustering, aggregate materialization, and vertical partitioning. Tradeoffs among different data types for record design.
- Query rewriting—using indexes appropriately, avoiding DISTINCT's and ORDER BY's, the appropriate use of temporary tables, and so on.
- Procedural extensions to relational algebra—embedded programming languages, stored procedures, and triggers.
- Connections—to hierarchical databases and to conventional programming languages.

4.2 TABLE SCHEMA AND NORMALIZATION

One of the first steps in designing an application is to design the tables (or relations) where the data will be stored. Once your application is running, changing the table design may require that you change many of your application programs. So, it is important to get the design right the first time.

Normalization is a rational guide to the design of database tables.

Preliminary definitions

A *relation schema* is a relation name and a set of attribute names. If you think of a relation as a table name, then its schema is the table name plus the column headers of that table. A *relation instance* for a relation R is a set of records over the attributes in the schema for R. Informally, a relation instance is the set of records (or rows or tuples, if you wish) in the table.

For example, table 4.1 is called Purchase and has attributes name, item, price, quantity, supplier, and year. The records are the four bottom rows.

Schemas can be good or bad

Consider the following two schema designs for information relating suppliers and their addresses to the parts on order and the quantity ordered of each part from each supplier.

Table 4.1 PURCHASE TABLE

name	item	price	quantity	supplier	year
Bolt	4325	15	60	Standard Part	1990
Washer	5925	13	60	Standard Part	1991
Screw	6324	17	54	Standard Part	1992
Nut	3724	15	80	Metal Part	1990

Schema design I:

- Onorder1(supplier_ID, part_ID, quantity, supplier_address)

Schema design II:

- Onorder2(supplier_ID, part_ID, quantity)
- Supplier(supplier_ID, supplier_address)

Let us compare these two schema designs according to three criteria. Assume that there are 100,000 orders outstanding and 2,000 suppliers altogether. Further assume that the supplier_ID is an eight-byte integer (64-bit machine) and the supplier_address requires 50 bytes.

1. *Space*: The second schema will use extra space for the redundant supplier_ID = 2000 × 8 = 16,000 bytes. The second schema stores will save space, however, by storing 2000 supplier addresses as opposed to 100,000 supplier addresses in the first schema. So, the second schema consumes $98,000 × 50 = 4,950,000$ bytes less space for address information. Adding these two effects together, the second schema actually saves 4,934,000 bytes under the given assumptions.

2. *Information preservation*: Suppose that supplier QuickDelivery has delivered all parts that were on order. The semantics of the relation Onorder1 dictate that the records pertaining to QuickDelivery should be deleted since the order has been filled. The problem is that the database would lose any record of QuickDelivery's address. Using the second schema, you would not lose the address information, because it will be held in the Supplier relation.

3. *Performance*: Suppose one frequently wants to know the address of the supplier from where a given part has been ordered. Then the first schema, despite the problems mentioned so far, may be good, especially if there are few updates. If, however, there are many new orders, i.e. many insertions, then including the supplier address in every Onorder1 record requires extra data entry effort or entails an extra lookup to the database system for every part ordered from the supplier. So, these two schemas present a tuning tradeoff. Starting with section 4.2.4 (p. 97) you will see how to make this tradeoff for your application.

Relation Onorder2 is *normalized*, whereas Onorder1 is *unnormalized*. What do these terms mean?

Intuitively, the problem of the first schema is that the relationship between supplier_ID and supplier_address is repeated for every part on order. This wastes space and makes the presence of a given supplier's address dependent on the presence of parts on order from that supplier.

We can formalize this intuition through the notion of functional dependencies. Suppose X is a set of attributes of a relation R, and A is a single attribute of R. We say that X *determines* A or that the functional dependency $X \rightarrow A$ holds for R if the following is true: For any relation instance I of R, whenever there are two records r and r' in I with the same X values, they have the same A values as well. The functional dependency $X \rightarrow A$ is *interesting* if A is not an attribute of X.

Suppose you discover that each supplier is to be associated with a single address. This implies that any two records with the same supplier_ID value have the same supplier_address value as well. Thus, supplier_ID $\rightarrow$ supplier_address is an interesting functional dependency.

Having defined a functional dependency, we can now define a *key*. Attributes X from relation R constitute a key of R if X determines every attribute in R and no proper subset of X determines every attribute in R. For example, in the relation Onorder1, supplier_ID and part_ID together constitute a key. In the relation Supplier, supplier_ID by itself constitutes a key. So a key of a relation is a minimal set that determines all attributes in the relation.[2]

Check yourself with the following:

- Do you see why supplier_ID by itself does not constitute a key of relation Onorder1?

  Answer. Because supplier_ID does not determine part_ID.

- Do you see why supplier_ID and supplier_address together do not constitute a key of Supplier?

  Answer. Because supplier_ID by itself determines all the attributes. That is, supplier_ID and supplier_address do not constitute a minimal set of attributes that determines all attributes.

A relation R is *normalized* if every interesting functional dependency $X \rightarrow A$ involving attributes in R has the property that X is a key of R.

Relation Onorder1 is not normalized because the key is supplier_ID and part_ID together, yet supplier_ID by itself determines supplier_address. It does not matter that supplier_ID is part of the key. For the relation to be normalized, supplier_ID would have to be the whole key.

Relation Onorder2 and Supplier are both normalized.

---

[2] There is an unfortunate confusion in database terminology regarding the word *key*. The key of an index is the attribute or sequence of attributes by which one can search the index. There may be many records in a given relation with the same value of a given index key. In normalization theory, a key of a relation R is a set of attributes such that no two records of any instance of R have the same values on all the attributes of that key. You must always use context to determine the sense in which "key" is meant. This chapter uses "key" in the sense of normalization theory.

4.2.1 Normalization by Example

Practice Question 1. Suppose that a bank associates each customer with his or her home branch, i.e., the branch where the customer opened his or her first account. Each branch is in a specific legal jurisdiction, denoted jurisdiction. Is the relation (customer, branch, jurisdiction) normalized?

Answer to Practice Question 1. Let us look at the functional dependencies. Because each customer has one home branch, we have

$$customer \rightarrow branch$$

Because each branch is in exactly one jurisdiction, we have

$$branch \rightarrow jurisdiction$$

So, customer is the key, yet the left-hand side of the functional dependency branch $\rightarrow$ jurisdiction is not customer. Therefore (customer, branch, jurisdiction) is not normalized. Its problems are exactly the problems of Onorder1 earlier:

Relation (customer, branch, jurisdiction) will use more space than the two relations (customer, branch) and (branch, jurisdiction). Also, if a branch loses its customers, then the database loses the relationship between branch and jurisdiction. (The bank directors may not care, but information scientists like to preserve information.)

Practice Question 2. Suppose a doctor can work in several hospitals and receives a salary from each. Is the relation (doctor, hospital, salary) normalized?

Answer to Practice Question 2. The only functional dependency here is doctor, hospital $\rightarrow$ salary. Therefore, this relation is normalized.

Practice Question 3. Suppose that we add the field primary_home_address to the previous question. Each doctor has one primary_home_address, but many doctors may have the same primary home address. Would the relation
(doctor, hospital, salary, primary_home_address) be normalized?

Answer to Practice Question 3. We have a new functional dependency.

$$doctor \rightarrow primary\_home\_address$$

Unfortunately, doctor is a proper subset of the key of the relation so the relation is unnormalized. The key is doctor and hospital together.

A normalized decomposition would be

(doctor, hospital, salary)
(doctor, primary_home_address)

Practice Question 4. Suppose that a new law forbids doctors from working in more than one hospital. However, nothing else changes. In that case, is (doctor, hospital, salary, primary_home_address) normalized?

Answer to Practice Question 4.   In this case, we have the following functional dependencies:

$$doctor \rightarrow primary\_home\_address$$
$$doctor \rightarrow hospital$$
$$doctor \rightarrow salary$$

So, doctor by itself is the key, and the relation is normalized.

Practice Question 5.   Suppose we have the situation of the previous question, but we add the hospital_address associated with each hospital. In that case, is (doctor, hospital, hospital_address, salary, primary_home_address) normalized?

Answer to Practice Question 5.   To the functional dependencies that we have already, we would add

$$hospital \rightarrow hospital\_address$$

Because doctor is still the key of the relation, we have a functional dependency involving the attributes of a relation in which the left-hand side is not the key of the relation. Therefore the relation is not normalized.

A possible decomposition would yield the relations

$$(doctor, hospital, salary, primary\_home\_address)$$
$$(hospital, hospital\_address)$$

Notice that these two relations would probably occupy less space than the single unnormalized one, because the hospital address would be represented only once per hospital.

4.2.2 A Practical Way to Design Relations

There are many algorithms to design normalized relations. In practice, such algorithms are far more complicated than necessary. An easier strategy is to find the *entities* in the application. Intuitively, entities make up what the application designer considers to be the "individuals" of the database. For example, doctors, hospitals, suppliers, and parts might be the entities of the applications we've spoken about so far. Usually, an entity has *attributes* that are properties of the entity. For example, hospitals have a jurisdiction, an address, and so on. There are two formal constraints on attributes.

- An attribute cannot have attributes of its own. Only entities can have attributes.
- The entity associated with an attribute must functionally determine that attribute. (For example, there must be one value of address for a given hospital.) Otherwise, the attribute should be an entity in its own right.

Each entity with its associated attributes becomes a relation. For example, the entity doctor with attributes salary, primary_home_address, and so on becomes a relation. Hospital is not part of that relation according to this design methodology, because hospital is an entity in its own right with attributes hospital_address, and so on.

To that collection of relations, add relations that reflect *relationships* between entities. For example, there is a relationship "Worksin" between doctors and hospitals. Its schema might be (doctor_ID, hospital_ID).

Three relations would result from this design strategy for an application concerning doctors and hospitals.

1. Doctor(doctor_ID, primary_home_address, . . .)
2. Hospital(hospital_ID, hospital_address, . . .)
3. Worksin(doctor_ID, hospital_ID)

Most CASE (computer-aided software engineering) tools, such as those from Ernst and Young, James Martin Associates, KnowledgeWare, SEMA Group, Peter Chen Associates, TRT-TI, Bachmann Engineering, and INFOSYS, begin with something similar to this "entity-relationship" design strategy.

4.2.3 Functional Dependency Test

In most cases, your relations will be normalized after you have used this entity-relationship methodology. To be sure, you can use functional dependencies. The two main conditions to check are that

- Each relation is normalized.
- The attributes constituting each "minimal" functional dependency are a subset of the attributes of some relation.

For example, if the functional dependency $AB \rightarrow C$ holds and is minimal, then attributes A, B, and C should all be attributes of some relation R.

Intuitively, a functional dependency is minimal if it is not implied by other functional dependencies, and it does not have too many attributes on the left-hand side. For an example of a redundant functional dependency, consider the three functional dependencies $A \rightarrow B$, $B \rightarrow C$, and $A \rightarrow C$. The third one is implied by the other two. That is, any table satisfying the first two will also satisfy the last one. Given these functional dependencies, we would construct two relations having schemas *(A, B)* and *(B, C)*, but no relation having schema *(A, B, C)* or *(A, C)*, because $A \rightarrow C$ is not minimal in this context.

Now let's see how a functional dependency can have too many attributes on its left-hand side. Suppose there are three functional dependencies $A \rightarrow B$,

$ABF \rightarrow C$, and $BD \rightarrow E$, then the second one has an unnecessary attribute on its left-hand side. The reason is that any table satisfying the first two functional dependencies will also satisfy $AF \rightarrow C$. (If two rows of the table have the same AF values, then they have the same B values because of $A \rightarrow B$ and the same C values because of $ABF \rightarrow C$.) On the other hand, the third functional dependency has no extra attributes on the left-hand side. So, the three corresponding minimal functional dependencies are $A \rightarrow B$, $AF \rightarrow C$ and $BD \rightarrow E$. This leads to the schemas *(A, B)*, *(A, F, C)*, and *(B, D, E)*, but not *(A, B, C, F)*.

If you are a mathematician at heart, you may want to read the rigorous but clear discussion of the preceding procedure in Dave Maier's book[3]. Serge Abiteboul, Rick Hull, and Victor Vianu will soon also publish a new book on database theory.

4.2.4 Tuning Normalization

Different normalization strategies may guide you to different sets of normalized relations, all equally good according to our criteria so far. Which set to choose depends on your application's query patterns.

Scenario: different normalization sets 1

Suppose that we have three attributes: account_ID, balance and address.

The functional dependencies are

- account_ID $\rightarrow$ address

and

- account_ID $\rightarrow$ balance

There are two normalized schema designs in this case.

- (account_ID, address, balance)

and

- (account_ID, address)
- (account_ID, balance)

The question is: Which design is better? Let us look at the query patterns.

In most U.S. banks, the application that sends a monthly statement is the principal user of the address of the owner of an account. By contrast, the balance is updated or examined much more often, possibly several times a day. In such

---

[3] David Maier, *The Theory of Relational Databases*. New York: Computer Science Press, division of W. H. Freeman, 1983.

a case, the second schema might be better, because the (account_ID, balance) relation can be made smaller. This offers three benefits.

1. A sparse clustering index on the account_ID field of the (account_ID, balance) relation may be a level shorter than it would be for the (account_ID, balance, address) relation, because the leaves of such an index will have only one pointer per data page, and there will be far fewer data pages.

2. More account_ID-balance pairs will fit in memory, thus increasing the hit ratio for random accesses.

3. A transaction that must scan a significant portion of account_ID-balance pairs will read relatively few pages.

In this case, two relations are better than one, even though the two relation solution requires more space.

Scenario: different normalization sets 2

Suppose that the address field in scenario 1 were actually divided into two fields, a street address and a zip code. Would the following normalized schema design make sense?

- (account_ID, street address)
- (account_ID, zip code)
- (account_ID, balance)

Because street address and zip code are accessed together or not at all in this application, dividing the address information among two relations hurts performance and uses more space.

In this case, having one relation (account_ID, street address, zip code) will give better performance than having two (account_ID, street address) and (account_ID, zip code).

The preceding examples show that the choices among different normalized designs depend critically on the application's access patterns. Usually, a single normalized relation with attributes XYZ, is better than two normalized relations XY and XZ, because the single relation design allows a query to request X, Y, and Z together without requiring a join. The two-relation design is better if and only if the following two conditions hold:

- User accesses tends to partition between the two sets most of the time. (80% of the time or more is a good rule of thumb, because joins are expensive.)
- Attribute Y values or attribute Z values or both are large (one-third the page size or larger).

Bond scenario

In certain cases, you may start with a vertically partitioned schema and then perform what may be called *vertical antipartitioning*. Here is an example.

Some brokers base their bond-buying decisions on the price trends of those bonds. The database holds the closing price for the last 3000 trading days. However, statistics regarding the 10 most recent trading days are especially important.

Consider therefore the following two schemas.

- (bond_ID, issue_date, maturity, . . .)—about 500 bytes per record.
- (bond_ID, date, price)—about 12 bytes per record.

  versus

- (bond_ID, issue_date, maturity, today_price, yesterday_price, . . . 10dayago_price)—about 600 bytes per record.
- (bond_ID, date, price)

Suppose we arrange for the second schema to store *redundant* information. That is both relations will store the data from the last 10 days of activity. This will cost a little extra space, but will be much better for queries that need information about prices in the last ten days, because it will avoid a join and will avoid fetching 10 price records per bond. Even if (bond_ID, date, price) is clustered by bond_ID and date, the second schema will save at least one disk access for such queries. It may save more depending on the number of overflow pages needed to store all the price records associated with a given bond.

It is possible to avoid redundancy by storing records in the (bond_ID, date, price) table only after they become more than 10 days old, but then queries that want the price on a given day or the average price over a range of 50 consecutive days (given as a parameter) become very difficult to write.

4.2.5 Tuning Denormalization

Denormalization, i.e., violating normalization, has only one excuse: performance. Even this excuse applies only to some situations. The schema design

$$Onorder1(supplier\_ID, part\_ID, quantity, supplier\_address)$$

is bad for performance when inserts are frequent. As mentioned earlier, the data entry operator must either enter or look up the supplier address when performing an insertion.

This schema design would help a query that returns the parts available from suppliers having some zip code, however.

As a general rule, denormalization hurts performance for relations that are often updated. However, denormalization may help performance in low-update situations. For that reason, some applications denormalize their archival data while keeping their online data normalized. (Updates can also introduce semantic errors as in the QuickDelivery scenario cited at the beginning of this section, thus hurting maintainability.)

In the next section, we will compare denormalization with a compromise design technique: table clustering.

4.3 CLUSTERING TWO TABLES TOGETHER

Some systems such as ORACLE offer the possibility to cluster two tables together based on the key of one of the tables. For example, suppose that there are two relations.

- Branch(branch_ID, city, balance, . . .)
- Account(account_ID, owner, balance, branch_ID, . . .)

Clustering would intermix these two tables, so there will be a single Branch record followed by all the Account records that match the Branch record. In that case branch_ID is said to be a *cluster key*. Here is how the layout might appear.

- Branch 1 record

  - Account 235 record
  - Account 981 record   *accounts at Branch 1*
  - Account 112 record

- Branch 2 record

  - Account 239 record
  - Account 523 record   *accounts at Branch 2*
  - Account 867 record

Clustering tables has its good and bad points.

- Queries on the cluster key are fast. Thus, a query that wants to find all accounts at a particular branch will execute quickly.
- Point queries on either Branch or Account that use indexes will behave as well as point queries using nonclustering indexes on the standard layout.
- Full table scans of the Account table will be somewhat slower than in a standard layout. Full table scans of the Branch table will be much slower than in a standard layout, because there may be many Account records between neighboring Branch records.

- Insertions may cause overflow chaining, slowing the performance of cluster key searches. In fact, if there are enough insertions, application performance may degrade badly.

Different systems will have different advice regarding the layout of clusters. However, here is good general advice.

- It is good to cluster on a key of a small table that is an attribute of a larger table. We did that in the preceding example, when we clustered based on branch_ID (the key of the smaller table Branch).
- Estimate the size in bytes of the records from the larger table (Account in the preceding example) corresponding to each record of the smaller table (Branch). If the estimate is too high, there will be wasted space and scans through one table or the other will be slow. If the estimate is too low, there will be excessive chaining.
- Make sure that the cluster is used properly. For example, in ORACLE version 5, it is important to mention the larger table first when writing a join query. For the account-branch example, this would suggest the following form for a select statement that seeks cities with people having large balances:

```
SELECT DISTINCT branch.city
FROM Account, Branch
WHERE Account.account_ID = Branch.branch_ID
AND   Account.balance > 500000
```

Digression regarding definitions

It is important to understand the similarities and differences between table clustering and index clustering.

- Both concepts force a certain organization on table records.
- A clustering index forces an organization onto the records of a single table and provides an index to access the records of that table. Table clustering forces an intermixing of the records between two different tables based on an attribute, essentially precomputing a join.
- As far as the larger table is concerned, the performance effect of table clustering is similar to having a clustering index on the cluster key field. For example, clustering Account with Branch on branch_ID gives similar performance to a clustering index on Account.branch_ID. The smaller table, by contrast, has no clustering index.

4.3.1 Clustering Versus Denormalization

To gain intuition concerning the relative merits of table clustering compared with denormalization, consider the following scenarios.

Basic mail order scenario

Suppose that an application supporting a mail order department store includes the following relations

- Sale(customernum, itemnum, quantity, date, price)
- Customer(customernum, customercity, customerstreet, customername)

There are two kinds of transactions on these relations.

1. *Record sale:* This involves an insertion into the Sale relation. There are an average of 10 sales per customer per month.

2. *Send bill to customer:* This happens once a month for each customer and entails summing the values of the sales for that customer and sending them to the customer address (which is the concatenation of customername, customerstreet, and customercity). The Sale records corresponding to that month are then deleted from the Sale relation.

Consider three relational organizations.

1. *Standard:* The Sale and Customer tables are stored separately. Both have a clustering index on customernum.

2. *Clustered:* The two tables are stored together with customernum as the cluster key. That is, each Customer record *r* is followed by all Sale records that have the same customernum as *r*. The organization of the table can be illustrated as follows:

- Customer record for customernum X

  - Sale record for customernum X
  - second Sale record for customernum X
  - third Sale record for customernum X
  - fourth Sale record for customernum X

- Customer record for customernum Y

  - Sale record for customernum Y
  - second Sale record for customernum Y

  and so on

3. *Denormalized:* Add the customer address to the Sale relation.

The denormalized organization uses by far the most space, because the customer address is added to each Sale record. Obtaining the customer at the time of each sale entails either extra key punch effort or an extra table lookup—by now a familiar refrain.

Table clustering will use the next largest amount of space, if one overestimates the space devoted to Sale records between succeeding Customer records. The table clustering organization is much faster for the Billing transaction, but a little slower for the Record Sale transaction. So, cluster the tables if sending bills is a bottleneck. Otherwise, use the standard organization.

Embellished mail order scenario

The marketing department decides that it would like to "mine" the sales information to determine which items to put in a brochure and where to send those brochures. Specifically, they want to issue queries that

- Correlate the sale of some specific item, e.g., safari hat, with the city where the customer lives.
- Find a correlation between different items bought at different times, e.g., do people frequently buy safari hats soon after buying khaki shorts?

So, they request that a new relation called Oldsale be created. When a bill is sent to the customer, the records deleted from Sale are placed in Oldsale. There are several possible organizations of Oldsale.

1. *Standard:* Oldsale has the same attributes as Sale. That is, Oldsale(customernum, itemnum, quantity, date, price). The Customer relation is not touched.

2. *Clustered:* Oldsale has the same attributes as Sale and an additional relation Oldcustomer has the same attributes as Customer. The two are clustered on customernum.

3. *Denormalized:* Oldsale acquires the customercity in addition to the attributes of Sale.

Because the queries will take far longer than the insertions and the insertions will be done on a customer-by-customer basis, the denormalized design is extremely attractive because it saves a join on the query that correlates customer city with the sale of a particular item. Neither of the other designs measures up.

We can draw three lesssons from these scenarios.

1. Insert- and update-intensive applications with few long queries should use a standard, normalized, design without table clustering.

2. If a certain join is computed frequently, insertions are rare, and most updates do not increase the size of records, then consider table clustering on the join field. (Updates that don't change record sizes will not disrupt the physical layout of the cluster.)

3. *Data mining* applications (complicated read-only activities, requiring many joins on a normalized schema) are the best candidates for denormalization.

4.4 DENORMALIZATION TROUBLESHOOTING

4.4.1 Situations

1. Your client has an insert-intensive sales application, but the system is not keeping up with the volume of orders. The Orders relation has the schema

• Orders (itemnum, customernum, quantity, timestamp)

with a clustering index using a B-tree based on timestamp. In addition, there is a nonclustering index based on customernum. An order transaction consists of inserting one or more records (one for each item ordered) into order and then checking a credit rating.

Every night the orders are batch sorted by product line and sent to the appropriate factories. You examine the situation and find that there is low disk utilization and a lot of processor idle time. Nevertheless, the system is not keeping up with orders.

Action. As new orders are entered, they are appended to the end of the Orders file because they have the highest timestamp value. This makes the last page of the Orders file a hot spot. All the inserts are effectively serialized because of contention for that last page. Use a hash structure as the clustering data structure or cluster on some nonsequential field (e.g., customernum).

2. The accounting department of a chain of convenience stores issues queries every 20 minutes to discover the total dollar amount on order from a particular vendor and the total dollar amount on order by a particular store. They have a normalized schema.

• Order(ordernum, itemnum, quantity, purchaser, vendor)
• Item(itemnum, price)

Order and Item each has a clustering index on itemnum.

Both "total amount" queries execute very slowly and disrupt normal insert processing into these relations. The database administrator believes he must denormalize Order to include the price. What do you suggest?

Action.   Denormalizing would eliminate one join. However, updating the price of an item would be complicated. Also, every insertion into Order may require a lookup in the (still present) Item table to discover the price. Another approach should at least be considered. First see whether these queries can be done less often. (If they can be executed during off-hours, then they should be.) If they must be done so often, then consider creating two additional relations.

- VendorOutstanding(vendor, amount), where amount is the dollar value of goods on order to the vendor, with a clustering index on vendor.
- StoreOutstanding(store, amount), where amount is the dollar value of goods on order by the store, with a clustering index on store.

This approach, known as *aggregate maintenance*, requires updates to VendorOutstanding and StoreOutstanding on every update of the Order table, so makes it more expensive to insert Order records. The benefit is that the "total amount" queries require a simple lookup with this approach. Thus, aggregate maintenance is worthwhile if the time saved for the lookup queries is greater than the extra time required by all updates between two lookups.

Using the denormalized approach, the Order table must be sorted by the vendor field or the store field. The massive sort would take a long time. This would probably be the worst approach.

3. An airline database stores information about airplanes and flights as follows:

Airplane(airplane_ID, dateofpurchase, model), with key airplane_ID.

Flight(airplane_ID, flight, seat, occupant), with key airplane_ID, flight, seat.

Would there be any performance-related advantage to denormalizing to

(airplane_ID, flight, seat, occupant, dateofpurchase, flight, model)

for the online portion of the database?

Action.   No. Denormalizing is unlikely to help. The number of updates on flights is likely to be much higher than queries relating specific flight-seat pairs to the date of purchase.

4.5 RECORD LAYOUT

Once you have determined the attributes of each relation, you face the far easier task of choosing the data types of the attributes. The issues are fairly straightforward.

- An integer is usually better to use than a float, because floats tend to force selections to perform range queries. For example, if attribute A is computed based on some floating point expression, then a selection to find records having value 5 in attribute A may require the qualification

```
WHERE A >= 4.999
AND A <= 5.001
```

  to avoid problems having to do with different machine precisions. Therefore, you should choose integer values for data such as salaries (record the salary in pennies) and stock prices.

- If the values of an attribute vary greatly in size and there are few updates, then consider using a variable-sized field.

  On most systems, a variable-sized field will be only a few bytes longer than the value it represents. A fixed-sized field has to be long enough for the longest field value. So, variable-sized fields give better space utilization. This makes them better for scans and for clustering indexes. The main cost is that the overhead of doing storage management for variable-sized fields can become significant if there are many updates. Especially disruptive is an update that makes a certain field much larger, e.g., changing the address of an Employee record from NULL to a rural postal address. Such an update may cause that field to be placed on another page (as in ORACLE) or may move the entire containing record to a new page (as in DB2).

4.6 QUERY TUNING

The first tuning method to try is the one whose effect is purely local. Most changes such as adding an index, changing the schema, or modifying transaction lengths have global and sometimes harmful side effects. Rewriting a query to run faster has only beneficial side effects.

There are two ways to see that a query is running too slowly.

1. It issues far too many disk accesses, e.g., a point query scans an entire table.

2. You look at its query plan and see that relevant indexes are not used. (The *query plan* is the method chosen by the optimizer to execute the query.)

Refer to chapter 7 or your system's tuning guide for information about these monitoring facilities. Here are some examples of query tuning and the lessons they offer. The examples use three relations:

- Employee(ssnum, name, manager, dept, salary, numfriends).

Clustering index on ssnum and nonclustering indexes on name and dept each. Ssnum and name each is a key.

- Student(ssnum, name, course, grade).

Clustering index on ssnum and a nonclustering index on name. Ssnum and name each is a key.

- Techdept(dept, manager, location)

Clustering index on dept. Dept is the key. A manager may manage many departments. A location may contain many departments.

1. It is important to make sure that the indexes that you think should be used are in fact being used. As we saw in sections 3.11 and 3.12 of chapter 3 (pp. 82 ff), many query optimizers won't use indexes in the presence of

- Arithmetic expressions:

```
WHERE salary/12 >= 4000
```

- Substring expressions:

```
SELECT *
FROM Employee
WHERE SUBSTR(name, 1, 1) = 'G'
```

- Numerical comparisons of different sized fields (e.g., int and smallint).
- Comparison with NULL.

2. In most systems, DISTINCT will entail a sort or other overhead, so should be avoided.

Query.   Find employees who work in the information systems department. There should be no duplicates.

```
SELECT DISTINCT ssnum
FROM Employee
WHERE dept = 'information systems'
```

There is no need for the keyword DISTINCT, since ssnum is a key of Employee so certainly is a key of a subset of Employee. (Because of the index on ssnum, this particular query may not encounter extra overhead as a result of the DISTINCT keyword, but some cases are not so obvious as we will see later in section 4.6.1, p. 113.)

3. Many subsystems handle subqueries inefficiently.

Query.   Find employee Social Security numbers of employees in the technical departments. There should be no duplicates.

```
SELECT ssnum
FROM Employee
WHERE dept IN (SELECT dept FROM Techdept)
```

might not use the index on Employee dept in some systems. Fortunately, the query is equivalent to the following one, which would use the index on Employee dept:

```
SELECT ssnum
FROM Employee, Techdept
WHERE Employee.dept = Techdept.dept
```

Note that if employees could belong to several departments, then the second query would require DISTINCT whereas the first one would not. Since ssnum is a key of Employee and dept is a key of Techdept, neither query needs DISTINCT (see section 4.6.2 p. 115).

4. The unnecessary use of temporaries can hurt performance for two reasons. First, it may force operations to be performed in a suboptimal order. Second, in some systems, the creation of a temporary causes an update to the catalog, perhaps creating a concurrency control hot spot.

Query.   Find all information department employees who earn more than $40,000.

```
SELECT * INTO Temp
FROM Employee
WHERE salary > 40000

SELECT ssnum
FROM Temp
WHERE Temp.dept = 'information'
```

Not only is there overhead to create the temporary, but the system would miss the opportunity to use the index on dept. A far more efficient solution would be the following:

```
SELECT ssnum
FROM Employee
WHERE Employee.dept = 'information'
AND salary > 40000
```

5. Complicated correlation subqueries may execute inefficiently, so perhaps should be rewritten. In that case, temporaries may help.

Query.   Find the highest paid employees per department.

```
SELECT ssnum
FROM Employee e1
WHERE salary =
   (SELECT MAX(salary)
    FROM Employee e2
    WHERE e2.dept = e1.dept
   )
```

This query may search all of e2 (that is, all of the Employee relation) for each record of e1 (or at least all the records in each department). In that case, this query should be replaced by the following query that uses temporaries.

```
SELECT MAX(salary) as bigsalary, dept INTO Temp
FROM Employee
GROUP BY dept
```

```
SELECT ssnum
FROM Employee, Temp
WHERE salary = bigsalary
AND Employee.dept = Temp.dept
```

Observe that you would not need DISTINCT, because dept is a key of Temp. In the terminology that we will develop later, Temp "reaches" Employee.

6. Temporaries may also help avoid ORDER BY's and scans when there are many queries with slightly different bind variables.

Queries.   For the salary ranges, $40,000 to $49,999, $50,000 to $59,999, $60,000 to $69,999, and $70,000 to $79,999, order the employees by ssnum. Thus, there are four queries.

Each query would have the form (with 40000 and 49999 replaced appropriately):

```
SELECT ssnum, name
FROM Employee
WHERE salary >= 40000
AND salary <= 49999
ORDER BY ssnum
```

That is, each would require a scan through Employee and a sort of the records that survive the qualification on salary. A better approach would do the following:

```
SELECT ssnum, name, salary INTO Temp
FROM Employee
WHERE salary >= 40000
AND salary <= 79999
ORDER BY ssnum
```

A typical query would then have the form:

```
SELECT ssnum, name
FROM Temp
WHERE salary >= 40000
AND salary <= 49999
```

The reformulation would require only

- A single ORDER BY of the records whose salaries satisfy the constraints of the four queries.
- Four scans without an ORDER BY statement of these selected records.

The big savings comes from avoiding a scan of the entire Employee relation for each query. This will reduce the necessary number of disk accesses.

7. It is a good idea to express join conditions on clustering indexes. Failing that, prefer a condition expressing numerical equality to one expressing string equality.

Query.   Find all the students who are also employees.

```
SELECT Employee.ssnum
FROM Employee, Student
WHERE Employee.name = Student.name
```

In this case, the join is correct because name is a key, but we can make it more efficient by replacing the qualification as follows:

```
SELECT Employee.ssnum
FROM Employee, Student
WHERE Employee.ssnum = Student.ssnum
```

This will speed up the query by permitting a merge-join, since both relations are clustered on ssnum.

8. Don't use HAVING when WHERE is enough.

For example, the following query finds the average salary of the information department, but may first perform the grouping for all departments.

```
SELECT AVG(salary) as avgsalary, dept
FROM Employee
GROUP BY dept
HAVING dept = 'information'
```

The following will first find the relevant employees and then compute the average.

```
SELECT AVG(salary) as avgsalary
FROM Employee
WHERE dept = 'information'
```

9. Study the idiosyncrasies of your system. For example, some systems never use indexes when different expressions are connected by the OR keyword.

Query. Find employees with name Smith or who are in the acquisitions department.

```
SELECT Employee.ssnum
FROM Employee
WHERE Employee.name = 'Smith'
OR Employee.dept = 'acquisitions'
```

Check the query plan. If no index is used, then consider using a union.

```
SELECT Employee.ssnum
FROM Employee
WHERE Employee.name = 'Smith'

UNION

SELECT Employee.ssnum
FROM Employee
WHERE Employee.dept = 'acquisitions'
```

10. Another idiosyncrasy is that the order of tables in the FROM clause may affect the join implementation. For example, in ORACLE version 5, the following query will scan in all the Student tuples and then use the index to access the appropriate Employee tuples.

```
SELECT Employee.ssnum
FROM Employee, Student
AND Employee.name = Student.name
```

By contrast, the following query will scan Employee and then use the index on Student.

```
SELECT Employee.name
FROM  Student, Employee
AND Employee.name = Student.name
```

If one relation is much smaller than the other, it is better to scan the smaller one. So, the ordering of the tables in the query can be important for performance (though the set of records in the answer won't change).

11. Views may cause queries to execute inefficiently.

Suppose we create a view Techlocation as follows:

```
CREATE VIEW Techlocation
AS SELECT ssnum, Techdept.dept, location
FROM Employee, Techdept
WHERE Employee.dept = Techdept.dept
```

The view definition can be read as if it were a table. For example,

```
SELECT location
FROM Techlocation
WHERE ssnum = 452354786
```

In this case, the database management system will process this query based on the definition of Techlocation. That is, the system will execute

```
SELECT location
FROM Employee, Techdept
WHERE Employee.dept = Techdept.dept
AND ssnum = 452354786
```

Thus, the use of a view cannot give better performance than a query against base tables. (If such a query is performed frequently and updates are rare, then it may be worthwhile to maintain the unnormalized relation Techlocation as a redundant base table. However, a view does not do that.)

A view can easily lead you to write inefficient or even incorrect queries, however. For example, consider the similar query:

```
SELECT dept
FROM Techlocation
WHERE ssnum = 452354786
```

This will be expanded to a formulation having a join:

```
SELECT dept
FROM Employee, Techdept
WHERE Employee.dept = Techdept.dept
AND ssnum = 452354786
```

Because dept is an attribute of Employee, the following less expensive query is possible:

```
SELECT dept
FROM Employee
WHERE ssnum = 452354786
```

The query against the view might lead to an incorrect response if the given employee does not work in a technical department.

4.6.1 Minimizing DISTINCTs

Although most of the preceding lessons are straightforward, the interrelated questions of minimizing DISTINCTs and eliminating certain kinds of nested queries can be subtle. This subsection concerns DISTINCT.

In general, DISTINCT is needed when

- The set of values or records returned should contain no duplicates.
- The fields returned do not contain (as a subset) a key of the relation created by the FROM and WHERE clauses.

In example 2, DISTINCT was not needed, because ssnum is a key of Employee and the selection condition retrieves a subset of Employee.

In example 3, DISTINCT was not needed, because an Employee record e will survive the join with Techdept only if e has the same department as some Techdept record t. Because dept is a key of Techdept, there will be at most one such record t, so e will be part of at most one record of the join result. Because ssnum is a key of Employee, at most one record in Employee will have a given ssnum value.

Generalizing from this example, we conclude that if the fields returned constitute a key of one table T and all other tables perform an equijoin with T by their keys, then the values returned will contain no duplicates, so DISTINCT will be unnecessary.

Technical generalization—notion of reaching

In fact, DISTINCT is unnecessary in more general situations. To describe those situations, we must resort to a little mathematics and graph theory. Call a table T *privileged* if the fields returned by the select contain a key of T.

Let R be an unprivileged table. Suppose that R is joined on equality by its key field to some other table S, then we say that R *reaches* S. We define *reaches* to be transitive. So, if $R1$ reaches $R2$ and $R2$ reaches $R3$, then we say that $R1$ reaches $R3$.

There will be no duplicates among the records returned by a selection, even in the absence of DISTINCT, if the following two conditions hold:

- Every table mentioned in the select line is privileged.
- Every unprivileged table reaches at least one privileged one.

The reason this works is the following. If every relation is privileged, then there are no duplicates even without any qualification. Suppose some relation T is not privileged but reaches at least one privileged one, say R. Then the qualifications linking T with R ensure that each distinct combination of privileged records is joined with at most one record of T.

Here are some examples to train your intuition.

- Note that the following slight variation of example 3 would return duplicates:

```
SELECT ssnum
FROM Employee, Techdept
WHERE Employee.manager = Techdept.manager
```

The reason is that the same Employee record may match several Techdept records (because manager is not a key of Techdept), so the Social Security number of that Employee record may appear several times. The formal reason is that the unprivileged relation Techdept does not reach privileged relation Employee.

- If the preceding example were changed slightly to make Techdept privileged

```
SELECT ssnum, Techdept.dept
FROM Employee, Techdept
WHERE Employee.manager = Techdept.manager
```

then the problem goes away, because each repetition of a given ssnum value would be accompanied by a new Techdept.dept, since Techdept.dept is the key of Techdept.

- In fact, the qualification isn't even necessary. That is, the following query would have no duplicates either.

```
SELECT ssnum, Techdept.dept
FROM Employee, Techdept
```

- If Techdept were not privileged in a query, however, then the query might produce duplicates as in the following example:

```
SELECT ssnum, Techdept.manager
FROM Employee, Techdept
```

- Finally, the reaches predicate may go through an intermediate relation yet still ensure that there are no duplicates. Recall here that name is a key of Employee. (It also happens to be a key of Student, though even if it weren't, there would be no duplicates in the result of the following query.)

```
SELECT Student.ssnum
FROM Student, Employee, Techdept
WHERE Student.name = Employee.name
AND Employee.dept = Techdept.dept
```

The formal reason is that both Employee and Techdept reach Student. However, let us try to show this directly. If a given Student's ssnum appeared more than once, then there would be some Student record s that survived twice in the qualification. That is, there are Employee records e and e' and Techdept records t and t' such that s, e, t and s, e', t' both survive the qualification. Because name is the key of Employee, however, $e = e'$. Because dept is the key of Techdept, only one record can join with e, so $t = t'$.

- Can you see why the following might have duplicates?

```
SELECT Student.ssnum
FROM Student, Employee, Techdept
WHERE Student.name = Employee.name
AND Employee.manager = Techdept.manager
```

4.6.2 Rewriting of Nested Queries

It is unfortunate but true that most query optimizers perform much less well on some types of nested queries than on the corresponding non-nested ones. The four major kinds of nested queries are

1. Uncorrelated subqueries with aggregates in the inner query.
2. Uncorrelated subqueries without aggregates.
3. Correlated subqueries with aggregates.
4. Correlated subqueries without aggregates.

Since the first three are the most common, we concentrate on them.

Uncorrelated subqueries with aggregates

Consider the following example. "Find all employees who earn more than the average employee salary."

```
SELECT ssnum
FROM Employee
WHERE salary > (SELECT AVG(salary) FROM Employee)
```

Virtually all commercial systems would compute the average employee salary first and then insert the result as a constant in the outer query. This type of query causes no particular performance problem.

Uncorrelated subquery without aggregates

Recall the example from earlier. "Find all employees in departments that are also in the Techdept relation."

```
SELECT ssnum
FROM Employee
WHERE dept IN (SELECT dept FROM Techdept)
```

This query might not use the index on dept in employee in many systems. Consider the following transformation:

1. Combine the arguments of the two FROM clauses.
2. AND together all the where clauses, replacing IN by =.
3. Retain the SELECT clause from the outer block.

This yields

```
SELECT ssnum
FROM Employee, Techdept
WHERE Employee.dept = Techdept.dept
```

The transformation will work for nestings of any depth, but sometimes we have to worry about duplicates.

Consider, for example, the following:

```
SELECT AVG(salary)
FROM Employee
WHERE dept IN (SELECT dept FROM Techdept)
```

This will be equivalent to

```
SELECT AVG(salary)
FROM Employee, Techdept
WHERE Employee.dept = Techdept.dept
```

because the same number of salary values result from the join as from the nested query. The reason is that the salary value from a given Employee record will be included at most once in both queries, because Techdept reaches (see section 4.6.1, p. 113 for the definition of reaches) Employee in this query.

By contrast, the following query:

```
SELECT AVG(salary)
FROM Employee
WHERE manager IN (SELECT manager FROM Techdept)
```

could yield a different value from

```
SELECT AVG(salary)
FROM Employee, Techdept
WHERE Employee.manager = Techdept.manager
```

because the second one may include an Employee record several times if that Employee's manager is the manager of several Techdepts. (As you can see, the reaches formalism is quite useful when duplicates matter. Duplicates do not matter for aggregates like MIN and MAX.)

The best solution would be to create a temporary relation, say Temp with key field manager. Then,

```
SELECT DISTINCT manager INTO Temp
FROM Techdept

SELECT AVG(salary)
FROM Employee, Temp
WHERE Employee.manager = Temp.manager
```

Correlated subqueries

Let us modify slightly the uncorrelated subquery from the preceding example.

"Find employees who earn exactly the average salary in their department where their department is a technical one."

```
SELECT ssnum
FROM Employee e1
WHERE salary = (SELECT AVG(e2.salary)
FROM Employee e2, Techdept
WHERE e2.dept = e1.dept
AND e2.dept = Techdept.dept)
```

In most cases, this query will be quite inefficient so should be transformed to:

```
SELECT AVG(salary) as avsalary, Employee.dept INTO Temp
FROM Employee, Techdept
AND Employee.dept = Techdept.dept
GROUP BY Employee.dept

SELECT ssnum
FROM Employee, Temp
WHERE salary = avsalary
AND Employee.dept = Temp.dept
```

This transformation can be characterized as follows:

1. Form a temporary based on a GROUP BY on the attribute (or attributes) of the nested relation that is (or are) correlated with the outer relation. (The correlation must be equality for this to work.) In the example, the attribute was dept. Use the uncorrelated qualifications from the subquery in the construction of the temporary. In the example, that was the qualification

```
Employee.dept = Techdept.dept
```

2. Join the temporary with the outer query. A condition on the grouped attribute replaces the correlation condition. In the example, the condition is

```
Employee.dept = Temp.dept
```

A condition between the comparing attribute and the dependent attribute of the grouping replaces the subquery condition. In the example, that corresponds to the replacement of

```
WHERE salary = (SELECT AVG(e2.salary)
```

by

```
WHERE salary = avsalary
```

All other qualifications in the outer query remain. There were none in this example.

By definition, the GROUP BY attribute(s) will constitute a key of the resulting temporary. Therefore, the temporary relation will always reach the outer relation. This eliminates any problem about duplicates. The correlation predicate was

```
WHERE e2.dept = e1.dept
```

in the example. Can you show by example why the transformation could be incorrect if the correlation predicate were not equality? (*Hint:* the grouping operator could create the wrong aggregate values.)

There is one more problem concerning empty sets and counting aggregates. Consider the following slight variation of the preceding query.

"Find employees whose number of friends equals the number of employees in their department where their department is a technical one."

```
SELECT ssnum
FROM Employee e1
WHERE numfriends = COUNT(SELECT e2.ssnum
FROM Employee e2, Techdept
WHERE e2.dept = e1.dept
AND e2.dept = Techdept.dept)
```

Construct a similar transformation to the preceding one:

```
SELECT COUNT(ssnum) as numcolleagues, Employee.dept INTO Temp
FROM Employee, Techdept
AND Employee.dept = Techdept.dept
GROUP BY Employee.dept
```

```
SELECT ssnum
FROM Employee, Temp
WHERE numfriends = numcolleagues
AND Employee.dept = Temp.dept
```

Can you see why the result of this transformation is not equivalent? *Hint:* consider an employee Helene who is not in a technical department.

In the original query, Helene's friend's list would be compared with the count of an empty set which is 0, so her record would survive the selection provided she has no friends. In the transformed query, her dept would not correspond to a dept value in Temp (because it would not correspond to a department value in Techdept). So she would not appear in the output of the second query no matter how few friends she has.

In the first query this would not have been a problem, because Helene's salary would never be equal to the average salary of an empty set (which is NULL in most systems).

For more details, see the papers of Richard A. Ganski and Harry K. T. Wong[4] and of Won Kim.[5] The Ganski and Wong paper extends the Kim paper and corrects a few bugs. These transformations can be very tricky.

4.7 PROCEDURAL EXTENSIONS TO RELATIONAL ALGEBRA

This section discusses three procedural extensions to SQL that can reduce overhead:

1. Procedural languages containing loops and conditionals associated with a database management system. This helps avoid third generation programming language (e.g., COBOL, PL/1, C) to database interactions.

2. Saving stored procedures to avoid recompilation expense.

3. Triggers to avoid polling.

4.7.1 Procedural Extensions to SQL

Because interactions between a conventional programming language and the database management system are expensive, a good performance strategy is to package a number of SQL statements into one interaction. The embedded procedural language that many systems offer includes control flow facilities such as if statements, while loops, goto's, and exceptions.

Here is an example in SYBASE-like syntax that determines whether Carol Diane is an ancestor of Nicholas Bennet. For the purposes of the example, assume a genealogical database containing at least the relation Parental(parent, child).

---

[4] R. A. Ganski and H. K. T. Wong, "Optimization of Nested SQL Queries Revisited," ACM SIGMOD Conference 1987, pp. 23-33.

[5] Won Kim, "On Optimizing an SQL-like Nested Query," *Transactions on Database Systems* vol. 7, no. 3, pp. 443-469, September 1982.

```
DECLARE Temp1, Temp2, Ancestor;

/* Temp2 will hold the latest generation discovered. */

INSERT Temp1
SELECT parent
FROM Parental
WHERE child = 'Nicholas Bennet';


WHILE EXISTS(SELECT * FROM Temp1)
BEGIN
  INSERT Ancestor
  SELECT * FROM Temp1;

  INSERT Temp2
  SELECT * FROM Temp1;

  DELETE Temp1 FROM Temp1;

  INSERT Temp1
  SELECT Parental.parent
  FROM Parental, Temp2
  WHERE Parental.child = Temp2.parent;

  DELETE Temp2 FROM Temp2;

END
IF ( EXISTS (
  SELECT *
  FROM Ancestor
  WHERE parent = 'Carol Diane'
))
 PRINT "Carol Diane is an ancestor of Nicholas Bennet."
ELSE
 PRINT "Carol Diane is not an ancestor of Nicholas Bennet."
```

Using the embedded procedural language reduces the number of calls from the application program to the database management system, saving significant overhead.

The main disadvantage is that many such languages are product-specific, so can reduce the portability of your application code.

4.7.2 Saving Query Plans

Query parsing and optimization is a second form of overhead to avoid. There are two aspects to this cost.

1. The compilation of simple queries requires from 10,000 to 30,000 instructions; compiling a complicated query may require from 100,000 to several million instructions. If this seems surprisingly high, remember that compilation requires parsing, semantic analysis, the verification of access privileges, and optimization. In fact, for simple queries that use indexes, compilation time can exceed execution time by a factor of three or more.

2. Compilation requires read access to the system catalog. This can cause lock-induced blocking if other transactions modify the catalog concurrently.

For these reasons, a well-tuned online relational environment should rarely if ever perform query compilations. (This means limiting the number of ad hoc queries as well.) Moreover, the *query plan* resulting from a compilation (telling which indexes will be used and which tables will be scanned) should be rapidly accessible. Many systems offer a procedure cache for this purpose. You should make sure that your cache is big enough for frequently executed queries. In some systems, avoiding recompilation requires holding cursors. Check your tuning guide to see what your particular system requires you to do in order to avoid recompilation.

Query plans will become obsolete if the relations upon which they work change significantly. Here are some changes that should induce you to recompile a query (after you update the catalog statistics):

- An index is added on an attribute that is important to the query. The query should be recompiled, so the new query plan will take advantage of this index. Some systems do this automatically, e.g. DB2, version 3.

- A relation grows from nearly empty to a significant size. The query plan for the nearly empty relation will not use any index on the grounds that it is cheaper to scan a nearly empty relation than to use an index to access it. So, once the relation grows, the query should be recompiled so it will use the index.

4.7.3 Triggers

A *trigger* is a stored procedure that executes as the result of an event. In relational systems, the event is usually a modification (insert, delete, or update) or a timing event (it is now 6 A.M.). The event that causes a trigger to execute its modification is called the *enabling event* and it is said to *fire* that trigger. The trigger executes as part of the transaction containing the enabling event.

There are three main reasons to use a trigger, only one of which has to do with performance:

- A trigger will fire regardless of the application that enables it.

This makes triggers valuable for auditing purposes or to reverse suspicious actions. For example, the following trigger rolls back transactions that try to update salaries on weekends. (We use SYBASE syntax here.)

```
CREATE TRIGGER nosalchange
ON Employee
FOR update
AS
IF update(salary)
AND datename(dw, getdate()) IN ('Saturday', 'Sunday')
BEGIN
  rollback transaction
  PRINT 'Nice try, buster!'
END
```

- A trigger can maintain integrity constraints of which the application is un-aware.

Referential integrity is the constraint that every value in some column A of table T should be present in column A' of table T'. For example, the following trigger deletes all accounts from a deleted branch.

```
CREATE TRIGGER killaccounts
ON Branch
FOR delete
AS
DELETE Account
FROM Account, deleted
WHERE Account.branch_ID = deleted.branch_ID
```

- The third use of a trigger is to respond to events generated by a collection of applications. In this case, triggers can provide substantial performance benefits.

Consider an application that must write into a table Monitortable the latest data inserted into a table Interestingtable. Without triggers the only way to obtain this data is to query the table repeatedly—i.e., to *poll*. The query might be of the form

```
INSERT Monitortable
SELECT *
```

```
FROM interestingtable
WHERE inserttime > :lasttimeIlooked

Update :lasttimeIlooked based on current time.
```

Polling introduces a tension between correctness and performance. If your application polls too often, then there will be unnecessary queries in addition to concurrency conflicts with inserters to Interestingtable. If your application polls too seldom, you may miss important data (perhaps some transactions delete recently inserted records from Interestingtable).

A better approach (known as an *interrupt-driven* approach) is to use a trigger to put the data directly into Monitortable when an insertion occurs. The trigger might have the form

```
CREATE TRIGGER tomonitor
ON Interestingtable
FOR insert
AS
INSERT Monitortable
SELECT *
FROM inserted
```

No tuning is necessary and no inserts will be missed.

Triggers do have one serious disadvantage: They can lead to a maintenance nightmare for two related reasons.

1. In the presence of triggers, no update can be analyzed in isolation, because the update may cause some trigger to cause a further modification.

2. The interaction between triggers can be confusing once the number of triggers becomes large. This is an issue because several triggers may be enabled by the same modification. The system must choose which one to execute first and whether to execute the others at all. (A system could, in principle, execute all enabled triggers simultaneously, but it is not clear what that would mean if several of the triggers modify the same data.)

4.7.4 Special Problems Concerning Trigger Performance

For most purposes, improving a trigger's performance entails the same analysis as improving any query's performance. For example, if the trigger updates the branch balance each time an account balance is updated, then one can conclude that one needs an index on branch ID. Trigger performance tuning presents two unique aspects, however

- A trigger occurs only after a certain combination of operations. Sometimes, one can make use of that information to suggest a special strategy. For example, suppose every update to the Sale relation requires a check on whether the customer credit is good. It may, then, be a good idea to cluster the Customer and Sale tables together on customer number. That way, when processing a sale, one will likely obtain the Customer record on the same page.

- A naive application developer may often write a trigger that executes too often or returns too much data. For example, consider a trigger that writes records to table Richdepositor each time an account balance increases over $50,000. Writing the trigger this way

```
CREATE TRIGGER nouveauriche
ON Account
FOR update
AS
BEGIN
  INSERT Richdepositor
  FROM inserted
  WHERE inserted.balance > 50000
END
```

has two problems. First, it will try to write into Richdepositor whether or not a balance has been updated. Second, suppose that some depositor Ariana Carlin already had a balance greater than $50,000 before the update took place. This trigger will then write Ariana Carlin into the Richdepositor table unnecessarily. It would be better to write the trigger this way

```
CREATE TRIGGER nouveauriche
ON Account
FOR update
AS
IF update(balance)
BEGIN
  INSERT Richdepositor
  FROM inserted
  WHERE inserted.balance > 50000
  AND deleted.balance < 50000
  AND deleted.account_ID = inserted.account_ID
END
```

4.8 INTERACTING WITH THE NONRELATIONAL WORLD

Two important interfaces to a relational database are those to your application program and to nonrelational database systems. The tuning considerations for these are straightforward in principle, but very important.

4.8.1 Tuning the Application Interface

Application interactions with the database system can occur by using a conventional (so-called third generation) programming language or a system-specific fourth-generation language. (A *fourth-generation language* (4GL for short) is a language that makes calls to the database system, usually through SQL statements. Normally, your database vendor will provide you with one. Different vendors offer different 4GL's, so using a 4GL hurts portability.)

How applications are written can have a large performance impact on a database system. Here are some hints and justifications.

- As discussed in the concurrency control section of chapter 2 (pp. 20 ff), a transaction should not encapsulate user interactions (e.g., manual screen updates), because such interactions lengthen the transaction significantly, thereby causing concurrency problems. Imagine, for example, that the operator decides to go to lunch while holding important locks. To avoid such nightmares, the application should divide an update into a read transaction, a local update (outside transactional boundaries), and a write transaction.

- If the application includes a transaction that updates most of the records in a table, then the transaction should specify a table lock from the start rather than allowing the table lock to result from lock escalation. This avoids unnecessary overhead to acquire page and record locks. (Be careful to whom you suggest this idea. Unsophisticated users may ask for table locks when they don't really need one.)

- Application programming languages offer looping facilities. Embedding an SQL SELECT statement inside the loop means that there will be application-to-database interaction in every iteration of the loop. A better idea is to retrieve a significant amount of data outside the loop and then to use the loop to process the data.

- The database system is good at retrieving data. It is less efficient at arithmetic, field validation, or string manipulation. For this reason, do such computation at the application level.

- Retrieve only needed columns. There are two reasons why this is usually a good idea, one obvious and one less so.

(a) The obvious reason is that retrieving an unneeded column will cause unnecessary data to be transferred.

(b) The subtle reason is that retrieving an unneeded column may prevent a query from being answered within the index. For example, if there is a nonclustering composite index on last name and first name, then a query that asks for all the first names of people whose last name is 'Codd' can be answered by the index alone, provided no irrelevant attributes are also selected.

4.8.2 Interfacing with a Nonrelational Database

Performance, application needs, or an existing software base may sometimes require that your relational system interface with a special-purpose database system. For example, one part of your database may use IBM's IMS and the rest of your system may use a relational system. Since this is seldom desirable, do this only if the following conditions hold:

1. You really need the performance. As mentioned at the beginning of this chapter, IMS/FastPath is about twice as fast as IBM's DB2 on transaction processing applications. The reason has little to do with algorithms, but a lot to do with engineering. IMS/FastPath applications are tied to the data and take advantage of its physical layout. This results in fewer layers of indirection for dereferencing pointers.

2. There would be little communication between the hierarchical and relational databases, e.g., perhaps once a day to dump the IMS database to a DB2 database.

Industrial experience has shown four main reasons to prefer a purely relational system over a hierarchical or network system.

1. Applications are easier to develop and to maintain using a relational system.

2. It is much easier to use SQL than to program within IMS or DBTG. Programming ease reduces the time to develop and debug new applications.

3. Relational systems have a richer repertoire of tuning options. For example, IMS/FastPath does not support nonclustering indexes.

4. Hardware can often overcome the speed disadvantage of relational systems. For example, Teradata and Oracle have announced products on multiprocessor platforms whose speeds exceed IMS/FastPath on a uniprocessor platform.

4.9 GENERAL TROUBLESHOOTING

Scenario 1

An airline manages 100 flights a day. In their database, there is a table for each flight (called Flight) containing a flight identifier, a seat identifier, and a passenger name. There is also a master table (called Totals) that has the total number of passengers in each flight. Each reservation transaction updates a particular Flight table and the Totals table. They have a performance bottleneck whose symptom is high lock contention. They try to resolve this by breaking each reservation transaction into two: one that updates the appropriate Flight table and the other that updates the Totals table. That helps but not enough.

Action. The Totals table may be a serialization bottleneck for all transactions because every flight reservation transaction must update that table and the table is small, possibly only a few pages in size. Therefore, there is going to be contention on that table. If you are using page-level locking, then consider reorganizing Totals, so each flight record is alone on a page and then establish a hash index on that table.

Notice that making Totals a view on Flight would not be useful, because it would not be updatable (data derived from an aggregate never is).

Scenario 2

Consider again the data mining application on behalf of the department store. Suppose that queries against the relation

Oldsale(customernum, customercity, itemnum, quantity, date, price)

take place during the day. Updates to Oldsale take place as a bulk load at night. In addition to the bulk load, there is a bulk delete of old records (the marketing group is concerned about purchases in the last few weeks only). To serve the daytime processing, there are indexes on customernum, customercity, and item. Load times are very slow, and the daytime performance is degenerating. What should you do?

Action. Drop the indexes at night while modifying the table and recreate them after the load and deletes have finished. Besides reducing index update overhead during the night, this will eliminate overflows, thereby giving better query performance during the day.

Scenario 3

Suppose you are given the following relation

Purchase(name, item, price, quantity, suppliername, year)

with a clustering index on name.

Table 4.2 PURCHASE TABLE

Name	Item	Price	Quantity	Suppliername	Year
Widget	4325	15	60	Standard Widget	1990
Widget	5925	13	60	Standard Widget	1991
Widget	6324	17	54	Standard Widget	1992
Woosit	3724	15	80	Standard Widget	1990

You want to compute the cost of items based on a first-in first-out ordering. That is, the cost of the first purchase of an item should be accounted for before the cost of a later item. Consider Table 4.2 which contains all the widget records in the Purchase relation. To account for the purchase of 98 widgets, we should account for 60 from the year 1990 (costing $900) and 38 from the year 1991 (costing $494) for a total cost of $1394.

We want to do this for all the data items. So, for each such data item :x, we return the data sorted by year.

```
SELECT *
FROM Purchase
WHERE item = :x
ORDER BY year
```

There are 10,000 different items, and we discover that each query scans the entire Purchase table and then performs a sort based on year. The application runs too slowly. What do you do?

Action.   If there are fairly few records for each item, then one possibility is to construct a nonclustering index on item. The query style won't have to change. Another strategy is to sort all the records into a temporary by (item, year). Then go through the table sequentially using a 4GL.

5

Tuning an Object-Oriented Database System

5.1 GOAL OF CHAPTER

Object-oriented database management systems (OODBs) constitute a fast-growing (though still small) segment of the database management market. This chapter has four goals.

1. To explain the appeal of the object-oriented approach and to identify applications for which object-oriented database systems may offer better performance than relational ones as commonly implemented. Figure 5.1 shows the architecture of an object-oriented database system.

2. To suggest ways to speed up object-oriented applications.

3. To identify ways in which relational systems are evolving to satisfy some of the same goals as these object-oriented systems.

4. To speculate on the prospectus for object-oriented systems.

5.2 THE COMPARATIVE ADVANTAGE OF OBJECT ORIENTATION

As of this writing, relational systems dominate the database management market. Such systems are efficient enough for most applications, familiar to a large programming community, and portable. Despite this state of affairs (cynics might say because of it), a small but determined community of researchers and practitioners believe that the object-oriented model should supersede the relational model, at least for some applications.

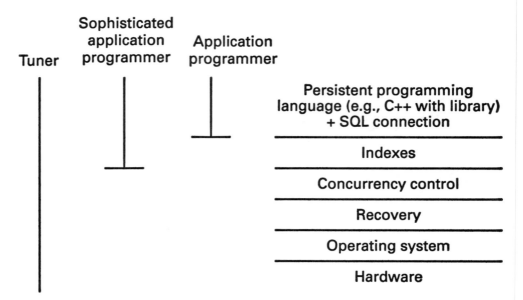

Figure 5.1   Architecture of Object-Oriented Database Systems with Tuning Responsibilities.

This section

- Explains the basic concepts of object-oriented database systems.
- Presents the software maintenance argument for object-orientation.
- Discusses applications in which object-oriented databases, as presently conceived, will offer better performance than relational ones.[1]

5.2.1 Basic Concepts

An *object* is a collection of data, an identity and a set of operations, sometimes called *methods*. For example, a newspaper article object may contain zero or more photographs as constituent objects and a text value. Typical operations will be to edit the article and display it at a certain width: *edit(), display(width)*. The system prevents programs using that object (perhaps with the exception of a privileged few) from accessing the internal data (e.g., the text) of the object directly. Instead, such programs must access the operations —or, in object orientese, "invoke the

---

[1] Two sympathetic surveys of object-oriented database products are *Communications of the ACM,* vol. 34, no. 10, October 1991—the entire issue.

R. G. G. Cattell, *Object Data Management: Object-Oriented and Extended Relational Database Systems.* Reading, Mass.: Addison-Wesley, 1991.

methods"—of the object (e.g., edit). Hiding the representation of an object is known as *encapsulation*.

A *class* is the definition of a data description (analogous to the relational notion of schema) and operations that will characterize a set of objects. For example, there may be a newspaper article class whose data description would consist of text, and a set of photographs and whose operation description would consist of the code for *edit* and *display*. There may be many objects belonging to class newspaper article, each denoting a different article.

Finally, many object-oriented systems have a concept of *inheritance* that permits class X to derive much of its code and attributes from another class Y. Class X will contain the data attributes and operations of class Y plus additional ones. For example, there may be a sports article class that derives its data description and operations from newspaper article, but then adds a table (of scores) and the operations *enlarge headline* and *display score*.

In summary, an object-oriented system is made up of objects, classes, and an inheritance hierarchy. Each object has an *identifier* allowing an object to be shared. For example, by making photographs objects in their own right, several related newspaper articles might share a single photograph. By contrast, text is not shared between articles so is treated as a value (Figure 5.2).

5.2.2 A Babel of OODB Languages

An implementer of the object-oriented model must choose a syntax for these ideas. As of this writing, approximately 20 languages have been proposed for object-oriented databases, though languages derived from C, C++, and Smalltalk seem to be in the ascendancy in the commercial market. (As of this writing, there are some 500,000 C++ licenses worldwide, making it the most widely distributed object-oriented language available.)

Language variations can lead to different working methods. For example,

- Products derived from Smalltalk such as GemStone are partially interpreted. This implies that users can add new classes while the application is running and then use them immediately. (This is analogous to the ability of a user of a relational database to define and use schema without performing any recompilations.) The ability to change code quickly in this manner is useful for prototyping, but interpretation tends to slow down execution.

- Products derived from fully compiled languages such as C++, by contrast, may require recompilation before a code change (e.g., the addition of a class) changes an application's behavior.

Recent systems offer the benefits of both language approaches: compiled code for production use and the ability to add classes dynamically during application development. For example, Servio Logic's GemStone allows users to

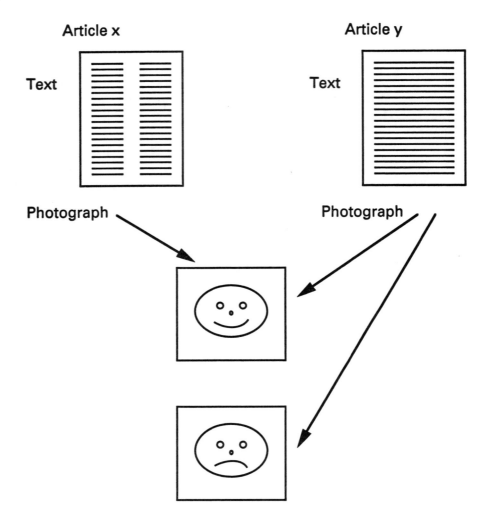

Figure 5.2   Article Objects with Text Subvalues and Photograph
Constituent Objects.

add "primitive" operations, which are operations implemented in C or assembly
code. This gives the benefit of compilation for the most frequently used operations. Similarly, several C++-based systems such as Ontologic's ONTOS, allow
new class definitions to be added at runtime and later invoked. Future releases
of C++ should make such facilities easier to provide, because they may provide

useful runtime information (e.g., symbolic linker and loader information) about classes.

5.2.3 Object-Oriented Approach Good for Databases?

True believers in the object-oriented approach believe it is the best approach for any large software product. They argue that all good software will have to change to remain useful. The notion of encapsulation, they say, permits this change to happen gracefully, thus enhancing human performance.[2]

This argument should ring familiar to relational system advocates who argued similarly when touting the virtues of the relational model in the early 1980s. Here was the basic refrain:

- A relational database offers *physical data independence*. This means that you can write your application knowing only the application schema. If you or the system administrator change the index structure or the clustering properties, the application will continue to work, though its performance may change. Changing the physical structure of a hierarchical or network database, by contrast, may render an application program obsolete.

Replace "physical data independence" by "encapsulation" and you have half of the software maintenance argument of the OODBers. The other half goes like this.

- The relational model is a special case of an object-oriented model. The relation is a class offering certain operations that are fixed by the system language SQL. The language is biased against records that are larger than a page, sorted sequences, and pointers. The object-oriented approach allows the *user* to construct an infinite number of classes, rather than being limited to relations and their operations. To see why this is useful, consider trying to implement *display(width)* with relational operators.

OODBers are an indefatigable lot. If they fail to convince you by database examples, they will appeal to your sense of analogy.

- "How does a car company arrive at new car designs?" they might ask rhetorically. "They don't throw out an old car design and start anew. Instead, they use some of the components from old car designs, e.g., fuel tank, suspension, or whatever, and discard or change others, e.g., the body. In order to be able to change one component more or less in isolation, that component must be an "object" in that the rest of the car uses its services, e.g., to dampen shocks,

---

[2] Bertrand Meyer presents an excellent exposition of this argument in his book *Object-oriented Software Construction*, Prentice-Hall 1988.

without regard to its internal structure. Thus, object-orientation is intrinsic to most engineering endeavors. Why not databases?"

- A second analogical argument appeals to a metaphor from the flashy world of electrical engineering: the metaphor of "impedance mismatch." In electrical engineering, if two attached wires have different impedances (impedance is a generalization of resistance), then a signal traveling from one to the other will reflect at the interface. Since reflections usually cause problems, handbooks recommend against such impedance mismatches between wires. How does this apply to databases, you might ask? Well, relational languages manipulate sets, whereas conventional languages like COBOL, C, Pascal, and FORTRAN manipulate records. These different orientations constitute a kind of impedance mismatch because the interface between the different kinds of languages is usually ugly and inefficient. Because object-oriented database systems offer a single language for both data access and computation, the impedance mismatch disappears, making for simpler and possibly more efficient code.

5.2.4 Which Application Is Right?

The largest present application of object-oriented databases is in engineering design, though many of the OODB vendors anticipate that newspaper layout will be a large future application. (In case you think that newspaper publishing is a low-technology enterprise, imagine a newspaper that tailors its articles, advertisements, and layouts to each city block to which it is distributed.)

For such applications, object-oriented database systems can offer a huge (500 fold in certain situations) performance improvement over relational systems. The main reason for this benefit is that most object-oriented database systems represent their objects in the same way on disk and in random access memory. In particular, the disk representation supports pointers.

Example: Pointers in Memory

Consider two data items i and j (let us not prejudice the discussion by calling them objects or records) where i has a reference to j. Here is the work needed to follow that reference assuming both data items are in random access memory (Figure 5.3).

- Relational systems support references through tuple identifiers. That is, record i would contain the key of record j. To find j, one would access an index using its key value. This may take several thousand machine instructions.

- Most object-oriented database systems, by contrast, would allow object i to

OODB : direct pointers in random access memory

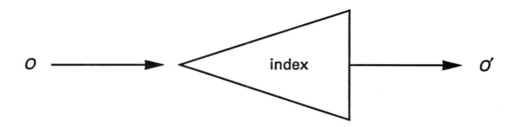

Relational : indirection through indexes

Figure 5.3   Pointer Dereferencing in an OODB Can Be 1000 Times Faster
Than in a Relational System

hold a pointer to *j*. To access *j* from *i*, an operation would merely dereference that pointer, requiring under 10 machine instructions. (Minimizing this
overhead is a topic of the next section.)

As the example shows, object-oriented database systems offer better performance for certain kinds of applications. There are, in fact, a set of application
attributes that should lead you to consider using an object-oriented database system.

- The application currently uses the file system, so it is not wedded to an
  existing database model.

  According to a survey done in 1988 by Michael Brodie of GTE Labs, only
  10% of computerized data is kept in databases. Most of the rest is kept in
  normal operating system files.

- The most natural data structure for the application is a graph with pointer
  dereferencing as the fundamental traversal method. The application will
  access the same data items many times in a short time period. Each access
  may be a function call of some complexity.

Circuit checking, cartography for urban and environmental planning, and hypertext are applications with these properties.

- The application requires special data structures.

Because OODBs provide efficient support for pointers and give the user the full power of a programming language, the user can create new data structures tailored to his or her application. For example, the implementer of a cartographic database could implement a two-dimensional data structure such as a Quad Tree or R+ Tree and enjoy good performance.

- The application has little data contention and may consist of a few long transactions.

In design applications, one designer designs and modifies a portion of the design without interference from other designers. Most accesses to hypertext and cartographic databases are reads. These are applications with little data contention. The transactions are long, because they involve human interaction.

- The application's data values may vary widely in size.

Relational systems are optimized for page-sized and smaller data. The largest pages are commonly 2, 4, or 32 kilobytes, depending on the system. Object-oriented systems boast of an ability to handle much larger sized objects as would be required for text, for example. I expect this advantage to diminish as relational vendors begin to offer special facilities for large objects as discussed in section 5.5 (p. 149).

Sample of existing applications

As of early 1992, here are the applications that object-oriented databases are being used for.

- A server for complex ("hypermedia") documentation supporting large machinery—for example, an M1A1 tank. The documentation integrates text, graphs, video, and voice. Different users can select different documents based on various criteria

  - Find components attached to the drive train.
  - Find parts made by manufacturer X.

- A database for a part-component explosion for an airplane manufacturer. This database must adapt to the needs of designers, machinists, and eventually the service organization. The data is complex and is difficult to encode into tables. Typical queries include

- Is there a path between mechanical linkage X and control panel Y going through linkage Z?
- Change all sensors of type A in any circuit responsible for flight control to type B. (Note that this is an update that requires graph traversal. Such updates are sometimes called *complex updates*.)

- A geographical database for urban planners. Such a database must serve many purposes. For example, to traffic planners roads are graph edges with flow capacities. To the road maintenance department, they are two-dimensional objects with varying widths and lengths. To the sewer department, a road and its underlying network of pipes and cables is three-dimensional. Typical queries include

- What is the nearest gas pipe to intersection X?
- Which water pipes are more than 30 years old in this geometric region?
- Are there alternate power line routes if the line between points X and Y is cut?

5.3 DESIRABLE PERFORMANCE FEATURES

Since object-oriented database technology is less mature than relational technology, different vendors offer quite different performance features. This section presents a list of features to look for and then discusses the controversies about some implementation strategies.[3]

1. Features that any database system should have:

- A variety of index possibilities, such as B-trees and hash structures, for unordered collections of objects.

   Use chapter 3 for guidance as to when to establish such indexes. Some systems such as ObjectStore permit users to describe the frequencies of various operations such as iteration, insertion, and removal; the system will then choose the structures.

- Index structures for ordered data types such as lists and sequences.

---

[3] See the following articles:

P. Butterworth, A. Otis, and J. Stein, "The GemStone Object Database Management System," *Communications of the ACM*, vol. 34, no. 10, pp. 64-77, October 1991.

O. Deux et al., "The O2 System," *Communications of the ACM*, vol. 34, no. 10, pp. 34-48, October 1991.

C. Lamb, G. Landis, J. Orenstein, and D. Weinreb, "The ObjectStore Database System," *Communications of the ACM*, vol. 34, no. 10, pp. 50-63, October 1991.

For example, large list types such as text data are often supported by a "positional" B-tree. In such a tree, the keys are the positions of the members within the list. This helps to make arbitrary insertions into and deletions from the list efficient while keeping the list sorted.

- Advanced features for recovery such as buffered commits and online database dumps as presented in chapter 2, section 2.3. Also, it should be possible to turn recovery off when it is not needed.

- A trigger facility.

2. Efficient pointer-following of data already in memory.

Since virtual memory pointers have no meaning on disk, every pointer in an object-oriented database system must have an in-memory representation as well as an on-disk representation. The two representations are different in most systems. When dereferencing a pointer of an object *o* in memory, the OODB system may discover that the pointer contains a valid virtual memory address (the good case) meaning that the object had already been brought into virtual memory. (The bad case occurs when the object is still on disk.) An important question to ask is how many instructions does the system execute in the good case. A well-designed system should make the good case very fast.

- One technique, implemented in Object Design's ObjectStore, is to dereference every pointer under the assumption that it contains a valid virtual memory address. If the pointer turns out to be invalid, it will cause an interrupt (a page fault) that will be caught by the object-oriented database system. If the pointer turns out to be valid, then it will be dereferenced without any test.
- A second technique is to give the user a way to tell the system not to perform the test, as is possible in Ontologic's ONTOS. This is risky, of course, and should be done only if the user knows that all referenced objects are already in memory.

3. Ability to do efficient online garbage collection in memory and on disk.

Systems that implement pointers can produce persistent objects that are no longer reachable from named objects of interest. A *garbage collector* eliminates such objects. A garbage collector must also perform storage compaction. All this must happen while the system continues to run (to provide 24-hour uptime). It should be possible to tune the frequency of garbage collection.

4. Allow users to move work from the database server to the user workstation and back again without changing application code, a kind of *execution site independence*.

Because many object-oriented applications involve substantial computation and little concurrency, a good system should allow the user to decide at log-in time whether to put server functionality such as database buffer management in the user workstation or at the server site (Figure 5.4). We will discuss the tuning implications of this decision subsequently (p. 148).

5. A variety of concurrency control mechanisms.

- *Check-out*: Since design applications are well suited to object-oriented database systems, many OODBs follow design conventions in their concurrency control. For example, they may allow a user to lock a large portion of the database for a long time ("check it out"). While holding it locked, the user may commit many transactions. Thus, the system offers a mechanism that decouples the length of time a lock is held from transaction com-

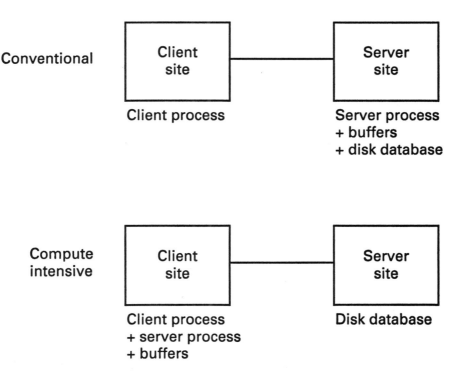

Figure 5.4   Application Can Move Buffers to Client Site Without Changing Functionality

mits. Having checked out data, the application program may process it at a client workstation.

- *Read-only queries*: Some systems, such as GemStone, provide a special mechanism that allows read-only queries to execute without using locking yet still obtain degree 3 isolation. An application like manufacturing needs this, because the planner must read a lot of data to make forecasts, whereas the production people perform a lot of short update transactions.

  Other systems allow readers to see uncommitted data at degree 0 isolation (see chapter 2, section 2.2.2, p. 20).

- *Lock granularity*: It should also be possible for the user to control the granularity of locking—from individual object to list of objects to page of objects to file of objects to the entire database. The system should also allow users to turn concurrency control off altogether.

- *Optimistic concurrency control*: When contention is rare but possible, a concurrency control method known as optimistic concurrency control (invented by H. T. Kung and J. T. Robinson of Carnegie-Mellon University) may help. The idea is to suppress all locking overhead, but then to check for the validity of a transaction when the transaction ends. The check supposedly entails less overhead than locking.

- *Gentle aborts and nested transactions*: Since transactions in object-oriented systems frequently include user interaction, discarding the updates of an aborted transaction may force users to lose significant work. For this reason, most object-oriented systems offer some kinder and gentler mechanism, such as to create a new version of data updated by an aborted transaction. What then happens to this version is up to the various users of the data.

  Other systems offer a form of transaction invented by Eliot Moss, now at the University of Massachusetts at Amherst[4] called *nested transactions*. A nested transaction divides a normal transaction into several subactions. When a subaction encounters a deadlock, it alone rolls back, thus minimizing the amount of work lost.

  That is usually enough, though it may not be in certain relatively rare

---

[4] J. E. B. Moss, *Nested Transactions: An Approach to Reliable Distributed Computing*. Cambridge, Mass.: MIT Press, 1985. P. K. Chrysantis and K. Ramamritham, also at University of Massachusetts at Amherst have characterized the various transactional models that have been proposed. Some of these may find their way into real systems.

cases. For example, suppose the first subaction of transaction T accesses x, the subaction encountering the deadlock accesses y, and transaction T' accesses y in its first subaction and x in its subaction that encounters the deadlock. Then one of the two transactions will have to roll back entirely.

6. The ability to specify strategies for prefetching data from disk into random access memory. These strategies may depend on the graph defined by interobject references.

For example, the ONTOS system gives the user three prefetching strategies:

- Do not prefetch i.e., fetch objects as needed.
- Prefetch all objects reachable from an accessed object.
- Prefetch a certain user-defined cluster on access to any member of that cluster.

The GemStone system, to give another data point, allows a filter called a "clamp set" that limits prefetching as follows:

- Prefetch objects reachable from an object through certain attributes only.
- Prefetch reachable objects up to a certain depth only.
- Prefetch reachable objects of certain classes only.

7. Ability to change the size of the unit of transfer between disk and the database buffers.

An experimental study conducted at O2 Technology[5] suggested that a larger unit of transfer was best for read-intensive queries with good locality of reference (i.e., nearby data tends to be referenced at nearly the same time) provided the database buffer is large enough. In other cases, small units of transfer, e.g., object sized, were best.

8. Ability to lay out objects on disk in a variety of ways. As we explain further in the next subsection, this can mean

- Placing every object of some collection in one contiguous section of storage ("clustering"). Such clustering can be recursive. For example, a father can be clustered with his daughters each of whom is clustered with her toys.
- Separating some parts of such an object into separate sections of storage, where the layout of each part can also be specified ("unclustering" and "vertical partitioning").

---

[5] D. J. DeWitt, P. Futtersack, D. Maier, and F. Velez, "A Study of Three Alternative Workstation-Server Architectures for Object-Oriented Database Systems," in *Proc. of the 16th VLDB Conference*, August 1990, pp. 107-121.

- Spreading a collection of objects of some class across several disks ("horizontal partitioning").

9. Efficient support for all sizes of objects.

Some object-oriented systems design their access methods for large objects. Smarter systems allow for large objects but offer special support for small ones such as clustering indexes (discussed in chapter 3). Studies by the OODB vendors have shown that application domains such as computer-aided design, manufacturing planning, process control and so on consist of a vast majority of small objects (usually between 30 to 100 bytes of user data) with a few (less than 5%) large objects (5 kilobytes or more).

One aspect of efficient support is the space overhead to store an object. This is usually from 20 to 50 bytes on disk and about 20 additional bytes in random access memory (mostly due to the representation of pointers).

10. Provision for physical data independence.

Your system should allow you to change organizational features such as clustering and system-provided data structures without changing the functionality of your application. A system that does not have this property may force you to rewrite your application when you change its data structures.

5.3.1 Controversial Features

Different object-oriented database vendors have adopted different strategies for representing references. There are two questions.

- Should an object identifier translate directly to a location on disk?
  - The designers of O2 from O2 Technology say, "Yes." They argue that a disk pointer avoids a level of indirection (to a table that converts logical object identifiers to disk addresses). If the object moves from its first location, it leaves a forwarding address. These forwarding pointers entail space and time overhead, so must eventually be eliminated.
  - GemStone designers say, "No." They argue that a disk address makes it more difficult to recluster objects, to handle objects that get bigger as a result of an update, or to perform storage compaction following garbage collection.

  My view is that the indirection will prove useful for any application that requires compaction. Other applications will benefit from the suppression of the layer of indirection.

- Should a reference to an object in virtual memory be a standard memory pointer or a logical address?

- ObjectStore says, "Standard memory pointer." Applications like circuit simulation use the processor intensively and involve a lot of graph traversal. Such applications cannot tolerate a penalty for dereferencing pointers.

Using standard memory pointers for persistent objects enjoys an important functional benefit, because it eliminates the need for an execution-time distinction between persistent and non-persistent objects. As a result, libraries designed to manipulate data from standard programming languages can apply to persistent data as well.

- Most other vendors say, "Logical address." They argue that the memory address strategy is the wrong approach in the case that several workstations share a large collection of objects, and each workstation updates a few. Since the virtual address spaces of different workstations are unrelated, there is no way to ensure "cache coherency" at least until data returns to stable storage. That is, it is difficult to obtain the latest copy of a given object given its virtual memory address. By contrast, it is straightforward to invalidate a local copy given a table that maps each identifier to a set of virtual memory addresses.

On balance, I think that the standard memory pointer approach will gain ascendancy for applications that perform frequent graph traversals.

5.4 SPEEDING UP SLOW APPLICATIONS

Many of the tuning techniques for object-oriented databases relate to the topics of chapter 2 (concurrency control recovery, operating system settings or hardware) or chapter 3 (indexes). We will not deal further with them here. However, there are two issues that are very specific to performance tuning for object-oriented systems.

- *Object layout*: How to lay out individual objects and how to lay out collections of objects on disk.
- *Computation layout*: What to do in the server and what to do in the user workstation.

This section discusses each in turn.

5.4.1 Object Layout

According to object-oriented doctrine, an object in an OODB is supposed to correspond to some real world object. For the purposes of this discussion, objects have *methods* (code stored with the class to which the object belongs) and *attributes* (data that is specific to each object of a class). Laying out an object, then, means specifying the placement of the contents of its attributes.

There are two kinds of attributes: *value attributes* and *object attributes*. Intuitively, a value attribute has the semantics of an attribute in a relational system, except that it can consist of an array, set, or list of a basic type (i.e., integer, string, float, and so on) in addition to just a single value of a basic type. By contrast, an object attribute has the semantics of a shared substructure in a programming language. Formally,

- An attribute A of class C is called an object attribute if

  (a) The contents x of attribute A can be accessed independently of an access to an instance of class C.

  (b) Different objects $o.A$ and $o'.A$ of class C (or other classes) can share the same constituent object x in the sense that if x changes, then $o.A$ and $o'.A$ will both be affected. (Specifically, if field $x.foo$ changes, then $o.A.foo$ and $o'.A.foo$ will change similarly.)

- An attribute A of class C is called a *value attribute* if it isn't an object attribute. That is, the contents of A can be accessed only through class C and changing $o.A$ has no effect on any $o'.A$ provided o and o' are different.

Example: Restaurant Database

Consider a database about restaurants and customers, and three attributes of the class restaurant: *name, town,* and *best customer*.

- It would probably be best to implement *name* as a value attribute, because changing the name of a restaurant should not affect any other restaurant.

- Whether *town* should be a value or object attribute depends on whether the database permits independent accesses to a town. If so, then *town* should be an object attribute. Otherwise, it should be a value attribute.

- The *best customer* attribute is potentially shared by many restaurants so it should be an object attribute. Also, a given customer Robert can be accessed whether or not he is the best customer of a given restaurant.

———

Let us now consider two ways of laying out the contents (whether value or object) of attribute A with respect to the structure representing object o and containing its *object header*. The header contains enough information to determine the object identifier (the systemwide unique integer that is associated with this object), the class, and size of the object.

1. *Cluster*: Place the contents of A close to the object header.

2. *Uncluster*: Place the contents of *A* in an arbitrary location on disk, normally at the end of some global heap-ordered file. (That is, each inserted element is placed at the end of the file as of the time of insertion.) Establish a pointer from *o* to those contents.

Now, we can discuss conditions in which one organization should be chosen over the other.

-

```
if A is a small value attribute then
   cluster the A value with o.
end if
```

-

```
if A is a large value attribute
   (more than half the page size) and
it is USUALLY used by application programs
   whenever o is accessed, then
        cluster A with o
    else
        uncluster A with respect to o
end if
```

-

```
if A is a value attribute and
its contents are very large
   (larger than the page size) and
it is ALWAYS used by application programs
   whenever o is accessed, then
        cluster A with o
    else
        uncluster A with respect to o
end if
```

-

```
if A is an object attribute and either
  its contents are larger than a page  or
  its contents are often accessed
     independently of class C or
  its contents are widely shared then
        uncluster A with respect to o
    else
        cluster A with o
end if
```

After considering each attribute, one at a time, this design methodology leads to a layout in which there is a single object structure containing the object header and the clustered attributes, with pointers to the unclustered attributes. This might be called an *octopus layout* (Figure 5.5).

Note on object clustering

Empirical observation suggests that it is rarely worthwhile to cluster the contents of an object attribute with an object header. Placing a new object at the end of a global heap-ordered file when it becomes persistent (the unclustered strategy) works very well. The reason is that objects become persistent at the moment they are reachable from other objects. So, even without explicit clustering, an inserted object will tend to be clustered with the object that first points to it. Such an organization behaves well for reads and certainly makes insertion easier.

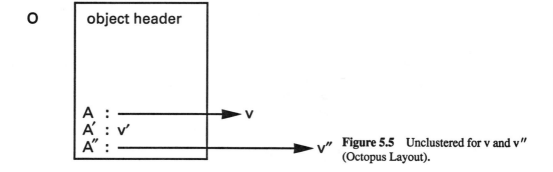

Figure 5.5   Unclustered for v and v″ (Octopus Layout).

(The organization may cause a concurrency control bottleneck, however, if many concurrent inserts take place at once. See chapter 3, section 3.6, pp. 69 ff.)

If you do decide to cluster a constituent object (the contents of an object attribute) with its parent object, you must decide with which object to cluster it in the case that it is shared. For example, if both the *restaurant* class and the *baker* class have *best customer* as a constituent object and both want to cluster *best customer* with objects of their type, there are two choices.

1. Cluster *best customer* with *restaurant*.

2. Cluster *best customer* with *baker*.

Which choice is better depends on access frequencies. If *best customer* is accessed more frequently through *restaurant*, then cluster it with *restaurant*. (Even in this case, if several restaurants have the same best customer, only one of them will benefit from this clustering.) Otherwise, cluster it with *baker*.

Roger King of the University of Colorado and Veronique Benzaken of O2 Technology have explored this issue further, but the question is far from resolved. My recommendation is to consider clustering when a constituent object has one parent, but not otherwise.

Vertical partitioning

A more sophisticated approach (available in only some systems) is to use *vertical partitioning*. In vertical partitioning, each object is divided into several *portions*. Each portion contains the object identifier and a header. Every other attribute is in exactly one portion. Vertical partitioning is better than an octopus layout when the following access pattern holds:

- Attribute sets X and Y have no attributes in common.
- Some accesses are to the object identifier and some set of attributes X.
- Nearly all other accesses are to the object identifier and some set of attributes Y.

In that case, establish two portions for each given object o: (object header, X) and (object header, Y). Each representation may have an octopus layout.

Horizontal partitioning

If there are many accesses against a large given collection of objects, then it may be worthwhile to partition the collection across several disks. This will help most when each access searches a single disk.

For example, if you partition the collection based on object identifier, but you access it based on name without an index, then your query will have to search all the disks. A far better approach would be to build an index on name (and perhaps partitioned based on name) that returns the object identifier. So, an access to an object would consist of two accesses: one to the name index and one to the object.

Laying out a single portion

Within a given portion (whether the result of a vertical partitioning or not), you must determine how to lay out the clustered attributes. The simplest rule of thumb is to place the most frequently accessed attributes closest to the object identifier. This tends to put such attribute contents on the same page as the object identifier at least for small objects.

The trouble with this simple rule of thumb is that one large attribute may crowd out several smaller attributes with slightly lower access frequencies. This leads to a slightly more sophisticated rule of thumb. Let the *access priority* of an attribute be its access frequency divided by its size.[6]

Rule of thumb: *the higher the access priority of a clustered attribute, the closer it should be to the object identifier.*

5.4.2 Computation Layout

In many OODB applications, e.g., design applications, users have powerful workstations on their desks. They use these workstations to perform compute-intensive graphics or numerical tasks. When those tasks involve the database, someone must decide where to do the work. In a system that supports execution site independence, this decision should not affect the application code.

- If a user must repeatedly access some set of objects X and there are few concurrent updates by other users of X, then it is best to place X in the database buffer on the user's workstation.

  This holds often for computer-aided design applications. The main danger of this strategy is that the database buffers may be corrupted by application programs in ways that would not otherwise be possible, e.g., by wild C pointers.

- In other cases—i.e., for small transactions that do little computation per disk access such as nonindexed queries or that update shared data—it is better for the server to hold the database buffers and for the client to communicate to the server through remote procedure calls. (This configuration is also the only one possible when accessing a database from a machine that cannot run

---

[6] This notion of access priority is similar to the notion of "heat" proposed by G. Copeland and his colleagues for the parallel database server Bubba, developed at MCC. G. Copeland, W. Alexander, E. Bougherty and T. Keller, "Data Placement in Bubba" in *Proc. of ACM SIGMOD Conference,* May 1988, pp. 99-108.

the code to manage buffers. For example, an MS-DOS client would use this mechanism to access a database that runs on top of UNIX.)

5.5 RELATIONAL SYSTEMS FIGHT BACK

Sales brochures from object-oriented vendors may lead you to believe that relational systems are frozen into obsolescence. They will tell you

- SQL is less powerful than a general-purpose (i.e., Turing-complete) programming language. They will omit any discussion of the procedural extensions (see chapter 4, section 4.7.1, p. 119) that overcome this deficiency.
- Relational systems are designed for business record processing. They will forget to mention that such systems have been used successfully for such varied applications as gene manipulation and computational linguistics.

Relational vendors, moreover, have not been sitting on their hands. Inspired by such forward-looking projects as the Pascal-R project (led by Joachim Schmidt at Hamburg) and the PostGres system (led by Mike Stonebraker at Berkeley)[7] vendors including INGRES, IBM, Hewlett-Packard and others have mapped out a strategy for the evolution of relational systems. There are two design rationales for that work.

- The relational model in general and SQL in particular constitute a good starting point for new database technology for the following reasons:
  - Data communication among heterogeneous hardware and software architectures consists of byte sequences. Relational tables can be encoded into and decoded from such sequences without loss of information. This is not easy with all implementations of interobject references.
  - The model and SQL enjoy a large, trained following.
  - There are many efficient implementations of SQL.
- SQL is as much of a *lingua franca* for database systems as English is for international human communication in the late twentieth century. Like English, SQL may not be the best such language, but it is the most widespread and can be extended in a straightforward way to meet the needs of new applications.[8]

[7] M. Stonebraker, G. Kemnitz, "The POSTGRES Next-Generation Database Management System," *Communications of the ACM,* vol. 34, no. 10, pp. 78-92, October 1991.

[8] Steve Rozen and I examined the need for extensions to the relational model for classical Wall Street applications based on Steve's experience working there. See the article by us entitled "Using a Relational Database on Wall Street: The Good, the Bad, the Ugly, and the Ideal," *Communications of the ACM*, vol. 32, no. 8, pp. 988-994, August 1989.

For concreteness, consider the extensions proposed by IBM Almaden's Starburst prototype designed principally by Guy Lohman, Laura Haas, Bruce Lindsay, Hamid Pirahesh, and Christoph Freytag, with important contributions from other researchers.[9]

- *Long fields*: For relational systems to support applications involving voice, video or image data, they must support large records. For example, consider a medical informatics application that wishes to store X-ray images in records along with the patient being treated, the attending doctor, the date and so on. Because relational systems, at least until recently, forced records to be smaller than a page, they would force such applications to adopt an artificial implementation. A typical implementation would store the name of the file containing the X-ray image in the record. The main problem with such an implementation is that the database management system's concurrency control mechanism will have no control over accesses to the file. Most commercial database systems have or will soon have support within the database management system for long records whose fields can be a gigabyte long or longer.

- *User-defined operations*: Database management systems that support the ability to store and retrieve long fields also support application-specific operations on them. For example, if the long field represents an image, then Starburst and new INGRES releases would permit the server to apply a user-defined rotate or enlarge operation within an SQL statement. A possible but badly performing alternative would be to retrieve the data from the long field into an operating system file, manipulate it in the application space, and then return it to the database. That would entail a huge amount of data transfer and many disk accesses to read and write the operating system file.

- *Inter-object references*: As pointed out earlier, direct support for references gives object-oriented systems a significant performance advantage for certain applications. By contrast, for applications that need only the ability to hold references and to traverse them occasionally, the relational model works quite well. As mentioned earlier, the representation of a reference from record X to record Y might consist of putting the key of Y into a field of X. Thus, the existence of references does not preclude the use of a relational system.

- *Support for recursion*: Finally, there is the issue of Turing-completeness, specifically the issue of support for recursion. To understand what recur-

[9] G. Lohman, B. Lindsay, H. Pirahesh, and K. Schiefer, "Extensions to Starburst: Objects, Types, Functions, and Rules," *Communications of the ACM*, vol. 34, no. 10, pp. 94–109, October 1991.

sion means in this context, imagine that your database contains a relation with fields parent and child. A typical recursive query would be to find all ancestors of Nicholas Green in the database. No single SQL I query will find them, because the number of joins needed to answer the question cannot be bounded in advance (that is, independently of actual record contents of the database). A user of a relational system would have to use a WHILE loop from a procedural extension (see the example in chapter 4, section 4.7.1, p. 120). This may be less efficient than maintaining some encoding of the transitive closure. Current workers in the area include R. Agrawal and G. Kiernan of IBM Almaden, Jagadish of AT&T Bell Labs, J-P Cheiney and C. de Maindreville of INRIA in France, M. Houtsma of AE Enschede in the Netherlands, P. Apers of the University of Twente, and S. Ceri of the University of Modena.

In summary, it is easy to extend SQL to the full power of a programming language. Procedural extensions already accomplish this. But power is not the real point—convenience and efficiency are. Object-oriented database languages based on programming languages such as C++ express operations on graphs more naturally and often more efficiently than SQL-based systems. However, this does not prevent extensible relational languages from satisfying many applications, e.g., in medical informatics or genetics, that use pointers but entail little graph traversal.

5.6 PROSPECTUS

Now that you've seen some examples and technical considerations, do you believe object-oriented databases have a future?

Here is what the typical believer will tell you

- Present database management systems are much too slow (factor of 500) for computationally expensive low concurrency applications, like electrical computer-aided design. These applications need memory speeds for graph traversal.
- For other applications, the impedance mismatch creates errors and forces unnatural implementations.
- Encapsulation is important for software maintenance.
- So, OODBs will come to replace many file system-based applications that cannot use relational databases.

If you then ask this advocate when this will happen, you might hear the familiar "Within 5 years or so."[10]

---

[10] Most technical start-ups think of their moment of glory as starting within 5 years from their founding.

The advocate may appeal to a historical parallel. Hierarchical and network databases took 15 years from conception (1960) to market importance (mid-1970s). Codd invented the relational model in 1970 and relational systems started to dominate the marketplace in the late 1980s. Smalltalk began the object-oriented stampede in 1980 (though Simula invented many of the basic concepts in the late 1960s). Does that mean the late 1990s will see significant commercial use of object-oriented databases? Maybe.

My view is that if object-oriented systems live up to their claims of improved maintainability, settle on a standard language (such as C++), achieve high performance across a variety of applications, and offer familiar amenities such as SQL access and continuous operation, then they will succeed. At the same time, extensible relational systems having support for gigabyte-long fields and special-purpose data types will find clients among those enterprises with a substantial investment in relational technology.

6

Choosing a System

6.1 GOAL OF CHAPTER

The most costly mistake a chief information officer can make is to choose the
wrong system for his or her organization. A system can be wrong because

- It does not provide sufficient transaction throughput.
- It offers more transaction throughput than necessary and is excessively expensive. (A transaction per second on a personal computer costs about $1000 at 1992 prices, whereas it costs around thirty times more on a mainframe.)
- It gives sufficient transaction throughput when first installed, but the organization discovers new needs that overwhelm the system.

The goal of this chapter is to help guide you to the proper choice of system,
thus avoiding the above mishaps.

The first step is to determine the needs. Many database consultants suggest
that a system designer think in contractual terms when specifying the performance
requirements of a system (the next subsection gives the main ingredients of such
a performance contract). The system can become overwhelmed, but at least the
system designer can defend his competence.

The trouble is, given a high performance system, users attempt to use a system for "unintended" purposes. A spectacular example of this occurred with the
computerized phone directory service (Minitel) in France when it was first installed. Previously computer-illiterate users found that they could send electronic

mail, an additional service provided by Minitel. Electronic mail became so popular that the system crashed because of overload several times.

Minitel is far removed from most database applications, but the situation reoccurs frequently in practice. When users discover that a database permits queries that they could never ask before, whether an analysis of stock trends or statistical queries about quasars, they will use them more than you expect.

One can summarize this phenomenon by the following rule of thumb: *Ten times the speed generates ten times the use. One hundred times the speed generates ten thousand times the use.* To put this directly, a requirements study based on interviews with potential users of new high-performance capabilities will understate actual use.

6.1.1 Determining Needs: Questions on the Way

A good design must survive the scrutiny of a lot of pointed questions. The goal of these questions is to determine the access patterns, the access frequency, and the data size. It is best to break the questions down into subquestions.

1. *Why*: Why should this application exist?

2. *What*: What kind of data will be accessed, what are the query types (see chapter 3), what will be returned to the application?

3. *How much*: How much data is there? Can it fit in random access memory? How fast will it grow?

4. *How fast*: What is the required transaction response time or application run time?

5. *How often*: What is the arrival rate of transactions, e.g., 100 transactions per minute or 3 per day? Which transactions will run concurrently?

6. *On which platforms*: A design may be more or less constrained depending on what has already been decided.

- Has the hardware been chosen? If your system must run on an old personal computer, then you may not have the same options as if it runs on a workstation. This may seem basic, but I have had the experience of discussing systems issues with a medical computing professional who told me after 20 minutes, "Oh, this must all run on Apple MacIntoshes." By the same token, a single mainframe with many disks may be ideally suited to I/O-intensive applications but not to graphic-intensive ones.
- Has the database management system been chosen? As chapters 4 and 5 should have convinced you, the different data models offer different comparative advantages.

7. *How secure*: Must there be authorization checks, auditing, or some other form of protection? Some forms of auditing are well handled by triggers.

8. *How relentless*: Is there time during the day to back up data? Is there time to reorganize the indexes?

9. *How distributed*: Is distribution inherent to the application (perhaps for geographical or political reasons)? In that case, what are the constraints on updates? Remember that many systems cannot support a transaction that performs updates on multiple sites. Must tables be partitioned for purposes of loading, access, or recovery?

6.2 GIVEN THE NEEDS, CHOOSE THE SYSTEM

There are lies, damn lies, and then there are benchmarks—Folklore

Suppose that you have somehow figured out your needs. That is, you know the main characteristics of your database and the kind of transaction mix you will expect. Now you must choose the system.

If your application already exists, then the test is straightforward in principle. You bring in each vendor's equipment or software, and try your application. A typical question that can be resolved this way is whether to substitute vendor X's SQL database management system for vendor Y's SQL database management system. Even this can be difficult for applications that use the nonportable features of X's SQL.

For applications that don't yet exist, one must extrapolate from other measures. Unfortunately, simple processor-based measures such as millions of instructions per second (MIPS) are insufficient. The reason is that the performance of database management systems depends not only on processing speed but also on database software algorithms, operating system overhead, the speed of secondary storage, and network latency. Performance also depends on the size and characteristics of the data, on the setting of tuning parameters, and on the kind of application (decision support, online transaction processing, or graph traversal). The question, then, is what measure to use.

In the subsequent sections we explore two main alternatives.

1. Create your own performance benchmark.

2. Use an existing benchmark that closely approximates your application.

6.3 DEVELOPING YOUR OWN BENCHMARK

Writing your own benchmark is a delicate compromise between realism and available time.[1] Having been brought up in a culture in which MIPS claims provided

---

[1] See the article of Tom Sawyer in *The Benchmark Handbook*, Jim Gray, Ed. San Mateo,

a simple, if often misleading, measurement criterion, designers of a home-brewed benchmark may underestimate the difficulty of their task. Benchmark designers also may feel obliged to provide a single number for fear that management will not understand anything more complicated. After all, managers must explain the results to innumerate upper management who must ultimately make a buy/no-buy decision.

A single number, however, can mislead you for at least two reasons.

- An application normally runs many different transaction types. At the very least, there are usually online and batch transaction types.
- If the single number offered is the average transaction throughput, you may end up with a system that exhibits a wide variance of response times. Variance is important. For example, users will overwhelmingly prefer a system that consistently gives 1-second response time to a system that usually gives subsecond response time and occasionally 30-second response time. So, a curve showing the frequency of different response times is essential.

6.3.1 What to Measure

For your benchmark to have any meaning at all, you must specify

- Your database.
- Your transactions.

It is essential to model the data well. If a test database doesn't reflect (in relational terms) the table sizes, column values, or data distribution of the real application, then the optimizer may behave one way on the test database and another way on the real database, giving you meaningless results. You can partially compensate for this by deliberately fudging the statistics in the catalog to simulate the properties of the real data, but this is tricky in some systems and may be impossible, e.g., in some releases of ORACLE.

In object-oriented systems, small size may give even more deceptive results than in a relational system, because an application that can store its buffer in a client site's random access memory will execute much faster than an application that must often make requests to server disks.

Specifying the transactions is more tricky, because transactions consist of four components (Figure 6.1).

- Terminal interactions.
- Local application programming logic.
- Communication (e.g., from client to server).

Calif.: Morgan-Kaufmann, 1991. You can find articles in that book about all the benchmarks mentioned in this chapter except order entry.

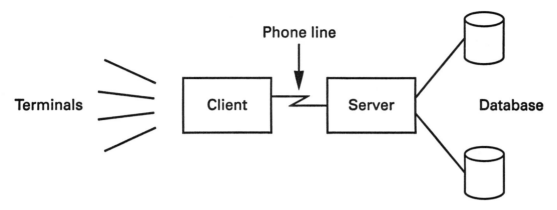

Figure 6.1   Terminal to Application Logic to Phone Line to Database.

• Database accesses.

Since your bosses are unlikely to give you access to an entire network, you will likely have to simulate the communication aspects. Here are some things to look out for.

• Correct simulation of the communication protocols.

Terminals that send every character to a host will create much more load than terminals that buffer their messages. The benchmark must correctly model the load of each terminal and the number of terminals.

• Appropriate simulation of arrival times.

Do jobs arrive with constant interarrival times or can jobs arrive in bursts? Occasional overloading can reveal functional problems such as lost messages, corrupted indexes, and even memory violation messages.

Application programming and terminal handling overhead at an underloaded client site can be ignored. Otherwise, it must be accounted for either by estimating or measuring its effects.

To characterize transactions with respect to database access, we are mainly interested in whether transactions perform accesses based on indexes or not and whether they perform updates or not. In particular, transactions can be characterized by

• The number of index-based reads per table.
• The number of index-based updates per table.
• The number of scanning reads per table.

• The number of scanning updates per table.

This level of abstraction may permit different transaction types to be combined. For example, if two different transaction types both perform four index-based reads and one index-based update, though on different tables, then consider summing their arrival rates and having them access a single table. The fewer the transaction types, the easier the comparison and reporting task. Combining transactions, however, may introduce two inaccuracies that you should avoid.

1. It may inflate the effect of concurrency control conflicts, since the combined transaction will access fewer tables than the original ones.

2. It may inflate the hit ratio for the same reason.

At the end, the goal will be to show, for each transaction type, the arrival rate and the response time.

6.4 USING A STANDARD BENCHMARK

If the previous discussion has convinced you that writing your own benchmark requires too much effort and presents too many opportunities for error, then you should consider using a standard benchmark. The main questions in this case are:

• Which benchmark to use.
• What that benchmark leaves out.

For the most part, the benchmarks concentrate on the database access question and largely ignore communication costs. Thus, it is your separate responsibility to guarantee that communication costs are not the bottleneck. The benchmarks differ along three dimensions.

• Transaction length: short or long.
• Transaction characteristics: update or read-only.
• Interaction with application logic: none or frequent.

Things to watch out for when running standard benchmarks are the following:

1. The benchmark is irrelevant to your application. For example, a transaction processing benchmark will tell you nothing about the performance of a decision support application and only a little about the performance of a circuit design application.

2. The vendor employs a special-purpose system for the benchmark whose features are not in the vendor's product.

If you can avoid these pitfalls, then a relevant benchmark can lead you to an appropriate choice of hardware and software assuming that your requirements estimate is correct.

6.5 TRANSACTIONAL APPLICATIONS

For the purposes of this discussion, *online transaction processing* denotes the execution of short (under 10 disk accesses with little computation), update-intensive programs. Demands on an online transaction processing system may vary greatly. A low end system may execute under 10 online transactions per second originating at a few terminals against a subgigabyte database. A high end system may execute 1000 of these short transactions per second originating at 100,000 terminals against a terabyte database.

Typical applications include

- *Telecommunications*: a typical database application here is billing. Proposed billing methods, such as billing by packet, may entail close cooperation between the database and communication switches. It may also entail cooperation among different industrial organizations. For example, a long distance call from Hawaii to Paris involves at least three different phone companies who must partition the revenue among them. Applications such as call forwarding, cellular telephones and autodialing require yet more sophisticated billing methods.

- *Airline reservations*: a classical application that has resulted in many special purpose features that have pushed database technology forward over the years. Here there must be communication between travel agents and the databases of airlines, hotels, and car rental companies.

- *Banking (or credit card services)*: many simple transactions here involve withdrawing, depositing, and transferring money.

- *Transportation*: worldwide express mail or transportation companies must adhere to strict delivery time constraints. This requires a tracking system that can locate any item, control vehicle routing, and so on. This depends conceptually on a centralized database that may be updated tens of thousands of times per hour.

- *Brokerage*: speed is essential for many applications in this domain. Ticker-tape information must flow to the proper broker at the proper time. Price histories and yields must be computed quickly. Databases must be kept consistent. For example, a brokerage house with offices (and databases) on the east and west coast incurred a multi-million dollar loss due to differences between prices posted in those databases for the same stock. A clever arbitrageur exploited those differences to sell to one branch while buying from another.

- *Process control*: this involves control of factory processes, warehouse inventory control, order entry and tracking.
- *Telemarketing*: in this application, operators receive calls from customers who order goods and are billed for them. In one application I am familiar with, if every teleoperator can spend one second less with every client, the application will save $10,000 per month.

The online transaction processing business (hardware and software) represents approximately $35 billion per year. The industry has set up its own standards organization called the Transaction Processing Performance Council. As of this writing, the council has specified and promulgated two online transaction benchmarks that simulate an idealized banking environment. The council is in the process of specifying a new transactional benchmark known as the order-entry benchmark.

6.5.1 Debit-Credit Benchmarks

The Transactional Processing Performance Council's two standard benchmarks for measuring throughput are called TPC/A and TPC/B. Both simulate a simple balance update in a banking application. They differ in the way they incorporate network communication. I will ignore this distinction and refer to the two benchmarks collectively as the TPC benchmarks. Please refer to Gray's book for details.

The TPC benchmark descriptions attempt to specify enough details of the benchmark to make cheating difficult, but not so much as to preclude clever implementations or new data models. A mark of the success of this approach is that when new products come out, their vendors routinely advertise their performance on these benchmarks.

Here is an example of some of the specifications that TPC makes and why:

- The basic procedure follows:

    (a) Read 100 bytes including account ID, teller ID, branch ID and balance information from the terminal.
    (b) Update a random account balance.
    (c) Write to a history file.
    (d) Update a teller balance.
    (e) Update a branch balance.
    (f) Commit the transaction.
    (g) Write 200 bytes to the terminal.

- The benchmarks specify properties of the terminal emulator, e.g., the "think time" should not be constant but should be based on a truncated negative exponential distribution. Systems with constant "think time" tend to have artificially high throughput.

- The program should use degree 3 isolation, and the hardware should be able to tolerate the failure of any single durable medium unit. This specification prevents systems from avoiding concurrency control and recovery overhead.

- Since each teller and each account is associated with a given branch, the benchmarks specify the probability that a given update applies to an account and teller at the same branch. This specification forces distributed systems to include intersite communication.

- The benchmarks specify that 95% of the transactions must complete within 2 seconds. Systems with arbitrarily long response times can achieve artificially high throughputs.

- Because one of the goals is to give a price per transaction per second, the benchmarks specify the pricing methodology.

- The results should be confirmed by an independent auditor. It's not that one shouldn't trust all vendors, but then again . . .

By tightly specifying the benchmark procedures, TPC ensures that comparisons have meaning. The main disadvantage is that the benchmarks are idealized to the point of irrelevance for many applications.

Jim Gray, a principal inventor of the precursor to these benchmarks, suggests adopting the cautious attitude one often takes when hearing the U.S. Environmental Protection Agency ratings for some car: "Your actual mileage may vary according to road conditions and driving habits. Use these numbers for comparison purposes only."

6.5.2 Order Entry

As of this writing, the order-entry benchmark is still a working draft, but many of its salient features have been outlined. Basically, the benchmark presents a mixture of read-only and update-intensive transaction types as might characterize a wholesale supplier. The supplier is assumed to have geographically distributed sales districts and associated warehouses. As in TPC/A and TPC/B, there are many ancillary constraints, e.g., concerning think time, isolation properties, auditing, and so on.

The database consists of nine tables: New-Order, Order-Line, Order, Customer, District, Warehouse, Stock, Item and History. Here are the main operations:

- *Payment transaction*: Reflects the effect of the receipt of a payment from a customer on the district and warehouse sales statistics. It involves three updates and one insertion, and occurs frequently with demanding response time requirements.

- *Order-status transaction*: Returns the status of an order. It involves three data retrievals, occurs relatively infrequently, but has stringent response time requirements.

- *Delivery batch*: Consists of processing ten orders by deferred execution. Each order is to be a separate transaction. When delivery is invoked, it returns as soon as all data is entered. It need only start executing within 60 seconds of being queued. Thus, its response-time requirements are relaxed.

- *Stock-level transaction*: Is a read-only database transaction that returns information about the quantity remaining of items recently sold. The transaction entails several joins and returns about 8000 records, representing a consumptive read-only transaction. Its response-time requirements are also relaxed.

Since there are several different kinds of transactions, the "business throughput" metric takes into account all transactions in the mix. (The council specifies how often each transaction should occur.)

6.6 RELATIONAL QUERY BENCHMARKS

Relational systems have the versatility to be used in a wide variety of situations: from transaction processing (row-at-a-time updates), to index-based joins, to multi-index decision support queries. The TPC and order-entry benchmarks offer a good test of an online transaction processing application. They test query optimization, join methods, and sort capabilities only to a small extent, however.

Relational benchmarks with wider coverage are the Wisconsin Benchmark, developed by David DeWitt and his colleagues at the University of Wisconsin at Madison, and its descendants:

- ANSI SQL Standard Scalable and Portable Benchmark for Relational Systems (AS^3AP).
- Set Query Benchmark.

6.6.1 Wide Coverage Benchmark

The AS^3AP query set, developed by Carolyn Turbyfill, Cyril Orji, and Dina Bitton, measures the following functionalities:

1. Select a single row using a clustered index.
2. Select a single row using a nonclustered index.
3. Select various percentages of rows using clustered and nonclustered indexes.
4. Select through multiple clauses, some of which should use their indexes and others of which should not.
5. Perform joins followed by selections.
6. Perform simple and group by aggregates.
7. Update single and multiple rows.

In addition a subset of these queries are proposed for multiuser queries. I would suggest this benchmark or the newer releases of the Wisconsin benchmark, for general relational systems without a significant telecommunications component.

6.6.2 Set Query Benchmark

The Set Query benchmark developed by Patrick O'Neil focuses on the opposite end of the spectrum from online transaction processing, namely, massive read-only transactions. Relative to the AS^3AP benchmark, the main difference is that this benchmark benefits from efficient scan performance and sophisticated index processing.

Sophisticated index processing means the ability to perform set manipulation on the results of different index queries. For example, the results of one index query may be intersected with the results of another one. In some cases, this manipulation benefits from unusual data structures such as bit maps to support negation queries.

Here is a typical application of set queries. Most organizations have some notion of customer. Large organizations, take breakfast cereal manufacturers for example, divide their customers into "segments," e.g., health-obsessed adults, sugar-obsessed kids, and sugar-obsessed kids with health-obsessed parents. Each segment returns a particular profit, has certain purchasing habits, and so on.

In some cases, statistical queries on the organization's own or someone else's database can help discern the characteristics of each segment. For example, the publisher of a fitness magazine may offer the following service to a cereal manufacturer: "We will give you the names of addresses of women on our subscriber list who responded to our special offer of biodegradable diapers four years ago." The cereal company may use this information to perform a direct mailing to advertise their new "Good-for-Kids Cereal."

This corresponds to a query of the form (let us say that *oldyear* indicates 4 years ago)

```
SELECT name, address
FROM subscribers
WHERE YEAR = :oldyear
AND SEX = 'F'
AND PRODUCT = 'diapers'
```

This will entail either a scan of the entire subscribers table or the intersection of the results of the queries on the indexes on YEAR, PRODUCT and possibly even SEX.

Besides straight selections, set queries may include aggregates. For example, document retrieval applications frequently count the number of documents that would be retrieved by a given query before deciding whether to retrieve those documents. Recall from chapter 3 that some systems such as SYBASE can answer these queries without going to the data tuples by using dense nonclustering indexes. (David DeWitt reports that some systems first implemented this feature in order to run the Wisconsin benchmark faster—there are no passive observers in this business.)

The Set Query benchmark includes joins to model applications that require correlations. For example, a clothing store may wish to determine which shoe brands are bought with which suit brands.

Set queries are important enough that certain products are designed specifically for them. Two such products for workstations and mainframes are Computer Corporation of America's MODEL 204 and Red Brick Systems's Gold Mine server. These products can achieve more than ten times the performance of mainstream relational database systems on many Set Queries against large (> 10 gigabyte large) databases. Their basic implementation approach is to build indexes on all attributes and to have the capability of handling even wild card queries, e.g., LIKE '%OLUMB%'. Red Brick also offers a modified SQL that offers facilities for moving sums, e.g., a rolling 12-month trend report. Of personal computer products, FoxBASE Version 2.0 from Fox Software performs very well on this benchmark.

Patrick O'Neil has listed some of the important capabilities a system should have in order to do well on the Set Query benchmark.

- Several join methods with the ability to take advantage of different combinations of indexes.
- Ability to perform the intersection of the results of different index selections, perhaps by performing boolean operations on bit maps (where each bit represents a tuple).
- Index compression (because set queries tend to run against large databases with many indexes).

Figure 6.2   Relationship between Benchmark and Application Area.

- Ability to perform intraquery parallelism. For example, if a query involves several joins, then it will often help to perform several of these joins in parallel or to apply parallelism to each join. Following the success of Teradata, several vendors have offered or will offer this capability.

Figure 6.2 summarizes the relationship between the benchmarks discussed in the last two sections and application areas.

6.7 BENCHMARKS FOR ENGINEERING DATABASES

By the early 1990s, workstations had become a principal tool for design applications, particularly engineering design applications. At the same time design software vendors concluded that transactional facilities had to be included as integral parts of their software applications. The confluence of these two effects led R. G. G. Cattell of Sun Microsystems to propose a benchmark for engineering databases.

As we noted in the chapter on object-oriented database systems, relational systems can be a factor of ten times to one hundred times too slow for many engineering applications, compared with modern object-oriented database systems. The main reason is that the object-oriented systems exploit the large main memories at client workstations and provide direct support for pointers.

Another important factor is that engineering applications typically perform operations of the following form:

1. Access data item.
2. Process it in the programming language.
3. Depending on the result of the processing, access the next data item.

An example would be the search for a lowest cost path through a graph.

So, for engineering applications, either the database management system must provide the functionality of a programming language or the interface between the programming language and the query language must entail low overhead.

6.7.1 Details of Cattell's Benchmark

These special application properties motivated Cattell's design. The database supporting the benchmark ranges in size from being small enough to fit into the random access memory on the client workstation to large enough to require extensive secondary storage on the server. The database has N parts and $3N$ connections with connections from each part to three other randomly selected parts. However random does not mean uniform. Ninety percent of the connections are selected among the one percent of the parts that have the numerically closest part IDs. For this reason, a clustering index on part ID will give some benefit.

There are two data types in the application.

- A part type having an ID, a type, an $x - y$ position, and a timestamp.
- A connection type having a source part ID, a target part ID, a length, and a type.

The single-user test (the most interesting one for this application) consists of three kinds of operations.

- *Lookup*: Find the parts corresponding to 1000 random part IDs. Call a procedure having the $x - y$ positions of each found part as parameters. The procedure has no body. (The call exercises the database to programming language interface.)
- *Traversal*: Find the parts connected to a randomly selected part within a distance of 7. That is, find all parts within seven connections from the given part. Again, call a null programming language procedure on each found part. The benchmark also includes a provision for reverse traversals.
- *Insert*: Insert 100 parts, each with three connections. Update indexes appropriately. Ensure degree three isolation properties.

Because the amount of data in the memory of the client workstation can have a large influence on performance, the performance can be very bad when this series of three operations runs the first time (a "cold start" effect). Therefore the benchmark is specified to be repeated ten times with only the randomly selected parts being different.

Database object code should already be in memory when the program begins.

6.8 SUMMARY

The first step in choosing a system is to determine its needs. If it is a new application, then consider multiplying your estimates or try to find a software and hardware architecture that will allow you to gain performance gracefully by purchasing new hardware.

If you decide to use a benchmark to measure new hardware or software, then buy Jim Gray's book on benchmarking and follow these recommendations:

1. If your application is already running, then test the prospective system on your application.

2. If your application is online transaction processing, then let TPC/A, TPC/B, or order-entry guide your purchase decision, provided your application is similar enough to the benchmark you use. "Similar enough" means the following: if system X has a better price/performance ratio on the benchmark than system Y, then X will also have a better price/performance ratio for your application.

3. If you have a general relational application then use AS^3AP or the new version of the Wisconsin benchmark.

4. If you have a read-only data mining application, then use the Set Query benchmark.

5. If you have a graph navigation application, then use the Cattell benchmark.

7

Performance Troubleshooting— What to Test, What to Do

7.1 GOAL OF CHAPTER

In an ideal world speeding up a slow system would consist of a simple three-step process:

1. Determine where the bottleneck is.
2. Figure out how to fix that bottleneck.
3. Fix it.

Unfortunately, troubleshooting is not so simple, because an apparent hardware bottleneck may result from many factors including query design. Fixing one factor may not break the bottleneck. So, troubleshooting is an iterative process:

```
Troubleshooting:
repeat
  monitor the system
  tune important queries
  tune global parameters
until satisfied or can do no more

if unsatisfied then
  add appropriate hardware
  start from the beginning
end if
```

There are two things to notice about this procedure

1. Troubleshooting usually leads you to look at one or more queries.

2. You should buy hardware only as a last resort. (See chapter 2, section 2.5, pp. 44 ff. for guidance about which hardware to buy.)

The goal of the first part of this chapter is to help you determine the location of bottlenecks by suggesting measurements to take. Depending on the outcome of those measurements, it will suggest a few possible reasons and solutions, then it will refer you to the part of the book that discusses the issue in depth.

The goal of the second part is to introduce you to some important utilities for measurement and performance improvement offered by database system vendors, operating system vendors and third-party tuning companies.

Note on the use of terms. For the purposes of this chapter, the whole database system consists of the database management system and the many user applications. Each user application consists of the code for one or more transactions. Each transaction consists of one or more queries. Local issues concern an individual application, transaction, or query. All other issues are global.

7.2 FINDING THE BOTTLENECK

The first goal is to distinguish between global problems (affecting all uses of the database) and query- or application-specific ones.

If you are presented with a problem affecting a single query or application, then consult section 7.2.2 directly. Otherwise, take an accounting summary to find out what is taking time. It is typical for a handful of transactions to cause 90% of the I/O statements to be executed. Look at each of these transactions and their queries as discussed in section 7.2.2.

If the preceding doesn't work, then you should look for global problems. Let's see what you might find.

7.2.1 Global Problems

Global problems arise because of insufficient hardware, poor operating system settings, or badly tuned or lock-greedy queries and transactions. Global measurements or inspection of configuration parameters can help identify the sources of the problem.

1. Poor operating system settings. Here are two typical problems. (See section 2.4 of chapter 2, pp. 37 ff. for detailed guidance.)

- The priority of the database server processes is lower than the priority of other applications; or different database management system processes have different priorities.

Either can cause priority inversion. It is always good to check for this.

- The database server has too little random access memory at its disposal.

  Check this if there are high paging levels in the database buffer.

2. Undisciplined application behavior for a production environment. Here are some examples.

- There are frequent DDL updates.

  You may have a rogue program developer who is creating test tables while the system is online. You should offer that person a separate test environment (logical partitioning).

- There is much query compilation activity or there is overhead caused by fetching code from disk.

  You may have a rogue user who loves to write ad hoc queries while the system is online. Or the size of the part of the database buffer that holds compiled queries may be too small (e.g., in ORACLE, this is determined by the parameter OPEN_CURSORS).

- There is a lot of index creation or maintenance activity.

  Maintenance and creation of indexes should be deferred to quiet periods. The same goes for the establishment of referential integrity constraints and the assignment of buffer pools to tablespaces.

- Checkpoints or database dumps occur frequently, slowing your system down.

  You should find out why the checkpoints or dumps are needed so often. (A checkpoint should not occur more frequently than every 20 minutes or so. A database dump should not occur more frequently than once or twice a day.) Making them less frequent may lengthen recovery times, thus reducing availability. Determine what recovery time is acceptable. This may require renegotiation with the system architects.

3. High disk utilization (greater than 50%) or response times greater than 30 milliseconds.

If some disks show high queueing delays, whereas others show no queueing, then try to balance the load. Again, see chapter 2 section 2.4.5, p. 44 for detailed guidance. It is important to

- Put the log on a separate disk.
- Use a buffered commit strategy.
- Use prefetching if your application performs many scans.

- Use raw partitions or extents to ensure there are few seeks (this is especially important for applications that do a lot of scanning).
- Ensure the data (and procedure) buffer is large enough but not too large. As discussed in chapter 2, section 2.4.2, p. 39 this means increasing the buffer size as long as the hit ratio increases without causing (much) additional paging. If there is paging, then either increase the amount of random access memory devoted to the buffer, reduce other uses of physical memory such as program text memory, locate the query that causes the paging and reduce the paging it causes, or consider buying hardware.
- Remove non-database applications that might be loading the disk.
- Put the nonclustering indexes on separate disks from the clustering index and the table data, if partitioning a single table into which there are many inserts. In other environments, partition everything (data and indexes) across several disks. See chapter 3, section 3.10, p. 81 for the rationale behind this advice.
- Consult chapter 2, section 2.5.2, p. 45 to determine how to use new disks should you decide to buy some.

4. High processor utilization.

- If one query uses the processing power, then try to tune it as discussed in the next subsection.
- Otherwise, ensure that the server does the work it should do and similarly for the client. See chapter 4, section 4.8.1, p. 125 and chapter 5, section 5.4.2, p. 148 for discussions about the kinds of work to put in the client as opposed to in the server. Here is a short list.

  (a) String manipulation in client.
  (b) Formatting and graphics in client.
  (c) Integrity constraints and triggers in the server.
  (d) Small lookup table in the client.
  (e) Joins in the server.

5. High network utilization.

- Make sure that message parameters such as the window size are set appropriately for your application.
- Then, find the application that makes the heaviest use of the network and rewrite its queries to move data around the network more efficiently. For example, if a large table moves across the network to the site of a smaller table for the purpose of performing a join, check your system's tuning guide to see whether you can reverse this situation.
- Try to rearrange your data so communication-intensive transactions can execute at a single site.

- Test any new network hardware you buy under as realistic conditions as possible. Network behavior can fluctuate widely in the presence of small differences in load.

6. Lock contention. An occasional suspension (a thread of control stops executing while waiting for a lock) is not bad. However, suspensions should happen less frequently than ten per minute on a well tuned system. Timeouts or deadlocks should basically never occur (see chapter 2 section 2.2.2, p. 26). Here are some frequent causes of lock contention and techniques for their elimination.

- You have many short transactions and your locking granularity is too coarse. Try using record locking if available. If you have long transactions, you are using record locking, and you encounter deadlocks, then perhaps you should use a coarser granularity of locking such as page-level or table-level—but do so with caution.
- Your transactions are too long. Make sure they include no user interaction (look carefully at the transactions produced by your 4GL programs) and see appendix A2 (p. 185).
- You have long reads or updates to counters. Take advantage of any special support your system offers for these access patterns. Also, remember to access hot-spot data items as late as possible in your transactions.
- Your transactions perform many updates on small tables. Remove indexes from those tables.
- You have indexed on a sequential key (see chapter 3, section 3.9, p. 80).

7. Other global problems resulting from poor setting of database parameters.

- The database server has too few or too many threads of control at its disposal. That is, there is a lot of processor idle time (too few threads) or thrashing (too many threads).

Adjust the appropriate tuning parameter up or down.

- There is contention on free lists (the lists keeping track of free pages in the database buffer).

You can solve this by creating as many free lists as there are server threads that access the database system.

- Sort times are too long due to excessive disk accesses.

If your file can fit into physical memory, then there should be only as many disk reads as it takes to read the file. You can achieve this by increasing the area in your buffer devoted to sorting.

7.2.2 Optimizing a Single Application

First understand what the application is supposed to do. That means asking

1. Its purpose—is it really important? Can it run at night?

2. Its performance requirements—throughput and response time. If it is interactive, then it should not read more than 5 to 10 pages. If it does, then there probably is an index problem.

3. Its actual performance—use your system's accounting facilities. Check its elapsed time and processor time. If all its time is spent in the processor, then the I/O subsystem is not the problem. It may be doing inappropriate operations (e.g., string manipulation) within the database system.

If it is I/O bound, then check to see whether prefetching is enabled. Also check to see whether the disks that it is using are overloaded.

If some query within the application appears to do much more work than it should, then examine its query plan (you will see how to do this in a few sample systems in a later subsection). This will tell you which indexes are being used and which are not. Now, try the following steps in order.

1. Rewrite the query using the hints in chapter 3, sections 3.11 and 3.12, pp. 82 ff, and chapter 4, section 4.6, pp. 106 ff and in your system's tuning manual.

2. Ensure that existing indexes are used properly. Here are some common reasons for problems (see chapter 3, section 3.11, pp. 83 ff for more details):

- The index that you thought existed doesn't.
- You haven't updated the catalog recently.
- A query specified the wrong predicate type, e.g., a float compared with an integer.
- A query used an arithmetic expression in an indexed field or compared an indexed field with NULL.

3. The index that you have is giving poor performance. In that case, try the following:

- You need a different kind of index than the one you have, e.g., you have a lot of inserts, but you are using a clustering B-tree index on a sequential key (see chapter 3, section 3.9, p. 80).
- You may have indexes that are rarely accessed. (A write-only index is not uncommon.) Remember that a nonclustering index is pure overhead during an insert.

- Your index should be restructured to eliminate overflow chains or empty nodes. This is an important issue for hash structures, ISAM structures, and clustering indexes of any kind. If your hash structure behaves badly, it may not have enough space or its hashing function should perhaps be changed.

4. Some queries use constructs such as ORDER BY, HAVING, DISTINCT, or subqueries in ways that make the query more expensive than necessary.

See chapter 4, section 4.6, p. 106 for methods of rewriting queries to eliminate these constructs without changing the meaning of the queries.

5. Accesses to one table of a multi-table cluster is slow.

The system may be spending time following overflow pointers. It may be good to reallocate the table clustering with more space between cluster key values of the smaller table (see chapter 4, section 4.3, pp. 100 ff).

6. The system spends a lot of time doing joins.

Consider an unnormalized schema if you have few updates or a multi-table clustered schema if you have frequent updates (see chapter 4, section 4.3, pp. 102 ff for a discussion of the tradeoff between these two).

7. The system spends a lot of time computing aggregates.

For example, the system may often have to calculate the total value of sales outstanding. In this situation, consider maintaining that value as a database relation and updating it (probably by using a trigger) whenever a new sale is recorded (see chapter 4, section 4.7.3, pp. 121 ff).

8. The application issues queries frequently to poll a change in some relation.

Use a trigger that executes whenever that relation is changed (again, see chapter 4, section 4.7.3).

9. You have a lot of trigger activity whenever there are updates.

The triggers may be maintaining redundant data such as aggregate data values or unnormalized relations. Make sure the triggers are supported by appropriate indexes. If you still have problems, then reconsider your denormalization decisions. Remember though that changing table organizations can be extremely disruptive to application software.

10. Your application suffers lock contention.

Look at point 6 in section 7.2.1, p. 172 of this chapter.

7.3 WILL A NEW DATABASE MANAGEMENT SYSTEM HELP?

Buying a new database management system is not normally considered a part of troubleshooting (which is why it is missing from the iterative process given in the introduction). Nevertheless, you might be forced to consider such a global change if you know that your database system will soon face radically new demands. This should lead you to two courses of action.

- You may benchmark your entire collection of applications on different software (see chapter 6).
- Before benchmarking, you may decide to consider other data models. Given current technology, you would do best to use a relational system unless

  - Your data has a natural representation in a graph structure, but an unnatural one in a tabular structure. In addition, many of your application's operations involve many pointer dereferences and repeated accesses to the same data item. Under these conditions, you should consider an object-oriented database system (see chapter 5, section 5.2, for more details).
  - Your use of the database is very stable and simple. In that case, you can consider a hierarchical model database such as IBM's TPF or a network model database that runs on your system.

If you restrict your search to a data model you have already selected, e.g., another relational system, then here are some facilities to look for that are not universally available:

- If your applications include online transaction processing (or have real-time constraints), then it should have (appendix A1, p. 183):

  - Record locking particularly for update-intensive environments (see chapter 2, section 2.2, p. 22 for more details).
  - Ability to place important data in random access memory.
  - Ability to control order in which locks are obtained to eliminate the possibility of deadlock.
  - Ability to give different transactions different priorities while avoiding priority inversion.
  - Ability to use buffered commit and to control checkpoint and dump frequency.

- Applications that work in response to database-changing events should have a trigger facility. This will avoid frequent polling to find those events (see chapter 4, section 4.7.3, p. 121).
- If you must perform long read-only queries concurrently with updates on the same data, then special support for long read-only queries (whereby these

queries require no read locks but still offer degree 3 isolation) will be useful (see chapter 2, section 2.2, p. 21).

- If your database applications use many different query types, ranging from short updates to range queries to multijoin queries, then look for a system with a rich set of data structures, e.g., hash, B-tree, ISAM, and possibly multidimensional search structures. Prefix compression should be possible within indexes (see chapter 3, section 3.4, p. 61 for more details).

- If you perform many point or multipoint queries, then you may save a disk access per query by using a clustering index that can be made sparse (see chapter 3, section 3.5 pp. 67 ff).

- If you do relatively few updates but many reads queries that do not retrieve all the attributes, then you would benefit from a system that answers queries based on dense indexes alone when possible (see chapter 3, p. 72).

- If your application is primarily decision support then you should look at facilities that are good for Set Queries (see chapter 6, section 6.6.2, p. 163).

  - Ability to perform boolean combinations of results of index selections based on tuple identifiers or bit arrays.
  - Multiple join methods to take advantage of different combinations of indexes.
  - Ability to perform several joins in parallel or to achieve parallelism within a join.

7.4 TUNING TOOLS FOR VARIOUS SYSTEMS

Here are some routines to call in the process of tuning. I have not tried to be exhaustive as I expect you to have your system tuning guide available. Instead, these commands constitute a useful subset for the systems discussed. Other systems, such as INFORMIX and DEC RDB, have similar monitoring facilities.

7.4.1 IBM DB2

The Instrumentation Facility (used in conjunction with the DB2 Performance Monitor) can be set to trace application-specific information as well as compute global statistics.

Accounting traces collect data related to specific transaction executions. For example, if there are seventeen transaction executions, then the DB2 performance monitor will generate seventeen reports. You can select the detail of information you want, e.g., Accounting class 1 is relatively undetailed. Each trace will contain information such as

- Elapsed time.

- Processor time.
- Number and type of SELECT, INSERT, UPDATE, and DELETE commands.
- Number of logical and physical page requests.
- Number of lock requests and commits.
- Queueing on locks and disks.

The DB2 Performance Monitor will then produce a two-line summary for every application executed, so you can locate the applications that take the most time. EXPLAIN will give the query plan for a given query.

Whereas accounting information gives application-specific information, statistics summarize information about all applications. The statistics give the total count as well as the rate of the following kinds of statements within a specific time interval (over all applications):

- Number of SELECT, INSERT, DELETE, and UPDATE commands.
- Data definition language statement, i.e., every query or modification of the catalog.
- Number of lock requests, deadlocks, lock escalations, and cursor opens and closes.
- Compilation and optimization activity.
- Hit ratio.

7.4.2 IBM SQL/DS

SQL/DS runs on the VM operating system (as opposed to DB2 which runs on MVS). Its main monitoring tool is REXXSQL.

SQL/DS also has a statistics gathering facility similar to (but with fewer options than) the DB2 accounting and statistics facilities.

7.4.3 INGRES

The INGRES Performance Monitor gives trace information about server execution, lock, and disk resources. For example, it provides a summary of locks held per locklist and per resource list. Because logs can frequently be a bottleneck, the performance monitor also offers a bar chart of log file utilization by process, by transaction, and by database.

SET is the verb that begins most tracing commands. Here are some of the major ones.

- io_trace—gives disk accesses for each query.
- lock_trace—displays lock waiting and ownership information.

- printevents—traces all significant database events.
- printgca—records all interactions between client and server.
- QEP *command*—gives the query execution plan including use of indexes, join strategies, and estimates used for the given SQL (or extended SQL) *command*.
- TRACE POINT *command*—gives debugging information for the given SQL (or extended SQL) *command*.

7.4.4 ORACLE

SQL*DBA MONITOR reports most useful global statistics. Here are some useful options.

1. PROCESS—shows which processes are using the database.
2. TABLE—shows which tables are being accessed.
3. LOCK—shows which processes own locks and which are suspended; waiting processes are highlighted in a graphical display.
4. STATISTICS—has several statistics-generating options, e.g., the USERS option gives cumulative information on a per-user basis, such as the number of cursors opened.
5. I/O—gives the hit ratio for each process.

SQL trace—generates statistics for each SQL statement including

- The number of times the statement is compiled and the number of times it is called.
- The elapsed time for compilation and execution on each invocation of that statement.
- The number of rows processed.
- The number of disk accesses.

VALIDATE—gives information about indexes, e.g., the structure of a B-tree.
EXPLAIN PLAN *statement*—gives the query plan used for *statement* including the way indexes are used and the order of different operations.

7.4.5 SYBASE

- sp_configure—gives the amount of buffer memory and space used for client-server connections and for procedures.
- sp_helpdb—lists the names of devices used by the database and how much space on them is allocated. This will tell you, for example, whether the log is on a separate device.

- sp_helpdevice—says how devices are defined, e.g., whether the device is a raw partition (if using UNIX).
- sp_help *mytable*—gives the column description and indexes of the table *mytable*.
- set showplan on, set noexec on—give the plan of queries without executing them, allowing you to experiment.
- set statistics io on—gives the number of table scans, logical accesses, and physical accesses for each table read.
- sp_lock and sp_who—gives information about locks.
- traceflag 1205—will dump deadlock information to the error log.

7.4.6 UNIFY

- lmshow—gives the lock usage of current transactions.
- shmmap—gives the size of the shared memory among the database processes and the amount of free space in that shared memory.
- tblstats—gives statistics about each table such as the number of rows it contains and the number of rows it contains per page.
- htstats—displays statistics about hash tables (very important in UNIFY).
- AMGR_LST_SCN—explains the query plan used by the system for a particular query.
- SQLSTATS—presents a variety of statistics including information about the use of indexes, the number of overflow links followed, locking behavior, and sorting statistics.

7.5 MONITORING STATEMENTS FOR MVS, VMS, AND UNIX

7.5.1 IBM MVS

Resource management facility (RMF) provides batch reports about system activity. This can tell you things like

- Disk utilization and which application (e.g., DB2 or some application program) is responsible for them.
- Disk (called DASD in IBMese) response times, queueing delays resulting from disk contention, seek times, rotational delays, and data transfer times.
- Paging and which application is suffering from the page faults (it is less serious if it is not the database management system).

- Processor utilization, divided by "group," e.g. all the DB2 work may be one group, CICS group may be another group, and so on.

7.5.2 UNIX

UNIX has many utilities. Here are the most useful ones for database applications.

- time—gives information about an application execution, giving total elapsed time, processor idle time, and time spent inside the operating system and time spent doing database server or client work. High idle times may mean that the system is disk or network bound. In that case, if your disks have low utlization, then you may have too few threads. High operating system time may suggest that your system is paging too much because the buffer has insufficient random access memory at its disposal.
- sar and vmstat—monitor disk accesses, memory utilization, paging, and swapping.
- ps—displays process status.
- prof—gives information about the execution path of programs.

7.5.3 DEC VMS

Here are some of the important utilities on VMS.

- MONITOR—gives general system load information depending on the option you select. For example, to find out about processor utilization, use MONI-TOR PROC.
- SHOW PROCESS /CONTINUOUS /ID=123—gives a real-time display of cumulative resource usage for a given process, in this example, 123.
- PCA—an optional product from Digital that gives a line-by-line listing of your program together with resource usage at each line. This may give some surprising results, e.g., that date arithmetic consumes enormous resources.

7.6 THIRD PARTY TOOLS

Many companies provide tools that you may find helpful in your tuning and administrative efforts. Here is a brief description of the products of two typical vendors.

7.6.1 ACE*Insight

Performance Technologies has a product called ACE*Insight that provides a kind of inverted index of a relational application (currently for ORACLE applications). It derives the following kind of information from the source code of an application:

- Which applications use which indexes and which tables. This can help to identify applications that will be affected if indexes are dropped or added, or if tables are changed.
- Locate statements with similar qualifications. This can help to identify candidate statements that can be combined.

7.6.2 BMC Software

BMC Software offers products to measure and improve database system performance for IBM software on mainframes, mostly DB2, IMS, and SQL/VS. They have approximately 4000 customers worldwide, most of the Fortune 100 variety.

TRW Credit Data is a typical customer. Their DB2 database holds 500 million records, 5% of which are updated each day. They back up an entire copy of their DB2 database every day and do frequent data reorganizations, all using BMC utilities.

BMC's basic products include

- Activity monitors that alert the user when unusual performance statistics arise. (The user can customize the alerters.)
- Utilities to speed up data copies.
- Utilities to restore cluster orderings to tables and to reorganize indexes.
- Data compression tools for disk storage and message transmission.
- Utilities to help IMS systems programmers reduce errors, e.g., by checking for dangling pointers when performing image copies.

BMC is thus typical of a variety of products that take information from a database management system and present it in a different (and possibly more informative) way than the native database management system. Also typical of such products is that they offer utilities to perform certain functions (e.g., data copies, index builds) better than the native database management system.

7.7 FINAL WORDS ABOUT TROUBLESHOOTING

Every database consultant has a different troubleshooting technique, sometimes influenced by local policies. For example, some consultants will always start by tuning application code, simply because that causes the fewest disruptions. Others start with the global view, under the theory that a bad operating system setting or clogged physical resource may have slowed down all database applications.

The most sophisticated troubleshooters try to preempt trouble altogether by looking for worrying historical trends. For example, they keep a historical record of monitored information about transaction elapsed times, processor times, paging requests, hit ratios, and so on in a relational table. Then they build a set of queries or triggers that warn them of radical changes in these parameters.

Still, all troubleshooters agree on three facts.

1. Troubleshooting requires tuning queries, indexes, lock contention, and logging.

2. It requires balancing the load between the client and the server.

3. It is challenging, exasperating, and fun.

May Murphy be absent. Good luck.

Appendices

A1. REAL-TIME DATABASES

A real-time database is one where some of the transactions must meet timing constraints. For most database applications these constraints are of a statistical nature, e.g., 90% of all transactions must complete within 1 second and 99% within 5 seconds. Such applications are known as *soft real-time* and apply to applications such as telemarketing, financial analysis, and even to certain kinds of industrial control.

Other real-time applications are characterized as "hard" if failure to meet a deadline can lead to catastrophe. The prototypical example is a jet aircraft control system that must keep an "inherently unstable" jet from crashing. Database applications in such domains require main memory databases, simplified locking, and either main memory recovery mechanisms or no recovery at all. Despite the differences, most of the guidelines offered below apply to hard real-time databases as well.

- Use main memory wisely, either by storing all important data in main memory or by placing some tables in favored buffers.

Many database management systems, such as DB2, allow database administrators to associate a buffer with specific tables. This is very useful in cases in which all timing constraints concern accesses to some table (or a few tables). If one table is critical, for example, then dedicating a large buffer to that table and a large enough slice of main memory to that buffer ensures that all important data is in main memory.

- Try to establish predictable lock patterns to avoid deadlocks and to minimize delays resulting from lock conflicts.

A real-time systems designer has the advantage of knowing what set of transactions is possible. He or she should use that information to chop transactions as discussed in Appendix A2 and in chapter 2 as well as to order the accesses within each transaction.

The question of order is essential to avoid deadlocks. One promising technique is to identify a total order among the variables that can be locked and lock them in that order. For example, if transaction type 1 locks X, Y, and Z and transaction type 2 locks W, X, and Z, and transaction type 3 locks Z and W, then they should all acquire locks in some order W, X, Y, and Z. That is, the acquisition order should be W before X; W and/or X before Y; and W, X, and/or Y before Z. This will eliminate the possibility of deadlock.[1]

- Give different transactions different priorities, but be careful.

To avoid the priority inversion problem cited in section 2.4.1 of chapter 2, pp. 38 ff, you must give the same priority to any two transactions that issue conflicting locks to the same data item. That is, if two transactions access some item X and at least one of them obtains a write (i.e., exclusive) lock on X, then the two transactions should run at the same priority.

On the other hand, if the above rule does not force you to give transaction T1 and T2 the same priority and T1 is time critical, then you might consider giving T1 higher priority.

- Make your data structures predictable. Usually this means some kind of balanced tree structure, such as a B-tree.

Overflow chaining can cause poor response times for tasks that must traverse those chains. (This will affect deletes even more than inserts, because a delete must traverse an entire chain even if the item to be deleted is not present.)

---

[1] A subtle problem can arise in systems in which the lockable units are larger than the data items of interest. For example, suppose that W, X, Y, and Z are records and the system uses page-level locking. Using the lock-ordering W, X, Y, and Z, you believe you have eliminated the possibility of deadlock. Unfortunately, however, W and Z are on the same page P1 and X and Y are on the same page P2. A transaction of type 1 may lock page P2 at the same time that a transaction of type 2 locks page P1. Each will seek to lock the other page, resulting in a deadlock.

- Minimize the overhead of the recovery subsystem.

   (a) Use the fastest commit options that are available. This includes options that delay updates to the database and that write many transactions together onto the log (which should be on its own disk). The only disadvantage to fast commit options is that they may increase recovery times from failures of random access memory. Minimize the chance of such failures by ensuring that your power supply is reliable.
   (b) Checkpoints and database dumps can cause unpredictable delays to real-time transactions so should be deferred to quiet periods.

A2. TRANSACTION CHOPPING

A2.1 ASSUMPTIONS

This appendix continues the discussion in chapter 2, pp. 16-20 about making transactions smaller for the purpose of increasing available concurrency. It uses simple graph theoretical ideas to show how to cut up transactions in a safe way. If there are no control dependencies between the pieces that are cut up, then the pieces can be executed in parallel. Here are the assumptions that must hold for you to make use of this material.

- You can characterize all the transactions that will run in some interval.

   The characterization may be parametrized. For example, you may know that some transactions update account balances and branch balances, whereas others check account balances. However, you need not know exactly which accounts or branches will be updated.

- Your goal is to achieve the *guarantees* of full isolation (degree 3 consistency). You just don't want to pay for it.

   That is, you would like either to *use* degree 2 consistency (i.e., write locks are acquired in a two-phased manner but read locks are released immediately after use) or to chop your transactions into smaller pieces. The guarantee should be that the resulting execution be equivalent to one in which each original transaction executes in isolation.

- If a transaction makes one or more calls to rollback, you know when these occur.

   Suppose that you chop up the code for a transaction T into two pieces T_1 and T_2 where the T_1 part executes first. If the T_2 part executes a rollback statement in a given execution after T_1 commits, then the modifications done by

T_1 will still be reflected in the database. This is not equivalent to an execution in which T executes a rollback statement and undoes all its modifications. Thus, you should rearrange the code so rollbacks occur early. We will formalize this intuition below with the notion of rollback-safety.

- Suppose a transaction T modifies x, a program variable not in the database. If T aborts because of a concurrency control conflict and then executes properly to completion, variable x will be in a consistent state. (That is, we want the transaction code to be "reentrant.")

- If a failure occurs, it is possible to determine which transactions completed before the failure and which ones did not (as for mini-batch transactions).

Suppose there are n transactions $T_1, T_2, \ldots, T_n$ that can execute within some interval. Let us assume, for now, that each such transaction results from a distinct program. Chopping a transaction will then consist of modifying the unique program that the transaction executes. Because of the form of the chopping algorithm, assuming this is possible will have no effect on the result.

A *chopping* partitions each T_i into *pieces* $c_{i_1}, c_{i_2}, \ldots c_{i_k}$. Every database access performed by T_i is in exactly one piece.

A chopping of a transaction T is said to be *rollback-safe* if either T has no rollback statements or all the rollback statements of T are in its first piece. The first piece must have the property that all its statements execute before any other statements of T. (As we will see, this will prevent a transaction from half-committing and then rolling back.)

A chopping is said to be *rollback-safe* if each of its transactions is rollback-safe.

Each piece will act like a transaction in the sense that each piece will acquire locks according to the two-phase locking algorithm and will release them when it ends. It will also commit its changes when it ends. Two cases are of particular interest:

- The transaction T is sequential and the pieces are nonoverlapping subsequences of that transaction.

  For example, suppose T updates an account balance and then updates a branch balance. Each update might become a separate piece, acting as a separate transaction.

- The transaction T operates at degree 2 consistency in which read locks are released as soon as reads complete.

  In this case, each read by itself constitutes a piece.[1] All writes together

---

[1] Technically, this needs some qualification. Each read that doesn't follow a write on the same

form a piece (because the locks for the writes are only released whe_
completes).

Execution rules:

1. When pieces execute, they obey the order given by the transaction. For example, if the transaction updates account X first and branch balance B second, then the piece that updates account X should *complete* before the piece that updates branch balance B *begins*. By contrast, if the transaction performs the two steps in parallel, then the pieces can execute in parallel.

2. If a piece is aborted because of a lock conflict, then it will be resubmitted repeatedly until it commits.

3. If a piece is aborted because of a rollback, then no other pieces for that transaction will execute.

A2.2 CORRECT CHOPPINGS

We will characterize the correctness of a chopping with the aid of an undirected graph having two kinds of edges.

1. *C edges*: C stands for *conflict*. Two pieces p and p' from different original transactions conflict if there is some data item x that both access and at least one modifies.[2] In this case, draw an edge between p and p' and label the edge C.

2. *S edges*: S stands for *sibling*. Two pieces p and p' are siblings if they come from the same transaction T. In this case, draw an edge between p and p' and label the edge S.

We call the resulting graph the *chopping graph*. (Note that no edge can have both an S and a C label.)

We say that a chopping graph has an *SC-cycle* if it contains a simple cycle that includes at least one S edge and at least one C edge.[3]

---

data item constitutes a piece. The reason for the restriction is that if a write(x) precedes a read(x), then the transaction will continue to hold the lock on x after the read completes.

[2] As has been observed repeatedly in the literature, this notion of conflict is too strong. For example, if the only data item in common between two transactions is one that is only incremented and whose exact value is insignificant, then such a conflict might be ignored. We assume the simpler read-write model only for the purposes of exposition.

[3] Recall that a simple cycle consists of

1. a sequence of nodes $n_1, n_2, \ldots, n_k$ such that no node is repeated and

chopping of $T_1, T_2, \ldots, T_n$ is *correct* if any execution of the
the execution rules is equivalent to some serial execution of
ons.

in the sense of the textbook.[4] That is, every read (respec-
·ery transaction returns (respectively, writes) the same value
and the same transactions roll back. Now, we can prove the

Theorem 1.   A chopping is correct if it is rollback-safe and its chopping
graph contains no SC-cycle.

Proof. The proof requires the properties of a serialization graph. Formally,
a serialization graph is a directed graph whose nodes are transactions and whose
directed edges represent ordered conflicts. That is, $T \rightarrow T'$ if T and T' both access some data item x, one of them modifies x and T accessed x first. Following
the Bernstein, Hadzilacos, and Goodman textbook, if the serialization graph resulting from an execution is acyclic, then the execution is equivalent to a serial
one. The book also shows that if all transactions use two-phase locking, then all
those who commit produce an acyclic serialization graph.

Call any execution of a chopping for which the chopping graph contains no
SC-cycles a *chopped execution*. We must show that

1. Any chopped execution yields an acyclic serialization graph on the given
transactions $T_1, T_2, \ldots, T_n$ and hence is equivalent to a serial execution of
those transactions.

2. The transactions that roll back in the chopped execution would also roll
back if properly placed in the equivalent serial execution.

For point 1, we proceed by contradiction. Suppose there were a cycle in
$T_1, T_2, \ldots, T_n$. That is $T \rightarrow T' \rightarrow \ldots \rightarrow T$. Identify the pieces associated
with each transaction that are involved in this cycle: $p \rightarrow p' \rightarrow \ldots \rightarrow p''$.
Both p and p'' belong to transaction T. Pieces p and p'' cannot be the same,
because each piece uses two-phase locking and the serialization graph on *pieces*
is acyclic by the result cited from the textbook. (A piece may abort because of
a concurrency control conflict, but then it will reexecute again and again until it
commits.) Because p and p'' are different pieces in the same transaction T, there

2. a collection of associated edges: there is an edge between n_i and n_{i+1} for $1 <= i < k$ and
an edge between n_k and n_1; no edge is included twice.

[4] P. A. Bernstein, V. Hadzilacos, and N. Goodman, *Concurrency Control and Recovery in
Database Systems*. Reading, Mass.: Addison-Wesley, 1987.

is an S edge between them in the chopping graph. Every directed edge in the serialization graph cycle corresponds to a C edge in the chopping graph because it reflects a conflict. So, the cycle in the serialization graph implies the existence of an SC-cycle in the chopping graph. By assumption, no such cycle exists.

For point 2, notice that any transaction T whose first piece p rolls back in the chopped execution will have no effect on the database, since the chopping is rollback-safe. We want to show that T would also roll back if properly placed in the equivalent serial execution. Suppose that p conflicts with and follows pieces from the set of transactions $W_1, \ldots W_k$. Then place T immediately after the last of those transactions in the equivalent serial execution. In that case, the first reads of T will be exactly those of the first reads of p. Because p rolls back, so will T.   ■

Theorem 1 shows that the goal of any chopping of a set of transactions should be to obtain a rollback-safe chopping without an SC-cycle.

Chopping graph example 1

Suppose there are three transactions that can abstractly be characterized as follows:

```
T1: R(x) W(x) R(y) W(y)
```

```
T2: R(x) W(x)
```

```
T3: R(y) W(y)
```

Breaking up T1 into

```
T11: R(x) W(x)
```

```
T12: R(y) W(y)
```

will result in a graph without an SC-cycle (Figure A2.1). This verifies the rule of thumb from chapter 2, section 2.2.2, p. 19.

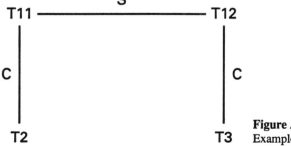

Figure A2.1 Chopping Graph Example 1: No SC-Cycle.

Chopping graph example 2

With the same T2 and T3 as in the first example, breaking up T11 further into

T111: R(x)

T112: W(x)

will result in an SC-cycle (Figure A2.2) so it may cause a bad execution.

Chopping graph example 3

By contrast, if the three transactions were

T1: R(x) W(x) R(y) W(y)

T2: R(x)

T3: R(y) W(y)

Then T1 could be broken up into

T111: R(x)

T112: W(x)

T12: R(y) W(y)

There is no SC-cycle (Figure A2.3). There is an S-cycle, but that doesn't matter.

Chopping graph example 4

Now, let us take the example from chapter 2, p. 18 in which there are three types of transactions.

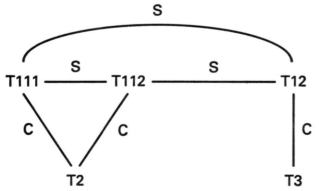

Figure A2.2 Chopping Graph Example 2: SC-Cycle.

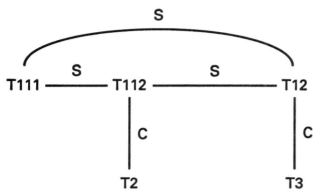

Figure A2.3   Chopping Graph
Example 3: No SC-Cycle.

- A transaction that updates a single depositor's account and the depositor's corresponding branch balance.
- A transaction that reads a depositor's account balance.
- A transaction that compares the sum of the depositors' account balances with the sum of the branch balances.

For the sake of concreteness, suppose that depositor accounts D11, D12, and D13 all belong to branch B1; depositor accounts D21 and D22 both belong to B2. Here are the transactions.

```
T1 (update depositor): RW(D11) RW(B1)
```

```
T2 (update depositor): RW(D13) RW(B1)
```

```
T3 (update depositor): RW(D21) RW(B2)
```

```
T4 (read depositor): R(D12)
```

```
T5 (read depositor): R(D21)
```

```
T6 (compare balances): R(D11) R(D12) R(D13) R(B1) R(D21) R(D22) R(B2)
```

Thus, T6 is the balance comparison transaction. Let us see first whether T6 can be broken up into two transactions.

```
T61: R(D11) R(D12) R(D13) R(B1)
```

```
T62: R(D21) R(D22) R(B2)
```

The lack of an SC-cycle shows that this is possible (Figure A2.4).

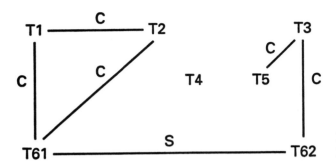

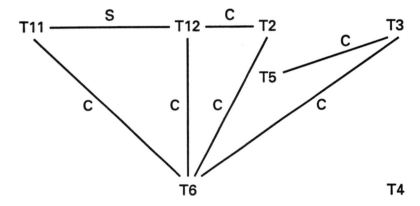

Figure A2.4   Chopping Graph Example 4: No SC-Cycle.

Figure A2.5   Chopping Graph Example 5: SC-Cycle.

Chopping graph example 5

Taking the transaction population from the previous example, let us now consider dividing T1 into two transactions giving the following transaction population (Figure A2.5).

T11: RW(D11)

T12: RW(B1)

T2: RW(D13) RW(B1)

T3: RW(D21) RW(B2)

T4: R(D12)

T5: R(D21)

T6: R(D11) R(D12) R(D13) R(B1) R(D21) R(D22) R(B2)

This results in an SC-cycle.

A2.3 FINDING THE FINEST CHOPPING

Now, one might wonder whether there is an algorithm to obtain a correct chopping. Two questions are especially worrisome.

1. Can chopping a piece into smaller pieces break an SC-cycle?

2. Can chopping one transaction prevent one from chopping another?

Remarkably, the answer to both questions is, "No."

Lemma 1. If a chopping is *not* correct, then any further chopping of any of the transactions will not render it correct.

Proof. Let the transaction to be chopped be called T and let the result of the chopping be called pieces(T). If T is not in an SC-cycle, then chopping T will have no effect on the cycle. If T is in an SC-cycle, then there are three cases.

1. If there are two C edges touching T from the cycle, then those edges will touch one or more pieces in pieces(T). (The reason is that the pieces partition the database accesses of T so the conflicts reflected by the C edges will still be present.) Those pieces (if there are more than one) will be connected by S edges after T is chopped, so the cycle will not be broken.

2. If there is one C edge touching T and one S edge leaving T (because T is already the result of a chopping), then the C edge will be connected to one piece p of pieces(T). If the S edge from T is connected to a transaction T', then p will also be connected by an S edge to T' because p and T' come from the same original transaction. So, the cycle will not be broken.

3. If there are two S edges touching T, then both of those S edges will be inherited by each piece in pieces(T), so again the cycle will not be broken.

Lemma 2. If two pieces of transaction T are in an SC-cycle as the result of some chopping, then they will be in a cycle even if no other transactions are chopped (Figure A2.6).

Proof. Since two pieces, say p and p', of T are in a cycle, there is an S edge between them and a C edge leading from each of them to pieces of other transactions. If only one piece of some other transaction T' is in the cycle, then combining all the pieces of T' will not effect the length of the cycle. If several pieces of T' are in the cycle, then combining them will simply shorten the cycle. ∎

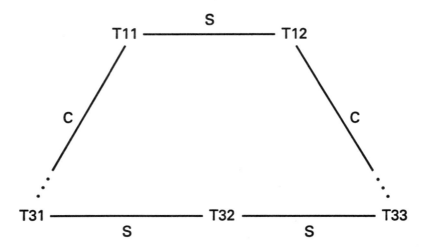

Figure A2.6   Putting Three Pieces of T_3 into One Will Not Make Chopping of T_1 OK, Nor Will Chopping T_3 Further.

These two lemmas lead directly to a systematic method for chopping transactions as finely as possible. Consider again the set of transactions that can run in this interval $\{T_1, T_2, \ldots, T_n\}$. We will take each transaction T_i in turn. We call $\{c_1, c_2, \ldots, c_k\}$ a *private chopping* of T_i, denoted private(T_i), if both of the following hold:

1. $\{c_1, c_2, \ldots, c_k\}$ is a rollback-safe chopping of T_i.
2. There is no SC-cycle in the graph whose nodes are $\{T_1, \ldots, T_{i-1}, c_1, c_2, \ldots, c_k, T_{i+1}, \ldots, T_n\}$. (If $i = 1$, then the set is $\{c_1, c_2, \ldots, c_k, T_2, \ldots, T_n\}$. If $i = n$, then the set is $\{T_1, \ldots, T_{n-1}, c_1, c_2, \ldots, c_k, \}$.) That is, the graph of all other transactions plus the chopping of T_i.

Theorem 2.   The chopping consisting of $\{private(T_1), private(T_2) \ldots, private(T_n)\}$ is rollback-safe and has no SC-cycles.

Proof

- *Rollback-safe*: the chopping is rollback-safe because all its constituents are rollback-safe.
- *No SC-cycles*: if there were an SC-cycle that involved two pieces of private(T_i,) then lemma 2 would imply that the cycle would still be present even if all other transactions were not chopped. But that contradicts the definition of private(T_i). ∎

A2.4 OPTIMAL CHOPPING ALGORITHM

Theorem 2 implies that if we can discover a fine-granularity private(T_i) for each T_i, then we can just take their union. Formally, the *finest chopping* of T_i, denoted FineChop(T_i), (whose existence we will prove) has two properties:

- FineChop(T_i) is a private chopping of T_i.
- If piece p is a member of FineChop(T_i), then there is no other private chopping of T_i containing p_1 and p_2 such that p_1 and p_2 partition p and neither is empty.

That is, we would have the following algorithm:

```
procedure chop(T_1 , ... , T_n)

  for each T_i
    Fine_i := finest chopping of T_i
  end for;
  the finest chopping is
      Fine_1 , Fine_2 , ... , Fine_n
```

We now give an algorithm to find the finest private chopping of T.

```
Algorithm FineChop:

initialization:

if there are rollback statements then
  p_1 := all database writes
      of T that may occur
      before or concurrently with any rollback
      statement in T
else
  p_1  := set consisting of
      the first database access;
end
P := x | x is a database access not in p_1;
P := P union {p_1};

merging pieces:

construct the connected components
of the graph induced by C edges alone
on all transactions besides T
and on the pieces in P
```

```
update P based on the following rule:

if p_j and p_k are in the same connected
component and j < k, then
  add the accesses from p_k to p_j;
  delete p_k from P
end if
```

```
call the resulting partition FineChop(T)
```

Figure A2.7 shows an example of a fine chopping of transaction T5 given a certain set of conflicts. Because there are no rollback statements, each piece starts off being a single access.

Note on Efficiency. The expensive part of the algorithm is finding the connected components of the graph induced by C on all transactions besides T and the pieces in P. We have assumed a naive implementation in which this is recomputed for each transaction T at a cost of $O(e + m)$ time in the worst case, where e is the number of C edges in the transaction graph and m is the size of P. Because there are n transactions, the total time is $O(n(e + m))$. Note

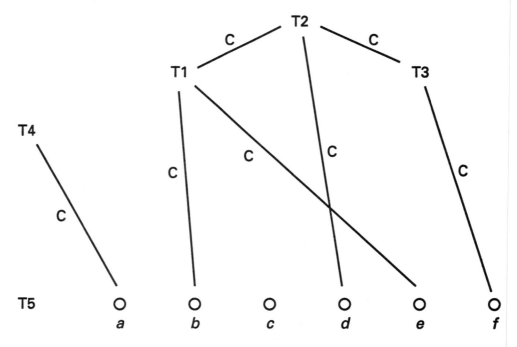

Figure A2.7   Assuming No Rollback Statements, T_5 Can Be Fine Chopped into $\{\{a\}, \{b,d,e,f\}, \{c\}\}$; If $\{b,d,e,f\}$ were Subdivided Further, There Would Be an SC-Cycle in Chopping Graph.

that the only transactions relevant to FineChop(T) are those that are in the same connected component as T in the C graph. An improvement in the running time is possible if we avoid the total recomputation of the common parts of the connected components graph for the different transactions.

Note on Shared Code.   Suppose that T_i and T_j result from the same program P. Since the chopping is implemented by changing P, T_i and T_j must be chopped in the same way. This may seem surprising at first, but in fact the preceding algorithm will give the result that FineChop(T_i) = FineChop(T_j). The reason is that the two transactions are treated symmetrically by the algorithm. When FineChop(T_i) runs, T_j is treated as unchopped and similarly for T_j. Thus, shared code does not change this result at all.

Theorem 3.   FineChop(T) is the finest chopping of T.

Proof. We must prove two things: FineChop(T) is a private chopping of T and it is the finest one.

- FineChop(T) is a private chopping of T:

    (a) *Rollback-safety*: By inspection of the algorithm. The initialization step creates a rollback-safe partition. The merging step can only cause p_1 to become larger.
    (b) *No SC-cycles*: Any such cycle would involve a path through the conflict graph between two distinct pieces from FineChop(T). The merging step would have merged any two such pieces to a single one.

- No piece of FineChop(T) can be further chopped:

    Suppose p is a piece in FineChop(T). Suppose there were a private chopping *TooFine* of T that partitions p into two nonempty subsets q and r. Because p contains at least two accesses, the accesses of q and r could come from two different sources.

    (a) Piece p is the first piece, i.e., p_1, and q and r each contain accesses of p_1 as constructed in the initialization step. In that case, p_1 contains one or more rollback statements. So, one of q or r may commit before the other rolls back by construction of p_1. This would violate rollback safety.
    (b) The accesses in q and r result from the merging step. In that case, there is a path consisting of C edges through the other transactions from q to r. This implies the existence of an SC-cycle for chopping *TooFine*.

A2.5 APPLICATION TO TYPICAL DATABASE SYSTEMS

For us, a typical database system will be one running SQL. Our main problem is to figure out what conflicts with what. Because of the existence of bind variables, it will be unclear whether a transaction that updates the account of customer :x will access the same record as a transaction that reads the account of customer :y. So, we will have to be conservative. Still, we can achieve substantial gains.

We can use the tricks of typical predicate locking schemes, however.[5] For example, if two statements on relation Account are both conjunctive (only AND's in the qualification) and one has the predicate

```
AND name LIKE 'T%'
```

whereas the other has the predicate

```
AND name LIKE 'S%'
```

they clearly will not conflict at the logical data item level. (This is the only level that matters because that is the only level that affects the return value to the user.) Detecting the absence of conflicts between two qualifications is the province of compiler writers. We offer nothing new.

The only new idea we have to offer is that we can make use of information in addition to simple conflict information. For example, if there is an update on the Account table with a conjunctive qualification and one of the predicates is

```
AND acctnum = :x
```

then, if acctnum is a key, we know that the update will access at most one record. This will mean that a concurrent reader of the form

```
SELECT ...
FROM Account
WHERE ...
```

will conflict with the update on at most one record, a single data item. We will therefore decorate this conflict edge with the label "1." If the update had not had an equality predicate on a key, then we would decorate this conflict edge with the label "many."

How does this decoration help? Well, suppose that the read and the update are the only two transactions in the system. Then if the label on the conflict is "1," the read can run at degree 2 isolation. This corresponds to breaking up the reader into n pieces where n is the number of data items the reader accesses. A cycle in the SC-graph would imply that two pieces of the resulting chopping conflict with the update. This is impossible, however, since the reader and update conflict on only one piece altogether.

In fact, even if many updates of this form are concurrent with the reader, the reader can be chopped in this way. To see that, we need to decorate the graph a bit more.

[5] K. C. Wong and M. Edelberg, "Interval Hierarchies and Their Application to Predicate Files," *ACM Transactions on Database Systems*, vol. 2, no. 3, pp. 223-232, September 1977.

We will label each transaction with the label with values "1" or "many" for each relation that it accesses. For example, the update above has the label "1, Account," whereas the read access has the label "many, Account." We will label the conflict edges similarly. So, the conflict edge will have the label "1, Account." Of course, there can be many labels on each conflict edge.

Now, we say that a transaction t that may contain binding variables is *bind-chop-safe* if one of the following two conditions holds (Figure A2.8):

1. Transaction t conflicts with a single other transaction and their conflict edge has a single label decorated with a 1.

2. Transaction t may conflict with many other transactions. However, for any cycle c (consisting of conflict edges only) that touches t, there must be a relation R such that both of the following hold:

- Every edge e in c has label $(1, R)$ as its only label.
- Every transaction t' other than t in c associates 1 with R (i.e., has label $(1, R)$), though t' may have other labels; t may have (many, R) as part of its label.

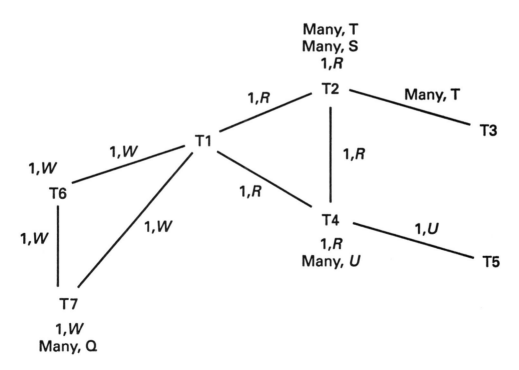

Figure A2.8   Transactions with Their Decorated Conflict Edges. In This Case, T_1 Can Be Executed at Degree 2, Yet Will Appear to Execute at Degree 3.

Theorem 4. If transaction t is bind-chop-safe, then t can be chopped into a set of pieces such that

- each piece holds at least one database access;
- the first piece holds all rollback statements; and
- no two pieces access the same data item.

(In particular, if t is a read-only query, then it can run at degree 2 isolation.)

Proof. Suppose there were a cycle in the SC-graph as a result of chopping t and some values of the bind variables. Such a cycle must connect two pieces p_i and p_j of the chopping by a path of conflicts through other transactions. Any such path must correspond to a cycle c consisting of edges labeled $(1, R)$ and nodes labeled $(1, R)$ for some relation R. That implies that the conflict carried by this path is on a single data item x. However p_i and p_j access different data items by construction. This contradiction implies that no such cycle is possible. ∎

A2.6 OTHER WORK ON THIS TOPIC

There is a rich body of work in the literature on the subject of chopping up transactions or reducing concurrency control constraints, some of which we review here. Such work nearly always proposes a new concurrency control algorithm and often proposes a weakening of isolation guarantees. (There is other work that proposes special-purpose concurrency control algorithms on data structures.)

The algorithm presented here avoids both proposals because it is aimed at database users rather than database implementors. Database users normally cannot change the concurrency control algorithms of the underlying system, but must make do with two-phase locking and its variants. Even if users could change the concurrency control algorithms, they probably should avoid doing so as the bugs that might result could easily corrupt a system.

The literature offers many good ideas, however. Here is a brief summary of some of the major contributions.

Farrag and Ozsu[6] of the University of Alberta consider the possibility of chopping up transactions by using "semantic" knowledge and a new locking mechanism. For example, consider a hotel reservations system that supports a single transaction Reserve. Reserve performs the following two steps:

1. Decrement the number of available rooms or roll back if that number is already 0.

2. Find a free room and allocate it to a guest.

---

[6] Abdel Aziz Farrag and M. Tamer Ozsu, "Using Semantic Knowledge of Transactions to Increase Concurrency," *ACM Transactions on Database Systems*, vol. 14, no. 4, pp. 503-525, December 1989.

If reservation transactions are the only ones running, then the authors assert that each reservation can be broken up into two transactions, one for each step. Our mechanism might or might not come to the same conclusion, depending on the way the transactions are written. To see this, suppose that the variable A represents the number of available rooms and r and r' represent distinct rooms. Suppose we can represent two reservation transactions by:

```
T1: RW(A) RW(r)
T2: RW(A) RW(r')
```

Then the chopping graph resulting from the transactions:

```
T11: RW(A)
T12: RW(r)
T21: RW(A)
T22: RW(r')
```

will have no cycles. By contrast, if $T2$ must read room r first, then the two steps cannot be made into transactions. That is, dividing

```
T1: RW(A) RW(r)
T2: RW(A) R(r) RW(r')
```

into

```
T11: RW(A)
T12: RW(r)
T21: RW(A)
T22: R(r) RW(r')
```

will create an SC-cycle as the accompanying figure shows. However, the semantics of hotel reservation tell us that it does not matter if one transaction decrements A first but gets room r' (Figure A2.9). The difficulty is applying this semantics. The authors note in conclusion that finding semantically acceptable interleavings is difficult.

Hector Garcia-Molina[7] suggested using semantics by partitioning transac-

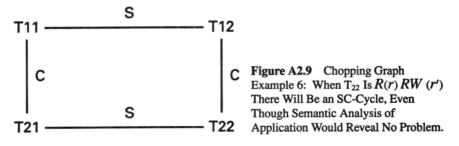

Figure A2.9 Chopping Graph Example 6: When T_{22} Is $R(r)\,RW\,(r')$ There Will Be an SC-Cycle, Even Though Semantic Analysis of Application Would Reveal No Problem.

[7] H. Garcia-Molina, "Using Semantic Knowledge for Transaction Processing in a Distributed Database," *ACM Transactions on Database Systems*, vol. 8, no. 2, pp. 186-213, June 1983.

tions into classes. Transactions in the same class can run concurrently, whereas transactions in different classes must synchronize. He proposes using semantic notions of consistency to allow more concurrency than serializability would allow and using counterstep transactions to undo the effect of transactions that should not have committed.

Nancy Lynch[8] generalized Garcia-Molina's model by making the unit of recovery different from the unit of locking (this is also possible with the check-out/check-in model offered by some object-oriented database systems). She groups transactions into nested classes with specified possible interleavings between them. Then she proposes a new scheduling mechanism that ensures that a specific order among conflict steps is maintained.

Rudolf Bayer[9] of the Technische Universitat of Munich showed how to change the concurrency control and recovery subsystems to allow a single batch transaction to run concurrently with many short transactions.

Meichun Hsu and Arvola Chan[10] have examined special concurrency control algorithms for situations in which data is divided into raw data and derived data. The idea is that the consistency of the raw data is not so important in many applications, so updates to that data should be able to proceed without being blocked by reads of that data. For example, suppose there are three transactions with the following read-write patterns:

```
T1: W(x)
T2: R(x) W(y)
T3: R(x) R(y) W(z)
```

Consider chopping each of these transactions into single accesses. There is an SC-cycle in such a chopping: R3(x) W1(x) R2(x) W2(y) R3(y). If reads only accessed current values, this would correspond to a cycle in the serialization graph. Their algorithm by contrast would allow the R3(y) to see the old state of y.

Some commercial systems such as ORACLE use this scheme as well of allowing reads to view old data. That facility would remove the necessity to use the algorithms in this paper for read-only transactions.

Patrick O'Neil[11] takes advantage of the commutativity of increments to release locks early even in the case of writes.

---

[8] N. Lynch, "Multi-level Atomicity—A New Correctness Criterion for Database Concurrency Control," *ACM Transactions on Database Systems*, vol. 8, no. 4, pp. 484-502, December 1983.

[9] R. Bayer, "Consistency of Transactions and Random Batch," *ACM Transactions on Database Systems*, vol. 11, no. 4, pp. 397-404, December 1986.

[10] M. Hsu and A. Chan, "Partitioned Two-Phase Locking," *ACM Transactions on Database Systems*, vol. 11, no. 4, pp. 431-446, December 1986.

[11] P. O'Neil, "The Escrow Transactional Mechanism," *ACM Transactions on Database Systems*, vol. 11, no. 4, pp. 405-430, December 1986.

Ouri Wolfson[12] presents an algorithm for releasing certain locks early without violating serializability based on an earlier theoretical condition given by Yannakakis.[13] He assumes that the user has complete control over the acquisition and release of locks. The setting here is a special case: the user can control only how to chop up a transaction or whether to allow reads to give up their locks immediately. As mentioned earlier, we have restricted the user's control in this way for the simple pragmatic reason that systems restrict the user's control in the same way. The restriction gives us a much more efficient algorithm (His is $O(n^2 \times m^2)$ whereas ours is $O(n \times (e + m))$, where n is the number of transactions in the given set, and e is the number of edges in the conflict graph of that set. Distributed transactions make no difference to our algorithm, but seem to take a factor of n^2 more time for his.) Also, our algorithm is provably optimal for the restricted class of choppings that we allow. His algorithm is correct, but not guaranteed to be optimal for complexity reasons.

Bernstein, Shipman and Rothnie[14] introduced the idea of conflict graphs in an experimental system called SDD-1 in the late 1970s. Their system divided transactions into classes such that transactions within a class executed serially whereas transactions between classes could execute without any synchronization. Their assumed concurrency control algorithm was based on locks and timestamps.

Marco Casanova's thesis[15] extended the SDD-1 work by representing each transaction by its flowchart and by generalizing the notion of conflict. A cycle in his graphs indicated the need for synchronization if it included both conflict and flow edges.

Shasha and Snir[16] explored graphs that combine conflict, program flow, and atomicity constraints in a study of the correct execution of parallel shared memory programs that have critical sections. The graphs used here are a special case of the ones used in that article.

[12] O. Wolfson, "The Virtues of Locking by Symbolic Names," *Journal of Algorithms*, vol. 8, pp. 536-556, 1987.

[13] M. Yannakakis, "A Theory of Safe Locking Policies in Database Systems," *Journal of the ACM*, vol. 29, no. 3, pp. 718-740, 1982.

[14] P. A. Bernstein, D. W. Shipman and J. B. Rothnie, "Concurrency Control in a System for Distributed Databases (SDD-1)," *ACM Transactions on Database Systems*, vol. 5, no. 1, pp. 18-51, March 1980.

[15] Marco Casanova, *The Concurrency Control Problem for Database Systems,* Springer-Verlag Lecture Notes in Computer Science, no. 116, 1981.

[16] D. Shasha and M. Snir, "Efficient and Correct Execution of Parallel Programs that Share Memory," *ACM Transactions on Programming Languages and Systems*, vol. 10, no. 2, pp. 282-312, April 1988.

Glossary

$\rightarrow$ See functionally determines (chapter 4).

2-3 tree B-tree whose maximum branching factor is 3 and minimum branching factor is 2. Should be used for small data structures that will remain in random access memory (chapter 3).

4GL See fourth generation language (chapter 4).

Abort See rollback (chapter 2).

After image The after image of a data item x with respect to transaction T is the value of x that T last writes (chapter 2).

Aggregate maintenance Maintenance of one or more redundant relations that embody an aggregate. For example, if the average of all salaries is frequently requested, then it may be worthwhile to maintain a relation containing that average and then to update it whenever a salary changes (chapter 4).

Atomicity guarantees Ignoring all of twentieth century physics, database theorists use atomicity to denote the indivisibility of transactions. That is, a transaction should appear to execute in isolation (without interleaving with other transactions) and in an all-or-nothing manner (either all its effects are registered with the database or none are) (chapter 2).

Attribute Name of the head of a column in a table (chapter 4).

B-tree The most used data structure in database systems. A B-tree is a balanced tree structure that permits fast access for a wide variety of queries. In virtually all database systems, the actual structure is a B+-tree in which all key-pointer pairs are at the leaves (chapter 3).

Batch transaction Transaction that performs many (possibly millions of) updates, normally without stringent response time constraints (chapters 2 and 6).

Before image The before image of a data item x with respect to transaction T is the value of x when T first reads it (chapter 2).

Bind variable Variable defined in some embedding programming language (usually, COBOL, PL/1, RPG, C . . .) that is used for communication with the database system. For example, if x is a bind variable, then a typical database query might include the expression R.A = :x, where x has been previously assigned a value in the embedding programming language (chapter 3).

Bottleneck System resource or query that limits the performance of an entire database application; breaking a bottleneck usually entails speeding up one or more queries or using partitioning (chapter 1).

Branching factor The average number of children of each nonleaf node in a B-tree or ISAM structure. The larger the branching factor, the fewer the levels. Compression is a technique for increasing the branching factor (chapter 3).

Buffer See database buffer (chapter 2).

Buffered commit strategy Logging and recovery algorithm in which a transaction's updates are not forced to the database disks immediately after commit but rather written when the write would cause no seek. This is almost always a good strategy to choose (chapter 2).

Catalog Place where data type and statistical information is held in a database management system. For example, the catalog may hold information about the number of records in a relation, the indexes on its attributes, and the data type of each attribute. It is important not to modify the catalog too often during busy periods. Otherwise, the catalog becomes a lock contention bottleneck (chapters 2 and 7).

Checkpoint Activity of backing up the log onto the database disks. This reduces the time to recover from a failure of main memory, but costs something in online performance (chapters 2 and 7).

Chopping See transaction chopping.

Class A data description and set of operations that characterizes some collection of objects. For example, an image class may define a data description consisting of a bit map and a set of operations including zooming, rotation, and so on (chapter 5).

Cluster key Attribute(s) that determine a table clustering. For example, Customer and Sale may be clustered based on the customer identifier in which case the Customer record with that identifier will be colocated with all Sales records having that identifier (chapter 4).

Clustering May refer to clustering index, to table clustering, or clustering attribute (chapters 3, 4, and 5, respectively).

Clustering attribute Object-oriented database attribute whose value is located close to the object header (chapter 5).

Clustering index Data structure plus an implied table organization. For example, if there is a clustering index based on a B-tree on last name, then all records with the same last name will be packed onto as few pages as possible (chapter 3).

CLV format Formatting method for optical disks whereby the outer tracks hold more data than the inner tracks. This implies that the most frequently accessed data should be slightly to the outside of the middle track to minimize seek time. By contrast, the most frequently accessed data on a magnetic disk should be in the middle (chapter 2).

Colocate Putting several objects or records close to one another on disk. For example, a clustering index based on a B-tree would tend to colocate records having lexicographically close keys, e.g., the records containing Smith and the records containing Smithe. By contrast, a hash-based clustering index will colocate the Smith records but not necessarily the Smiths with the Smithes (chapter 3).

Commit Every database transaction completes either by committing or aborting. When a transaction commits, the database management system guarantees that the updates of that transaction will be reflected in the database state even if there are failures (provided they are failures that the database system can tolerate) (chapter 2).

Complex update Series of updates that entail graph traversal. Such updates favor object-oriented systems with direct support for pointers over relational systems for two reasons. First, dereferencing is expensive in relational systems. Second, each update will tend to require a distinct client-server interaction, because the precise items to be updated depend on the data so cannot be anticipated in a single set retrieval. Such interactions tend to be cheaper in object-oriented database systems as currently implemented (chapter 5).

Composite index Index whose key is a sequence of attributes, e.g., last name, first name, city (chapter 3).

Compression See key compression (chapter 3).

Concatenated index See composite index (chapter 3).

Concurrency control Activity of synchronizing the database accesses of concurrent transactions to ensure some degree of isolation. Weaker degrees of isolation can result in higher performance but may corrupt the data (chapter 2).

Concurrent Activities (in this book, transactions) A and B are concurrent if there is some point in time t where both have begun and neither has completed (chapter 2).

Cursor stability Assurance given by a database management system's concurrency control algorithm that while a transaction holds a cursor, it holds its locks on the data associated with that cursor (chapter 2).

Cylinder Cylinder i is the set of all track i's for a given disk spindle. Because all the disk heads will be on the same track of all platters, reading track i on one platter after reading track i on another requires no head movement (i.e., no seek). Therefore, it is good to keep frequently scanned data on the same cylinder. This argues for large extents (chapter 2).

Database buffer Repository of databases pages in virtual memory (though, for performance reasons, most should be held in random access memory). Ideally, most database reads will be to pages held in the buffer, thus eliminating the need for a disk access. Database writes can be stored in the buffer and then written asynchronously to the database disks, thus saving seeks, in a strategy known as buffered commit (chapter 2).

Database cache See database buffer (chapter 2).

Database disks Stable storage is divided into two parts: the database disks and the log. The log contains the updates of committed transactions and the database disk contains the initial database state (or value of last database dump) modified by some of those committed transactions (chapter 2).

Database dump State of the database at some point of time. The current state of the database is equal to the value of the last database dump plus all the transactions committed since then (chapter 2).

Database state At any time, the database state is the result of applying all committed transactions (in the order of commitment) to the last database dump. The database state can be physically reconstructed from the database disks and the log or, in some cases, from the database dump and the log (chapter 2).

DBMS page replacements Activity of replacing pages in the database buffer by other pages when no free pages are available. A non-zero value of this parameter indicates either that the buffer is too small or that there are too few asynchronous write daemons (chapter 2).

Data item Unit of locking when discussing concurrency control and a unit of logging when discussing the recovery subsystem. Common data items are records, pages, and tables in relational systems; objects, pages, and class extents in object-oriented systems (chapter 2).

Data mining Application that issues complicated queries on the database to find obscure but perhaps profitable correlations. For example, one might find that people who buy suitcases frequently buy walking shoes soon afterwards (chapter 4).

Data page Page of a file containing records; by contrast, a data structure index page contains keys and pointers (chapters 3 and 4).

DDL Data definition language. The language used to manipulate catalog data. It is usually a bad idea to execute DDL updates during online transaction processing, because the catalog may then become a locking hot spot (chapters 2 and 7).

Deadlock Property of a set of transactions in which each transaction waits for another in the set, so none can proceed. Two-phase locking allows deadlock, unless users design transactions specifically to avoid it (chapter 2).

Denormalization Activity of changing a schema to make certain relations unnormalized for the purpose of improving performance (usually by reducing the number of joins). Should not be used for relations that change often or in cases where disk space is scarce (chapter 4).

Dense index Index in which the underlying data structure has a pointer to each record among the data pages. Clustering indexes can be dense in some systems (e.g., ORACLE). Nonclustering indexes are always dense (chapter 3).

Dereference Refers to the operation of obtaining the object or record pointed to by a pointer. For example, if object X points to object Y, then dereferencing the pointer in X yields Y. When references are logical (e.g., record identifiers), the dereferencing operation may take 1000 instructions even in the absence of disk accesses (chapter 5).

Determines See functionally determines (chapter 4).

Dirty data Data item x is dirty at time t if it has been modified by some transaction that has not yet committed (chapter 2).

Disk (movable head) Device consisting of one or more spindles, each of which consists of a set of platters stacked one on top of the other with a head positioned at the same track of each platter (except the top and bottom platters). Only one head can read or write at a time (chapter 2).

Disk head Device for reading or writing data on a disk. It is held by an arm that moves the head from one track to another along a single platter (chapter 2).

Durable media Media such as disks, tapes, etc. that will not lose data in the event of a power failure. Random access memory can be made durable if it has battery backup (but then the length of this durability is limited by the energy storage capacity of the battery) (chapter 2).

Encapsulation Facility of a language whereby the internal data of an object can be accessed only through its methods (i.e., its operations). In this way, the internal data structures of the object can be changed without functionally affecting users of that object (chapter 5).

Entity Notion from the Entity-Relationship model. Entities denote the objects of interest, e.g., employee, hospital, doctor. An entity has attributes that it must functionally determine. An attribute must not have attributes of its own (otherwise it should be promoted to entity status) (chapter 4).

Equality join query Join in which the join predicate is equality. For example, R.A = S.B is an equality join, whereas R.A > S.B is not (chapter 3).

Equality selection Clause of the form R.A = 5, that is, a relation-attribute pair compared by equality to a constant, constant expression or to a bind variable (chapter 3).

Equivalent executions Two executions E and F of transactions are equivalent if they consist of the same transactions, the same database accesses, every database read returns the same value in E and F, and the final writes on each data item are the same (chapter 2).

Escalation See lock escalation.

Exclusive lock See write lock (chapter 2).

Execution site independence Ability to move computation between server site and client site without changing the input/output behavior of a computation. This is useful for low contention/high computation activities and is provided in many commercial object-oriented database systems (chapter 5).

Extent Contiguous area on disk used as a unit of file allocation (chapter 2).

Extremal query Query that obtains the records or parts of records with the minimum or maximum of a set of values. For example, the following query finds the maximum salary in the employee relation. SELECT MAX(salary) FROM employee (chapter 3).

Fail-stop failure Failure in which a processor stops. The failure may destroy the processor's random access memory but not its disk storage. Such failures characterize hardware failures of machines that have redundant error-detecting circuitry, perhaps in the form of an extra processor. Software failures may not be fail-stop (chapter 2).

Fanout See branching factor (chapter 3).

Field See attribute.

Finer-grained locking A-level locking is said to be finer grained than B-level locking if A is a smaller unit of storage than B. For example, if records are smaller than pages, then record-level locking is finer-grained than page-level locking (chapter 2).

Foreign key Relationship between two tables in a relational system. The best way to define it is by example. Suppose Suppart has fields supplier_ID, part_ID, quantity, and there is another relation with information about supplier. Then Supplier.supplier_ID is a foreign key for Suppart.supplier_ID. Every supplier_ID value in Suppart is in some tuple of Supplier (chapter 4).

Fourth generation language Language used mostly for data entry and report production that makes calls to the database system, usually through SQL statements (chapter 4).

Free list List data structure that indicates which pages in the database buffer can be used for newly read pages without interfering with other transactions or overwriting data that should be put on the database disks (chapter 2).

Frequency-ordered linked list Linked list in which frequently accessed nodes are near the root of the list (chapter 3).

Functional dependency A is functionally dependent on B if B functionally determines A (chapter 4).

Functionally determines "X determines A" holds for a given table T if, in every relation instance I of T, whenever two records r and r' have the same X values, they also have the same A values. (X is one or more attributes, and A is a single attribute) (chapter 4).

Garbage collection The elimination of data objects that are not reachable (through pointers) from a persistent root (chapter 5).

Granule See data item (chapter 2).

Group commit Logging strategy in which the updates of many committing transactions are written to the log at once. This reduces the number of writes to the log (chapter 2).

Grouping query Query that partitions some set of records according to some attribute(s) usually in order to perform some aggregate on those partitions. Each partition has records with the same values in those attributes. For example, the following query finds the average salary in each department. SELECT AVG(salary) as avgsalary, dept FROM employee GROUP BY dept (chapter 3).

Hash structure Tree structure whose root is a function, called the hash function. Given a key, the hash function returns a page that contains pointers to records holding that key or is the root of an overflow chain. Should be used when point or selective multipoint queries are the dominant access patterns (chapter 3).

Head See disk head (chapter 2).

Heap A table organization based on insertion order. That is, each newly inserted record is added to the end of the table. Records are never moved between pages. May cause a locking bottleneck when there are many concurrent inserts (chapter 3).

Heisenbug Failure that appears once, corrupts no data, and never reappears. Studies have shown that the vast majority of software failures that appear in well-written mature systems are Heisenbugs (chapter 2).

Hit ratio Number of logical accesses satisfied by the database buffer divided by the total number of logical accesses (chapter 2).

Horizontal partitioning Method of partitioning a set of records (or objects) among different locations. For example, all account records belonging to one branch may be in one location and the records belonging to another branch may be in another location (chapters 4 and 5).

Hot spot Data item that is the target of accesses, some of them writes, from many concurrent transactions (chapter 2).

Hot table Table that is accessed by many concurrent transactions, some of which write it (chapter 3).

Identifier An integer that uniquely identifies an object or record within a database system. This is a generalization of the notion of address from normal programming languages. An object with an identifier can be shared ("pointed to") by other objects (chapters 4 and 5).

Idle time Wall clock time less the user and system time. Usually, this is time spent waiting for disks, networks or other tasks (chapter 2).

Impedance mismatch Performance and software engineering problems caused by the fact that a set-oriented language must interface with a record-oriented language. This term was popularized by David Maier to characterize the situation that occurs when programmers use a set-oriented language such as SQL embedded within a record-oriented language such as COBOL, C, RPG, etc. (chapter 5).

Index Data organization to speed the execution of queries on tables or object-oriented collections. It consists of a data structure, e.g., a B-tree or hash structure, and a table organization (chapter 3).

Inheritance Facility whereby one class A can be defined based on the definition of a class B, plus some additional operations. For example, a map image class may inherit from an image class and add the operation locate_city. (chapter 5).

Interesting functional dependency "X determines A" (or $X \rightarrow A$) is interesting if A is not an attribute in X (chapter 4).

Interior node In a data structure characterized by a tree, e.g., a B-tree or ISAM structure, an interior node is anything other than a leaf node or overflow page (chapter 3).

Internal node See interior node.

Interrupt-driven Action is interrupt-driven if it occurs whenever a certain event occurs. It should entail negligible overhead until that event occurs (chapter 4).

ISAM structure Balanced tree structure with a predetermined number of levels. Interior nodes of an ISAM structure never change, but there may be overflow chains at the leaves. Use ISAM when range queries are important and there are few updates (chapter 3).

Isolation Degree 3 isolation is the assurance given by a concurrency control algorithm that in a concurrent execution of a set of transactions, whichever transactions commit will appear to execute one at a time. Lesser degrees give lesser guarantees (chapter 2).

   Degree 0 isolation Write locks held while writes occur, no read locks. So, reads can access dirty data and writes can overwrite other transactions' dirty writes (chapter 2).

   Degree 1 isolation Write locks acquired in two-phase manner, no read locks. So, reads can access dirty data, but writes cannot overwrite other transactions' dirty writes (chapter 2).

   Degree 2 isolation Write locks acquired in two-phase manner, read locks held while reads occur. So, reads cannot access dirty data, but reads are not repeatable (chapter 2).

   Degree 3 isolation Read and write locks acquired in two-phase manner. So, transactions that commit appear to execute one at a time (chapter 2).

Item See data item (chapter 2).

Join attribute In a join clause of the form R.A = S.B, A is the join attribute of R and B is the join attribute of S (chapter 3).

Join query Query that links two or more table instances based on some comparison criterion. For example, the following query finds all students who have a higher salary than some employee: SELECT studname FROM students, employee WHERE student.salary > employee.salary. The two table instances may come from the same table. For example, the following query finds employees who earn more than their manager: SELECT e1.name FROM employee e1, employee e2 WHERE e1.manager = e2.ssnum AND e1.salary > e2.salary (chapter 3).

Key When talking about an index, the key is the set of attributes the index is defined on, e.g., A is the key of an index on A; by contrast, in normalization theory, a key of a table is a minimal set of attributes such that no two distinct records of the table have the same value on all of those attributes. Notice that the two notions are quite different. (chapter 3).

Key compression Encoding of keys in the interior nodes of B-trees and hash structures to make them shorter. This improves the branching factor at the cost of somewhat more processor time when updating or scanning (chapter 3).

Link implementation A data structure has a link implementation if every leaf node has a pointer to its right neighbor. This can improve the performance of range queries and, in a few systems, even the performance of concurrency control (chapter 3).

Linked list Data structure that one can access by beginning at a distinguished location called the root and follow pointers from the root to the first node, the first node to the second and so on (chapter 3).

Load An insertion of many records into a table. If a load occurs in isolation then no locks are needed and indexes should be dropped for best performance. Also, if the load inserts records in sorted order into a B-tree, then check to make sure that your system performs splits in a way that achieves high utilization (chapters 2, 3, 4).

Lock escalation Certain systems have the property that they will use a certain granularity of locking, say record-level locking, for a transaction T until T has acquired more locks than some user-specified threshold. After that point, the system obtains coarser granularity locks, say page-level locks, on behalf of T. The switch to coarser granularity locks is called lock escalation (chapter 2).

Locking Denotes the activity of obtaining and releasing read locks and write locks (see corresponding entries) for the purposes of concurrent synchronization (concurrency control) among transactions (chapter 2).

Log Section of stable storage (normally disk) that contains before images or after images or both for the purposes of recovery from failure. It should always be possible to recreate the current logical state of the database (up to the last committed transaction) by combining the log and the active database disks or (possibly) by combining the log and the last database dump (chapter 2).

Logging Denotes the activity of storing either before images or after images or both on a log for recovery purposes (chapter 2).

Logical logging Technique that consists of writing the operation that caused an update as opposed to the pages modified by the update, e.g., the recorded operation might look like: insert into tycoon (780-76-3452, Yamain, Robert, . . .) (chapter 2).

Logical reads and writes Page reads and writes requested by applications. Some of these may be satisfied by accesses to the database buffer (chapter 2).

Lookup table Small, read-only table used by many applications. For example, a table that translates codes to city names. Should not be put in the database system, but rather kept in application space for best performance (chapter 3).

Merge-join Join technique in which the two join arguments are sorted on their join attributes and then a merge-like procedure takes place in which matching tuples are concatenated and output. For example, if the tuples of R are (1, 1), (2, 4), (2, 3) and the tuples of S are (2, 5), (2, 1) and they are joined on their first attributes, then the four tuples (2, 4, 2, 5), (2, 4, 2, 1), (2, 3, 2, 5) and (2, 3, 2, 1) would be output in that order (chapter 3).

Method An operation that can be applied to one or to a few objects in an object-oriented system (chapter 5).

Minibatch A long batch transaction may use up all the memory in the database buffer, causing poor performance because of paging. Minibatch is the style of programming that consists of chopping such a long batch transaction into smaller ones. It is important to check whether this causes a violation of desired isolation properties (chapter 2, appendix).

Minimal (1) For sets: no smaller set satisfies some given required properties; and (2) for functional dependencies: a set of functional dependencies without redundancies and whose left-hand sides are the minimal sets possible that express the same dependency information (chapter 4).

MIPS Millions of instructions per second. This measure of processor speed is of limited relevance to the performance of a database system, which depends on factors such as the efficiency of the disk subsystem and software algorithms (chapter 6).

MIPS penalty Overhead resulting from communication that an application encounters when it runs on a distributed or parallel system (chapter 2).

Mirrored disks Set of disks that are synchronized as follows: each write to one disk goes to all disks in the mirrored set; reads can access any of the disks (chapter 2).

Multidimensional data structure Tree data structure that is useful for spatial queries, e.g., find all cities in some range of latitudes and longitudes (chapter 3).

Multiple inheritance Ability to inherit definitions from more than one class (chapter 5).

Multipoint query Equality selection that may return several records. Such queries always benefit from clustering indexes and will benefit from non-clustering indexes if the query is selective (chapter 3).

Node When speaking about a graph structure such as a circuit or a data structure such as a hash structure, B-tree or ISAM structure, a node is a section of storage that may have pointers to other nodes or that is pointed to by pointers in other nodes or both (chapters 3 and 5).

Nonclustering index Dense index that puts no constraints on the table organization. See, for contrast, clustering index (chapter 3).

Nonsequential key Opposite of sequential key (chapter 3).

Normalized Relation R is normalized if every interesting functional dependency "X functionally determines A," where A and the attributes in X are contained in R, has the property that X is the key or a superset of the key of R (chapter 4).

Number of levels In a B-tree and ISAM structure, the number of different nodes on any path from the root to a leaf. In the case of an ISAM structure, the leaf may have overflow pointers. These are not counted in the count of the number of levels (chapter 3).

Object Collection of data, an identifier, and operations (sometimes called methods) (chapter 5).

Object attribute Attribute in an object containing a reference to another object (i.e., an object identifier). Contrast with value attribute (chapter 5).

Object identifier An integer uniquely associated with a single object (chapter 5).

Object-level logging Property of a logging algorithm for an object-oriented database system in which the data items written to the log are objects (chapter 2).

Octopus layout Method of laying out an object or a vertical partition of an object wherein certain attribute contents are clustered with the object identifier and object header, whereas other attribute values are laid out elsewhere (chapter 5).

Online transaction processing Denotes the class of applications where the transactions are short, typically ten disk I/Os or fewer per transaction, the queries are simple, typically point and multipoint queries, and the frequency of updates is high (chapter 7).

Operating system paging Activity of performing disk reads to access pages that are in the virtual memory of the database buffer but not in random access memory. For a well-tuned buffer, this should be negligible (chapter 2).

Ordering query Query that outputs a set of records according to some sorted order on one or more attributes. For example, the following query orders the records in the employee relation from lowest salary to highest salary. SELECT * FROM employee ORDER BY salary (chapter 3).

Overflow chaining In ISAM structures and hash structures (with the exception of certain exotic hash structures such as extendible hashing), when an insertion applies to a full page p, a new page p' is created and a pointer from p to p' is added. This is called overflow chaining (chapter 3).

Page-level lock A page-level lock on page p will prevent concurrent transactions from modifying p. If the lock is a write lock, then the lock will prevent concurrent transactions from accessing p altogether (chapter 2).

Page-level logging Property of a logging algorithm in which the smallest data items written to the log are pages (chapter 2).

Parent object If object o contains an attribute whose contents is a reference to object o', then o is a parent object of o' (chapter 5).

Partition A division of a set into disjoint subsets whose union yields the set. For example, if $\{a, b, c, d, e\}$ is a set then one partitioning is $\{\{c, e\}, \{d, a\}, \{b\}\}$ (chapter 3).

Persistent object One that exists after the execution of the program that creates it (chapter 5).

Physical data independence Assurance given by a database system that changing a data structure (e.g., adding, dropping or reorganizing a B-tree, or replacing a B-tree by a hash structure) will not change the meaning of any program. SQL gives this assurance to the extent that an SQL query will have the same input/output behavior regardless of the indexes that support the query. Object-oriented systems offer a generalization of this property known as encapsulation (chapters 4 and 5).

Physical reads and writes Those logical reads and writes that are not satisfied by the database buffer and that result in accesses to secondary storage (chapter 2).

Point query Equality selection that returns a single record. Such queries benefit from indexes (chapter 3).

Poll Repeatedly access a data location or table to see if it has been changed in a certain way. Much less efficient than using an interrupt-driven mechanism such as a trigger (chapter 4).

Positional B-tree Kind of B+ tree to support ordered objects to which there may be inserts and deletes. Objects may be retrieved by their position in the list. Supplied by many object-oriented database systems (chapter 5).

Prefix compression Technique used in the interior nodes (the nonleaf ones) of a B-tree or ISAM structure to reduce the length of the key portion of each key-pointer pair. For example, if three consecutive keys are Smith, Smoot, and Smythe, then only Smi, Smo, and Smy need be stored (chapter 2).

Prefix match query Query on the prefix of a given sequence of attributes. For example, if the sequence is lastname, firstname, then lastname = 'DeWitt' AND firstname LIKE 'Da%' would be a prefix match query as would lastname LIKE 'DeW%'. By contrast, firstname LIKE 'Da%' would not be a prefix match query, because firstname is not a prefix of lastname, firstname (chapter 3).

Primary index See clustering index (chapter 3).

Priority inheritance Scheme to avoid lock-induced priority inversion by allowing a low priority thread that holds a lock to acquire the priority of the highest priority thread waiting for that lock (chapter 2).

Priority inversion Scheduling anomaly in which a higher priority thread waits for lower priority one. This can occur in first-in first-out queues and in situations in which there are locks (chapter 2).

Privileged Table T is privileged in a select if the fields returned by the select contain a key of T. For example, if ssnum is a key of Employee, then any statement of the form SELECT ssnum, . . . FROM Employee . . . WHERE . . . privileges Employee. Important when trying to eliminate the keyword DISTINCT (chapter 4).

Query plan The plan produced by an optimizer for processing a query. For example, if there is an index on R.B and on S.D, then a smart optimizer will apply the index on S.D and then scan the result from S against the index on R.B in the query SELECT R.A FROM R, S WHERE R.B = S.C AND S.D = 17 (chapter 3).

Random access memory Electronic (solid state memory) whose access times are in the range of 10-100 nanoseconds no matter where the previous access took place. Frequent synonyms are real memory and main memory.

Range query Selection of the form R.A >= 5 AND R.A <= 10. That is, a selection on an interval containing more than one value (chapter 3).

Reaches Table S reaches a table T if S is joined by equality on one of its key fields to T. If dept is a key of Techdept, then Techdept reaches Employee in the query SELECT . . . FROM Employee, Techdept WHERE Techdept.dept = Employee.dept. Important when trying to eliminate the frequency of DISTINCT, see privileged (chapter 4).

Read lock If a transaction T holds a read lock on a data item x, then no other transaction can obtain a write lock on x (chapter 2).

Record Row in a relational table containing null or non-null values of all the attributes of that relation schema (chapter 4).

Record-level lock A record-level lock on record r will prevent concurrent transactions from modifying r. If the lock is a write lock, then the lock will prevent concurrent transactions from accessing r altogether (chapter 2).

Record-level logging Property of a logging algorithm for a relational database system in which the data items written to the log are relational records (chapter 2).

Redo-only Property of a logging algorithm in which a transaction T performs no updates to the database disks before T commits (chapter 2).

Redo-undo Property of a logging algorithm in which a transaction T may perform updates to the database disks before T commits. The implication is that before images must be held on the log while T is active (chapter 2).

Relation instance Set of records that conform to some relation schema (chapter 4).

Relation schema Relation name and a set of attributes, or, equivalently, a table name and a set of column headers. Each attribute has a data type. In normalization theory, the functional dependencies on the attributes of the schema are considered to be part of the schema (chapter 4).

Relationship Notion from the Entity-Relationship model. A relationship links two entity types, e.g., the relationship Works-In links entity types employee and organization (chapter 4).

Repeatable reads Assurance given by a concurrency control algorithm that if a transaction T issues two reads to the same data item x without modifying x in between, then the two reads will return the same value (chapter 2).

Response time Time it takes to get a response after submitting a request (chapter 6).

Rollback (verbal form: to roll back) Action of undoing all effects of a transaction that has not yet committed. Rollback may result from internal program logic (e.g., roll back the purchase if cash is low) or from a deadlock in the concurrency control subsystem (chapter 2).

Rotational delay Time required to wait for the proper portion of the track to pass underneath the head when performing a read or write. Around 10 milliseconds for magnetic disks (chapter 2).

Scan See table scan (chapter 3).

Secondary index See nonclustering index (chapter 3).

Seek Head movement required to position a head over a given track (chapter 2).

Seek time Time required to do a seek (around 10 milliseconds for most magnetic disks depending on the distance that must be traveled) (chapter 2).

Selectivity A selection, e.g., R.C = 5, has high selectivity if it returns few records (viz., far fewer records than there are pages in R). Point queries have extremely high selectivity, whereas multipoint queries may or may not have high selectivity (chapter 3).

Semijoin condition Property of a join between two tables R and S such that no fields of one of the tables, say S, are in the result. For example, SELECT R.A, R.B FROM R, S WHERE R.C = S.E. If S is indexed on E, then the data records of S never need to be accessed. Some systems take advantage of this (chapter 3).

Sequential key Key of an index whose values are monotonic with the time of insertion, i.e., later insertions get higher valued keys (chapter 3).

Shared-disk Hardware configuration in which each processor has its private random access memory but all disks are shared. This is a very common configuration for database systems (chapter 2).

Shared lock See read lock (chapter 2).

Shared memory See database buffer (chapter 2).

Shared-nothing Hardware configurations in which each processor has its private random access memory and disks (chapter 2).

Single inheritance The restriction to inheritance from a single class (chapter 5).

Sparse index Index in which the underlying data structure contains exactly one pointer to each data page. Only clustering indexes can be sparse (chapter 3).

Split When an insertion occurs to a full B-tree page p, a new page is created and the tree is locally restructured so the new page and p are at the same distance from the root (chapter 3).

Stable storage That portion of memory that tolerates assumed failures. For example, if one assumes that disks will never fail (perhaps because disks are mirrored), then disk storage is stable (chapter 2).

Subobject The contents of an object attribute in an object-oriented database system. For example, article may have photograph as a subobject. Several objects may share the same subobjects and subobjects may have an existence that is independent of any of their parent objects. Same as constituent object (chapter 5).

Swizzling Method for achieving inexpensive dereferences of inter-object references when the source and target objects are in virtual memory (chapter 5).

System time The processor time some activity takes while executing operating system code (chapter 2).

Table In technical usage, a table is the same as a relation (chapter 4).

Table clustering The interleaving of two tables for the purpose of reducing the cost of a join. For example, each customer record might be followed by the sales records pertaining to that customer (chapter 4).

Table-level lock A table-level lock on table t will prevent concurrent transactions from modifying t. If the lock is a write lock, then the lock will prevent concurrent transactions from accessing t altogether (chapter 2).

Table scan Examination of every record of every page of a table (chapters 3 and 4).

Tablespace Physical portion of disk storage containing either an index or one or more tables.

Thread Unit of execution consisting of a program counter, a possibly size-limited stack with references to a shared address space and program text (chapter 2).

Throughput The number of transactions that complete per unit time when the system is in steady state.

Tickerplant Database system that takes stock and bond ticks and distributes them to a collection of brokers. Each broker receives the ticks concerning those stocks and bonds in which he or she is interested. Tickerplants are a typical example of quasi-realtime transaction processing, because the goal of the system is never to miss a tick (chapter 2).

Tightly-coupled Hardware configuration in which all processors share random access memory and disks (chapter 2).

Track Narrow circle on a single platter of a disk. If the disk head over a platter does not move, then a track will pass under that head in one rotation. The implication is that reading or writing a track does not take much more time than reading or writing a portion of a track (chapter 2).

Transaction Unit of work within a database application that should appear to execute atomically (i.e., either all its updates should be reflected in the database or none should; it should appear to execute in isolation). In IBM protocols, transactions are known as logical units of work (chapter 2).

Transaction chopping The division of a transaction into smaller transactions for the purposes of reducing concurrency control-induced contention or buffer contention (chapter 2, appendix).

Trie A special kind of tree structure that is good for an in-memory lookup table that supports prefix queries (chapter 3).

Trigger Stored procedure that performs an action when some table is updated in a certain way, e.g., whenever there is an insertion to table T, print the tuples that are inserted (chapter 4).

Tuple See record (chapter 4).

Two-phase commit Algorithm for terminating transactions that are distributed over many sites (specified by the LU6.2 protocol in the IBM world). A distributed system that does not provide two-phase commit cannot reliably support transactions that cause updates at multiple sites. Two-phase commit entails an overhead of between two and four messages per transaction per site (chapter 2).

Two-phase locking Algorithm for concurrency control whereby a transaction acquires write locks on data items that it will write, read locks on data items that it will only read; a transaction obeying two-phase locking will never obtain a lock after releasing any lock (even on another data item). Two-phase locking can encounter deadlock (chapter 2).

Unbuffered commit strategy Logging algorithm in which a transaction's updates are forced to the database disks immediately after commit. This implies that there will be many random writes to those disks, thus hurting performance. Its main advantage is that recovery from random access memory failures is somewhat faster than using a buffered commit strategy (chapter 2).

Unnormalized Opposite of normalized (chapter 4).

Usage factor The percentage of a page that can be utilized, yet still permit a further insertion. This influences utilization (chapter 2).

User In the context of this book, a user is someone who uses a database management system as opposed to a developer of the database management system itself. That is, a user may be a database administrator or an informed application developer.

User time The processor time some activity takes while executing non-operating system code (chapter 2).

Utilization That percentage of an index or data page that actually has data on it as opposed to free space. For example, a B-tree has an average utilization of about 69% (chapter 3).

Value attribute Attribute in an object containing a value, as opposed to an object reference. If a program changes the value of that attribute in an object o, no other object o' is affected (chapter 5).

Vertical anti-partitioning Technique for storing small sets in a single record. For example, if one relation contains the attributes (bond, descriptive information) and another one contains (bond, date, price), then vertical anti-partitioning may consist of putting some of the prices (e.g., the last ten days' worth) with the descriptive information (chapter 4).

Vertical partitioning Method of dividing each record (or object) of a table (or collection of objects) such that some attributes, including a key, of the record (or object) are in one location and others are in another location, possibly another disk. For example, the account ID and the current balance may be in one location and the account ID and the address information of each tuple may be in another location (chapters 4 and 5).

Wall clock time Time some activity takes as recorded by an external observer looking at a clock (chapter 2).

Write lock If a transaction T holds a write lock on a data item x, then no other transaction can obtain any lock on x (assuming degree 2 or 3 isolation) (chapter 2).

Bibliography

1. E. Adams, "Optimizing Preventive Service of Software Products," *IBM Journal of Research and Development*, vol. 28, no. 1, 1984.

2. R. Bayer, "Consistency of Transactions and Random Batch," *ACM Transactions on Database Systems*, vol. 11, no. 4, pp. 397-404, December 1986.

3. P. A. Bernstein, V. Hadzilacos, and N. Goodman, *Concurrency Control and Recovery in Database Systems*, Reading, Mass.: Addison-Wesley, 1987.

4. P. A. Bernstein, D. W. Shipman, and J. B. Rothnie, "Concurrency Control in a System for Distributed Databases (SDD1)," *ACM Transactions on Database Systems*, vol. 5, no. 1, pp. 18-51, March 1980.

5. P. Butterworth, A. Otis and J. Stein, "The GemStone Object Database Management System," *Communications of the ACM*, vol. 34, no. 10, pp. 64-77, October 1991.

6. Marco Casanova, *The Concurrency Control Problem for Database Systems*, Springer-Verlag Lecture Notes in Computer Science, no. 116, 1981.

7. R. G. G. Cattell, Ed., *Communications of the ACM*, vol. 34, no. 10, October 1991.

8. R. G. G. Cattell, *Object Data Management: Object-oriented and Extended Relational Database Systems*, Reading, Mass.: Addison-Wesley, 1991.

9. D. Comer, "The Ubiquitous B-Tree," *ACM Computing Surveys*, vol. 11, no. 2, pp. 121-137, 1979.

10. G. Copeland, W. Alexander, E. Bougherty, and T. Keller, "Data Placement in Bubba," in *Proc. of ACM SIGMOD Conf.*, May 1988, pp. 99-108.

11. Chris Date, *A Guide to the SQL Standard, 2nd Ed.*, Reading, Mass.: Addison-Wesley, 1989.

12. O. Deux et al., "The O2 System," *Communications of the ACM*, vol. 34, no. 10, pp. 34-48, October 1991.

13. D. J. DeWitt, P. Futtersack, D. Maier, and F. Velez, "A Study of Three Alternative Workstation-Server Architectures for Object-Oriented Database Systems," in *Proc. of the 16th VLDB Conference*, pp. 107-121, August 1990.

14. Ramez Elmasri and Sham Navathe, *Fundamentals of Database Systems*, Benjamin/Cummings, Redwood City, Calif., 1989.

15. Abdel Aziz Farrag and M. Tamer Ozsu, "Using Semantic Knowledge of Transactions to Increase Concurrency," *ACM Transactions on Database Systems*, vol. 14, no. 4, pp. 503-525, December 1989.

16. R. A. Ganski and H. K. T. Wong, "Optimization of Nested SQL Queries Revisited," in *ACM SIGMOD Conference*, pp. 23-33, 1987.

17. Hector Garcia-Molina, "Using Semantic Knowledge for Transaction Processing in a Distributed Database," *ACM Transactions on Database Systems*, vol. 8, no. 2, pp. 186-213, June 1983.

18. Georges Gardarin and Patrick Valduriez, *Relational Databases and Knowledge Bases* Reading, Mass.: Addison-Wesley, 1989.

19. Jim Gray, "A Census of Tandem System Availability, 1985-1990," *IEEE Trans. on Reliability*, vol. 39, no. 4, pp. 409-418, 1990.

20. Jim Gray, Ed., *The Benchmark Handbook*, San Mateo, Calif.: Morgan-Kaufmann, 1991.

21. Jim Gray and Frank Putzolu, "The 5 Minute Rule for Trading Memory for Disc Accesses and the 5 Byte Rule for Trading Memory for CPU Time," in *ACM SIGMOD Conference*, pp. 395-398, 1987.

22. Jim Gray and Andreas Reuter, *Transaction Processing: Concepts and Techniques*, San Mateo, Calif.: Morgan-Kaufmann, 1992.

23. Hans-Ulrick Heiss and Roger Wagner, "Adaptive Load Control in Transaction Processing Systems," in *Proceedings of the 17th International Conference on Very Large Data Bases*, Barcelona, September 1991, pp. 47-54.

24. M. Hsu and A. Chan, "Partitioned Two-Phase Locking," *ACM Transactions on Database Systems*, vol. 11, no. 4, pp. 431-446, December 1986.

25. T. Johnson and D. Shasha, "Utilization of B-trees with Inserts, Deletes, and Modifies," in *8th ACM SIGACT-SIGMOD Conference on Principles of Database Systems*, pp. 235-246, March 1989.

26. Won Kim, "On Optimizing an SQL-like Nested Query," *Transactions on Database Systems*, vol. 7, no. 3, pp. 443-469, September 1982.

27. Hank Korth and Avi Silberschatz, *Database System Concepts - 2nd ed.* New York: McGraw-Hill, 1991.

28. Nancy Lynch, "Multi-level Atomicity - A New Correctness Criterion for Database Concurrency Control," *ACM Transactions on Database Systems*, vol. 8, no. 4, pp. 484-502, December 1983.

29. C. Lamb, G. Landis, J. Orenstein, D. Weinreb, "The ObjectStore Database System," *Communications of the ACM*, vol. 34, no. 10, pp. 50-63, October 1991.

30. G. Lohman, B. Lindsay, H. Pirahesh and K. Schiefer, "Extensions to Starburst: Objects, Types, Functions and Rules," *Communications of the ACM*, vol. 34, no. 10, pp. 94-109, October 1991.

31. David Lomet and Betty Salzberg, "The hB-tree: A Multiattribute Indexing Method with Good

Guaranteed Performance," *ACM Transactions on Database Systems*, vol. 15, no. 4, pp. 625-658, December 1990.

32. David Maier, *The Theory of Relational Databases*, New York: Computer Science Press, division of W. H. Freeman, 1983.

33. Bertrand Meyer, *Object-oriented Software Construction*, Englewood-Cliffs, N.J.: Prentice-Hall, 1988.

34. C. Mohan, "ARIES/KVL: A Key-Value Locking Method for Concurrency Control of Multiaction Transactions on B-Tree Indexes," in *16th Very Large Data Base Conference*, San Mateo, Calif.: Morgan-Kauffman, pp. 392-405, 1990.

35. J. E. B. Moss, *Nested Transactions: An Approach to Reliable Distributed Computing*, Boston, Mass.: MIT Press, 1985.

36. J. Nievergelt, H. Hinterberger and K. C. Sevcik, "The Grid File: An Adaptable Symmetric Multikey File Structure," *ACM Transactions on Database Systems*, vol. 9, no. 1, pp. 38-71, March 1984.

37. Patrick O'Neil, "The Escrow Transactional Mechanism," *ACM Transactions on Database Systems*, vol. 11, no. 4, pp. 405-430, December 1986.

38. Christos Papadimitriou, *The Theory of Concurrency Control*, New York: Computer Science Press, division of W. H. Freeman, 1986.

39. R. Ramesh, A. J. G. Babu and J. Peter Kincaid, "Variable-Depth Trie Index Optimization: Theory and Experimental Results," *ACM Transactions on Database Systems*, vol. 14, no. 1, pp. 41-74, March 1989.

40. S. Rozen and D. Shasha, "Using a Relational Database on Wall Street: The Good, the Bad, the Ugly, and the Ideal," *Communications of the ACM*, vol. 32, no. 8, pp. 988-994, August 1989.

41. D. Shasha and M. Snir, "Efficient and Correct Execution of Parallel Programs that Share Memory," *ACM Transactions on Programming Languages and Systems*, vol. 10, no. 2, pp. 282-312, April 1988.

42. M. Stonebraker and G. Kemnitz, "The POSTGRES Next-Generation Database Management System," *Communications of the ACM*, vol. 34, no. 10, pp. 78-92, October 1991.

43. Y. C. Tay, *Locking Performance in Centralized Databases*, Orlando, Fl.: Academic Press, 1987.

44. Jeff Ullman, *Principles of Database and Knowledge-Based Systems*, New York: Computer Science Press, division of W. H. Freeman, 1988.

45. Gottfried Vossen, *Data Models, Database Languages and Database Management Systems*, Reading, Mass.: Addison Wesley, 1991.

46. Ouri Wolfson, "The Virtues of Locking by Symbolic Names," *Journal of Algorithms*, vol. 8, pp. 536-556, 1987.

47. K. C. Wong and M. Edelberg, "Interval Hierarchies and Their Application to Predicate Files," *ACM Transactions on Database Systems*, vol. 2, no. 3, pp. 223-232, September 1977.

48. Mihalis Yannakakis, "A Theory of Safe Locking Policies in Database Systems," *JACM*, vol. 29, no. 3, pp. 718-740, 1982.

Index

Biography

Dennis Shasha is an associate professor at New York University's Courant Institute where he does research on transaction processing, real-time algorithms, and pattern matching. He also consults at UNIX System Laboratory, where he has worked on the TUXEDO database system and the design of kernel enablers for transaction processing systems. In addition, he has consulted for the database groups of various Wall Street brokerage houses and for the Ellis Island Restoration Commission.

He received his BS from Yale College in 1967, then worked three years for IBM designing circuits and microcode for the 3090 while obtaining his master's from Syracuse University. He obtained his doctorate from Harvard University in 1974.

This is his first professional reference book, but he has written two other books about a mathematical detective named Dr. Jacob Ecco: *The Puzzling Adventures of Dr. Ecco* and *Codes, Puzzles, and Conspiracy*, both published by W. H. Freeman, New York.